A History of

AFRICAN AMERICANS

in North Carolina

Sylvia Conner, a seamstress, was a free black woman who resided in New Bern during the Civil War. She had been enslaved before Union troops captured and occupied the town. Tintype (June 5, 1863) from the collection of Tryon Palace, New Bern.

A History of
AFRICAN AMERICANS
in North Carolina

Second Revised Edition

Jeffrey J. Crow & Paul D. Escott & Flora Hatley Wadelington

Office of Archives and History
North Carolina Department of Cultural Resources
Raleigh
2022

Second Revised Edition, Fifth Printing, 2022

978-0-8652-6351-2

Printed by Friesens in Canada.

Distributed by the University of North Carolina Press, Inc.
www.uncpress.com

Contents

Maps, Tables, and Illustrations

Foreword

In 1992, Jeffrey J. Crow, Paul D. Escott, and Flora J. Hatley (now Flora J. Hatley Wadelington) produced a one-volume survey of the history of black North Carolinians. When this work first appeared, it represented the culmination of a concerted effort to better represent the history of African Americans in the state. For this second revised edition, Dr. Crow updated the tenth chapter, the appendixes, and the suggested readings. He would like to acknowledge Matthew Brown, Michael Hill, Josh Howard, Anne Miller, and Ansley Wegner for their research assistance.

Dr. Crow serves as deputy secretary of the North Carolina Office of Archives and History; he wrote the first, second, third, seventh, and tenth chapters. Dr. Escott is Reynolds Professor of History at Wake Forest University; he wrote the fourth, fifth, and sixth chapters. Mrs. Hatley Wadelington (a former employee of Archives and History) is an assistant professor of history and teaches at Shaw University and St. Augustine's College in Raleigh; she wrote the eighth and ninth chapters. Stephen E. Massengill (a former employee of the Archives and Records Section) compiled the appendix showing black and purportedly black legislators who served in the North Carolina General Assembly from 1868 to 1900. Two former members of the Historical Publications Section's Advisory Editorial Committee—Raymond Gavins of Duke University and John David Smith of the University of North Carolina at Charlotte—read and suggested revisions to the original manuscript.

Several members of the Historical Publications Section staff contributed to the work, both in its original printing and one or both of the two revised editions. Robert M. Topkins (a former editor with the section) edited the original manuscript, prepared the index, researched the illustrations, and saw the book through press. Sandra T. Hall (a former employee with the section) and Susan M. Trimble prepared electronic versions of the text, maps, and appendixes. In addition, Mrs. Trimble designed and typeset the second revised edition, assisted in revising the index, and helped design the cover, along with Bill Owens. Lisa D. Bailey assisted with the proofreading of all editions. I proofread the revised editions, modified the index, and saw the second one through press.

This second revision joins six other titles published by the section that are devoted specifically to North Carolina's African American heritage. The section would especially like to acknowledge the financial assistance provided by the African American Heritage Commission.

The inaugural publication of *A History of African Americans in North Carolina* in 1992 embodied what Dr. William S. Price Jr., previous director of the former Division of Archives and History, called "a launching pad for what will occur in years to come." Nearly twenty years later this book still stands as a testament to "the state's proud legacy of black heritage."

Donna E. Kelly, *Administrator*
Historical Publications Section

I

Colonial Origins of Slavery in North Carolina

Even before Sir Walter Raleigh planted an English colony on Roanoke Island in the 1580s, Africans had visited North Carolina's shores. In 1526 Lucas Vásquez de Ayllón, a Spanish explorer and slave trader, led an expedition of five hundred men and women from the West Indies to settle in the vicinity of Cape Fear. Among the adventurers were several black slaves. The expedition ultimately ended in disease, starvation, and failure, but the short-lived Spanish colony on the banks of the Cape Fear River was a harbinger of future efforts.

With the planting of the Raleigh colonies on the North American continent between 1584 and 1590, Sir Francis Drake inadvertently furnished North Carolina with its first permanent black inhabitants. Drake raided the Spanish-held West Indies in 1585 and 1586 and acquired numerous prisoners, including Moorish galley slaves and soldiers, a group of Negro slaves (to whom he promised their freedom), and approximately three hundred South American Indians. Drake then sailed to Roanoke Island to relieve the Ralph Lane colony. Departing Roanoke for England in June 1586, Drake evidently freed the Indian and Negro captives, although he kept the Moorish prisoners. What became of the South American Indians and West Indian slaves is not known, but they probably melted into the local Indian population.

Permanent settlement of Carolina began in the mid-seventeenth century. Settlers from Virginia pushed into present-day North Carolina in the 1650s. By 1663 the number of settlers in the Albemarle region exceeded five hundred. It is possible, though not known for certain, that the Virginians brought a few slaves with them. Meanwhile, events in England assured that North Carolina would become a slave colony.

In 1663, soon after his restoration to the English throne, Charles II granted eight Lords Proprietors a huge tract of territory south of Virginia.

The Lords Proprietors sought easy profits by renting lands and selling a wide variety of commodities. They recognized that a slave colony in Carolina held the greatest commercial promise.

A group of colonists from Barbados agreed. The Barbadians wished to settle in Carolina and bring their slaves with them. They pressed the Lords Proprietors to establish a headright system under which the heads of all households would be allotted acreage on the basis of the number of people who accompanied them. The proprietors assented by granting "the Owner of every Negro-Man or Slave, brought thither to settle within the first year, twenty acres, and for every Woman-Negro or Slave, ten acres of Land; and all Men Negro's, or slaves after that time, and within the first five years, ten acres, and for every Woman-Negro or slave, five acres."

Moreover, the Lords Proprietors made certain that the Negro's status was fixed and distinctive. Carolina's Fundamental Constitutions, drafted in 1669, stated explicitly (Article 110): "Every freeman of Carolina, shall have absolute power and authority over his negro slaves, of what opinion or religion soever." The document also provided for religious toleration for slaves but noted that conversion to Christianity in no way altered a Negro's servitude.

The commercially minded Lords Proprietors and Barbadian planters thus prepared the way for slavery's introduction into Carolina. As one proprietor bluntly stated upon purchasing sows for the early settlement at Albemarle: "we may have a quantity of Hoggs flesh wch will soonest come to bare to send to Barbados wch will p[ro]duce us Neagroes & Sarvts: to rayse a plantacon."

Because of North Carolina's treacherous coast and lack of good harbors, the large plantations envisioned by the Lords Proprietors and Barbadian planters took root in South Carolina, where many of North Carolina's principal rivers reach the sea. The northern province's other rivers empty into the shallow sounds of the Outer Banks. Thus, while slavery expanded rapidly in South Carolina, it grew more slowly in the northern precincts. Still, the headright system accomplished its purpose. In 1702, for example, John Shaw of Perquimans Precinct received 74 acres for two Negroes—Dick and Will. The following year Col. William Wilkeson of the same precinct converted eight headrights into 400 acres; among his headrights were two Indian slaves and one mulatto slave. Maj. Gen. Thomas Pollock of Chowan Precinct received 640 acres on February 26, 1711/12, for headrights that included eleven Negroes: London, Joe, Tom, Betty, Jenny, Tatte, Pompey, Tom, Scipio, Bowman, and Moll.

By 1710 Pasquotank and Currituck counties reported 308 Negroes and 1,871 whites. The number of blacks in the whole colony was estimated in 1712 at only 800. South Carolina, by comparison, was already 50 percent black in 1708 with 4,100 slaves. By 1720 the number of slaves there grew to 18,000, fully three times the number of whites.

Before 1730 most slaves in North Carolina lived in the tobacco-growing region of the colony's northeast. With the establishment of rice growing and the naval stores industry in the southeast, however, slavery expanded much more quickly. Between 1730 and 1767 the black population grew from approximately 6,000 to 40,000. While much of that growth resulted from natural increase, more than half of it probably represented slave imports, particularly during the period 1755–1767.

Slaves had been shipped directly from Guinea to Virginia and North Carolina as early as the 1680s, but most of the colony's slave trade originated elsewhere. With its dangerous coastline, North Carolina depended on overland trade from Virginia and South Carolina to meet its needs in slaves and other commodities. In 1733 Gov. George Burrington complained: "Great is the loss this Country has sustained in not being supply'd by vessels from Guinea with Negroes; in any part of the Province the people are able to pay for a ships load; but as none come directly from Affrica, we are under a necessity to buy, the refuse refractory and distemper'd Negroes, brought from other Governments. . . ." A majority of the 70,000 to 75,000 slaves who entered South Carolina between 1735 and 1775 were reexported, with Georgia and North Carolina, in that order, the principal destinations. When the first federal census was taken in 1790, North Carolina reported 100,572 slaves and 288,204 whites.

The distribution of slaves in North Carolina followed agricultural patterns. The tobacco culture spread westward from the Albemarle region in a line of counties parallel to the Virginia border. Large Negro populations existed in Northampton, Halifax, and Warren counties, where on the eve of the American Revolution 40 to 60 percent of the households owned slaves. The size of slaveholdings farther west was relatively insignificant. In Orange County (1755) and Anson County (1763), only about 10 percent of the households owned slaves.

The Lower Cape Fear region, on the other hand, had the greatest concentration of slaves. The area was settled in the 1720s by planters from South Carolina who brought rice culture and slaves with them. In New Hanover County in 1763 approximately 55 percent of the households owned slaves. Slaves, moreover, constituted 73 percent of the taxables in

New Hanover County in 1767 and more than 80 percent in Brunswick County in 1769. Just as significantly, slaveholdings in the Lower Cape Fear were concentrated in relatively few hands. In the 1770s fully 90 percent of the slaves were owned by masters with 10 or more slaves; 73 percent were owned by masters with 20 or more bondsmen.

Slave labor underpinned the naval stores industry and rice culture of the Lower Cape Fear. Slaves could be employed efficiently throughout the year making tar, pitch, and turpentine. Although the cultivation of rice was confined to perhaps no more than 500 acres of the Cape Fear, 95 percent of the crop cleared the port of Brunswick in 1771.

As shown in the Lower Cape Fear region, slavery was tied closely to the production of commercial crops. Where tobacco, rice, naval stores, and, to a lesser extent, grain flourished, slaves performed the requisite labor. Those areas included the coastal counties from the Albemarle to the Cape Fear, Piedmont counties as far west as Guilford, and inland counties along major waterways such as the upper Cape Fear.

By the American Revolution, slavery was firmly entrenched in North Carolina. As the institution grew, white North Carolinians searched for means to regulate slaves' behavior and ensure a stable work force. Ever cognizant of the endemic tensions between master and slave, whites sought personal security from the potential for slave revolts and an orderly system of permanent laborers to create a prosperous economy.

The activities of blacks themselves and the possibility of their acting independently of the master class's interests contributed to whites' concerns. In 1715 one North Carolinian, alarmed by suggestions that slaves should be armed for defense against French and Spanish attacks, declared: "there must be great Caution used, lest our Slaves when arm'd might become our Masters." Ten years earlier whites had complained in a petition to the Lords Proprietors about voting irregularities involving blacks. The petitioners reported: "in the year 1703 when a new General Assembly was to be chosen, . . . the Election was managed with very great partiality and Injustice, and all sorts of people, even servants, Negroes, Aliens, Jews and Common sailors were admitted to vote in Elections." In 1715 the General Assembly forbade such practices in a law stating "that no person whatsoever Inhabitant of this Government born out of the Allegiance of his Majesty and not made free no Negro Mullatto or Indians shall be capable of voting for Members of Assembly. . . ."

That same year North Carolina enacted its first slave code. "An Act Concerning Servants and Slaves" attempted for the first time to define the social, economic, and even physical place of the Negro population. Blacks could not leave their "Plantations without a Ticket or White servant along with them. . . ." Whites were authorized to "apprehend all such Servants & Slaves as they conceive to be runaways or travell without a Tickett or that shall be seen off his Master's ground Arm'd with any Gun, Sword or any other Weapon of defence. . . ." Any runaway slave absent for more than two months could be killed with impunity. Slaves accused of a crime or offense were to be tried by three justices of the precinct court and three slaveholders. Owners of executed slaves could be compensated by the General Assembly through poll taxes collected from slaveholders. Executions of slaves were to be held publicly "to the Terror of other Slaves."

The 1715 law also discouraged miscegenation. A white indentured woman who bore "a Bastard child" with a Negro, mulatto, or Indian father had her term of service extended two years or paid a fine of £6 to the Anglican church wardens. Similarly, the law forbade the intermarriage of any white man or woman "with any Negro, Mulatto or Indyan Man or Woman under the penalty of Fifty Pounds for each White man or woman." Clerics and magistrates likewise could not "celebrate such a marriage."

Slaves who had performed "honest & Faithful service" could be freed by masters, but no owner could manumit "Runaway or Refractory Negroes." Emancipated slaves had to leave the province within six months or be sold back into slavery for five years.

Suspicious of slave gatherings, the lawmakers prohibited any Negro "Meeting House upon the Acct. of Worship or upon any pretence." This provision of the 1715 law tended to blunt Anglican missionaries' efforts to convert slaves to Christianity. Despite the protection of a slave's status by the Fundamental Constitutions, many slave owners refused to permit the baptism of their bondsmen for fear the slaves would thereby become free.

The 1715 law could not suppress all forms of black assertiveness. In 1723 the General Assembly responded to complaints "of great Numbers of free Negroes, Mulattoes, and other persons of mixt Blood" moving into the province and intermarrying with whites. The lawmakers redefined taxables as all males and females over twelve years of age, whether free Negroes or mulattoes, who traced their African ancestry as far back as three generations. Furthermore, any white person who married a Negro, mulatto, or mustee was subject to the same tax.

Within two decades white Carolinians were compelled to revise the slave code once more. Frightened by the 1739 slave revolt on the Stono River some twenty miles from Charles Town, North Carolina lawmakers passed the colony's most elaborate slave code in 1741. The new law revealed the types of black initiatives that disquieted whites. Whites were forbidden to sell to or trade with slaves or servants unless their masters had given consent. Similarly, slaves could not raise horses, cattle, or hogs for their own benefit. The prohibition on slaves' carrying arms was extended to include hunting or ranging "in the Woods." Slaves whose names were submitted in writing by their masters to the county court were excepted from this provision, as were slaves "wearing Liveries."

The 1741 act focused especially on runaway slaves, slave insurrections, and manumissions. In so doing it prescribed harsh punishments. If a slave could not "speak English, or through Obstinacy" would not declare the name of his or her owner, the Negro was to be shuttled from county to county until the owner was found. In each county the runaway was to receive thirty-nine lashes from the sheriff or constable. If the owner were not located, the slave was hired out by the province with "an iron Collar" inscribed with "the letters P. G. [Public Gaol]." Because runaway slaves often lurked about "Swamps, Woods and other Obscure Places, killing Cattle and Hogs, and committing other Injuries," magistrates were empowered to issue proclamations against such slaves. If the runaways failed to surrender immediately, they could be killed or destroyed without accusation of any crime.

Under the 1741 law three or more slaves found guilty of conspiring to rebel were to be put to death. The composition of tribunals judging slave offenses was altered to include four instead of three slaveholders and two instead of three magistrates. Emancipation of slaves was made exceedingly difficult. Henceforth, only the county court could free slaves "for meritorious Services," which it alone determined.

In 1753 the General Assembly instituted slave patrols to examine Negroes' quarters for weapons at least four times a year. The lawmakers admitted that the 1741 statute had "proved ineffectual to restrain many slaves . . . from going armed, which may prove of dangerous consequences."

During the French and Indian War, the lawmakers, disconcerted by the financial drain of the conflict, substituted castration of black male offenders for execution. Since compensation to masters for executed slaves comprised a sizable proportion of the assembly's expenditures between 1748 and 1772, the lawmakers passed a law in 1758 that led to the castration of sixteen black men between 1759 and 1764, when the law was repealed.

While North Carolina lawmakers searched for effective means to suppress the black population in the countryside, restraints against urban slaves were even more difficult to enforce. Slaveholders bewailed the lack of security in towns such as Edenton and Wilmington. Ebenezer Pettigrew, who owned a large plantation near Albemarle Sound, urged Edenton authorities to institute a night guard because blacks were too "numerous there to have uncurbed liberty at night, night is their day."

As early as 1745 the General Assembly empowered Wilmington commissioners to monitor the role of slaves in the markets. To sell produce, slaves needed to carry tickets from their masters; lawmakers hoped to prevent "all Irregular Mobbs & Caballs by Negroes and others. . . ." Slaveholders recognized that in the marketplace bondsmen could sell, bargain, and negotiate to their own, not their masters', benefit. Rather than turn over their earnings to masters, slaves might keep all or part of the money. In some cases masters allowed slaves to arrange their own housing and subsistence, but the absence of direct supervision permitted too many abuses, in the whites' view.

In 1765 Wilmington commissioners promulgated a set of even stricter ordinances, including a ten o'clock curfew each night. The ordinances insisted on tickets from masters stating the slaves' names and business; forbade slaves from hiring out themselves or arranging their lodging for more than one day at a time; ordered that slaves' wages be paid directly to masters; and prohibited three or more blacks from gathering in "Streets, alleys, Vacant Lots," or houses for the purpose of "playing, Riotting, Caballing."

These measures, like earlier ones, proved ineffectual. In 1772 the Wilmington commissioners demanded the removal of all slaves living separately from their masters, but the practice of slaves' keeping independent households continued until the Civil War. In 1785 the General Assembly even resorted to the use of badges for all Negroes, slave and free, in Wilmington, Washington, Edenton, and Fayetteville. Under this law free Negroes had to register with town commissioners, pay a fee, and wear a "badge of cloth . . . to be fixed on the left shoulder, and to have thereon wrought in legible capital letters the word FREE."

The 1785 statute pointed to a major anomaly in the South's preferred system of race relations. Free Negroes constituted about 5 percent of North Carolina's black population by the time of the American Revolution. More than 5,000 free Negroes were recorded in the 1790 census. Before the Revolution most free Negroes were mulattoes or mixed bloods. Writing in 1835, William Gaston, justice on the state supreme court, noted "that previous to the Revolution there were scarcely any emancipated Slaves in this State; and that the few free men of color that were here at that time, were chiefly Mulattoes, the children of white women."

During the colonial period the percentage of free Negroes varied from region to region within the province. The Lower Cape Fear, where slave labor was most intensive, possessed the fewest free Negroes—perhaps no more than 1.5 percent of the Negro population. The Albemarle region (4.6 percent) was close to the colony-wide figure. In contrast the western counties, where slavery was less prevalent, supported a large free Negro population—approximately 11.6 percent of the Negro population.

Mixed in with slaves and free Negroes was a small number of Negro indentured servants. In the decades before the Revolution the percentage of white servants in the unfree population ranged from approximately 23 percent in the Albemarle region to more than 48 percent in Cumberland County. For North Carolina as a whole the percentage was 24. Nonwhite servants comprised 18 percent of the overall servant population in the Albemarle region, 16.7 percent in the Lower Cape Fear, and only 2.2 percent in the western region. What these figures suggest is that prior to the Revolution the scarcity of labor and limited number of slaves necessitated different types of labor: free persons, servants, and slaves. Despite restrictive legislation, especially on emancipation, taboos on miscegenation, and attempts to limit the free Negro population, control of the black population remained imperfect and failed to suppress various kinds of black autonomy.

Interracial marriage, though outlawed, was not uncommon. The Reverend John Blacknall of Edenton, an Anglican priest, was fined £50 in 1725 for marrying "Thomas Spencer a White man and a molatto Woman named Martha paul. . . ." Two years after the enactment of the 1741 law concerning servants and slaves, the vestry of St. John's Parish in Beaufort ordered "that Christian Finny Who has been Lawfully Convicted of Bringing forth Two Mulatto Children be Immediately sold at Public Vendue by the Church Wardens for the use of the parish. . . ." Finny, a white servant, had cohabited "with a Negroe Belonging now to Capt. Godby. . . ." Finny's term of servitude was extended two years. Among North Carolina's planter and merchant class, however, sexual bans were more relaxed. When Josiah Quincy, a Massachusetts revolutionary, visited the colony in 1773, he noted: the "enjoyment of a negro or mulatto woman is spoken of as quite a common thing: no reluctance, delicacy or shame is made about the matter."

As in the case of interracial sexual relations, other aspects of free Negroes' lives were ambiguous and contradictory. Free blacks served in the militia with no apparent discrimination until the nineteenth century, when they were limited to being musicians. While it is not clear whether or not free blacks actually voted before the Revolution, there were no absolute prohibitions against it if other requirements were met. The North Carolina Constitution of 1776 made no distinction between the races for suffrage. Before their disfranchisement, free blacks voted in North Carolina from the Revolution until 1835.

But free blacks also suffered numerous forms of discrimination. The 1723 act imposing a tax on the spouses and children of free blacks was especially oppressive, since no other spouses and children were taxed. Petitions to the General Assembly in the 1760s and 1770s requested the repeal of the burdensome statute. Signed principally by whites, the petitions from Northampton, Edgecombe, and Granville counties characterized free blacks and mulattoes as "persons of probity and good Demeanor [who] . . . cheerfully contribute towards the discharge of every public Duty"—that is, service in the militia, roadwork, and perhaps even voting.

Just as frequently, however, tensions afflicted the relations between the races. Since whites, free blacks, servants, and slaves all competed in the labor market, disputes and distrust generated friction. Whites in Bladen County in 1773 denounced a group of twenty "free Negars and Mulattus" who had "traitorously assembled together." Ocracoke pilots bitterly complained about free Negroes and slaves who piloted vessels up several rivers and back again "to the Great prejudice and Injury" of white pilots. The white watermen spoke ominously of the "Great Confusion and Irregularity [that] daily Insue from the Insolent and Turbilent disposition and behaviour of such Free negroes and Slaves," whom they hoped to bar from piloting.

Free Negroes also faced the constant threat of enslavement. In 1778 at Broad Creek on the Neuse River two masked men broke into the home of Ann Driggus, a free Negro woman, beat her with clubs, "wounded her terribly and carried away four of her children, three girls and a boy. . . ." The oldest girl escaped. The Perquimans County court in 1799 ordered three men to post a £1,000 bail bond and to pay £500 in damages to Dolley James, a free black whom they kidnapped and held for seven days with the intent "to Convey her into foreign parts & Sell & Dispose of her as a Slave. . . ."

Thus, a black's status as free did not assure permanent liberty, and all blacks, slave or free, confronted a host of legal disabilities and discriminations. Moreover, societal norms and prejudices affected blacks as much as written legal prescriptions. John Brickell, writing in 1737, astutely noted the extralegal ways in which slaves were disciplined. "I have frequently seen them whipt to that degree," he said, "that large pieces of their Skin have been hanging down their Backs; yet I never observed one of them shed a Tear, which plainly shows them to be a People of very harsh and stubborn Dispositions." Tobacco planters sometimes forced their slaves to eat tobacco worms "when they have been negligent in their Tobacco Fields, and have not carefully gathered them from amongst the Tobacco Leaves. . . ." Habitual runaway slaves and servants "have Neckyoaks put on them, which they constantly wear. . . ."

Brickell described how whites dispensed summary justice against slaves: "if a *Negroe* cut or wound his Master or a Christian with any unlawful weapon, such a *Sword*, *Scymiter*, or even a *Knife*, and there is Blood-shed, [and] if it is known among the Planters, they immediately meet and order him to be hanged, which is always performed by another Negroe, and generally the Planters bring most of their Negroes with them to behold their fellow Negroe suffer, to deter them from the like vile Practice." Brickell defended such draconian measures as necessary to prevent slave insurrections.

Occasionally, authorities in Great Britain and men of conscience in North Carolina attempted to ameliorate harsh conditions for slaves. In the 1730s and 1750s the king instructed the colony's royal governors to enact a law restraining "inhuman severity . . . by ill masters or their overseers" against servants and slaves. The Crown wanted a law making it punishable by death to kill Indians or Negroes willfully, as well as a "fit penalty" for maiming them. No such law passed, but in 1773 William Hooper, a Whig lawyer with homes in Wilmington and Hillsborough, drafted a bill making the murder of a slave equivalent to the murder of a freeman. The bill passed both houses but was rejected by royal governor Josiah Martin. In 1774, however, the bill passed. Thenceforth, it was a crime to kill a slave unless the murdered Negro tried to defend himself.

In 1784 Hooper again tried to improve living conditions for slaves. He introduced a bill to provide slaves with limited protection from arbitrary treatment by masters. For reasons of "humanity and the policy and interest" of slave owners, the bill enjoined slaveholders to furnish "wholesome and competent diet and Cloathing," limited whippings to twenty-five lashes, since "immoderate correction is a dishonour to a free Country and a disgrace to humanity," and promised slaves the same punishments as whites. For example, a slave who committed a crime for which a white would hang could not be put to death in any other way. This bill too failed to pass.

Though North Carolina never developed a full-fledged plantation system similar to those of South Carolina and Virginia, it did follow social, economic, and legal paths that firmly established slavery in the colony by the mid-eighteenth century. In 1790, 31 percent of all Tar Heel families owned slaves. Particularly in areas of advancing economic maturity, such as the Lower Cape Fear and tobacco-producing areas of the northern Piedmont, individual holdings in slaves were increasingly concentrated on large plantations. By 1771 fully 62 percent of the slaves in North Carolina lived on plantations with ten or more slaves. Such a concentration of slaves had one salutary effect for blacks. It allowed them to create a black community and interior life separate from the strict oversight of whites and to develop concomitantly a collective consciousness to lighten slavery's oppression.

II

Black Life and Labor before 1800

Negroes were in the vanguard of the colonists who settled America. The first blacks who arrived in the Carolinas came from the West Indies. Consequently, most spoke English, had been born or lived in the sugar islands, and understood European customs and culture. For them the adjustment to the New World proved less traumatic than that of later generations of freshly imported Africans.

In the early years of the eighteenth century, white slaveholders lived on small farms, held few slaves, engaged in mixed farming and stock raising, and worked on roughly equal terms with their bond servants. A kind of "sawbuck equality" existed as slave and master worked side by side or opposite each other at a whipsaw. As late as the 1790s, Henrietta Liston, wife of the British minister to the United States, noted that North Carolina was still like a "new Settlement." She commented: "I viewed the Master, giving his assistance with his slaves, to hew wood, & clear the ground, with a certain degree of respect."

Once planters began concentrating on exportable staples—tobacco, rice, and naval stores—and expanded their holdings in slaves, a division of labor and specialized jobs became more prevalent. Blacks performed many different tasks and provided crucial know-how to the agricultural economy. To cultivate rice, for example, required harsh, constant labor. But blacks from the west coast of Africa were noted rice farmers as well as "cattle chasers." In the Carolina lowlands blacks cleared cypress and gum forests and removed logs, stumps, and other obstructions. At least thirty slaves were needed to work a rice plantation because much of the labor was performed by hand. Janet Schaw, a Scottish visitor to the Lower Cape Fear, commented in 1775: "The rice too is whitening, . . . but there is no living near it with the putrid water that must lie on it, and the labor required for it is only fit for slaves, and I think the hardest work I have seen them engaged in." Each slave was expected to produce four or five barrels of rice averaging 500 pounds each—roughly the produce of two acres. Black hands broke the soil with a hoe, used a gourd to sow the seeds, harvested the crop with a sickle, flailed the rice for threshing, and polished the white grains with a mortar and pestle.

If the cultivation of rice required backbreaking labor, agricultural techniques were hardly more advanced elsewhere in the province. Janet Schaw noted that the stalks from the previous year's crop had never been removed and that "the only instrument used is a hoe, with which they at once till and plant corn." She continued: "To accomplish this a number of Negroes follow each other's tail the day long, and have a task assigned them, and it will take twenty at least to do as much work as two horses with a man and boy would perform." Four decades earlier, however, John Brickell wrote admiringly of how blacks were "very industrious and laborious in improving their Plantations, planting abundance of *Corn*, *Rice* and *Tobacco* and making vast quantities of *Turpentine*, *Tar*, and *Pitch*, being better able to undergo fatigues in the extremity of the hot weather than any Europeans."

The naval stores industry to which Brickell alluded was ideally suited to slave labor. Slaves "boxed" a pine tree by cutting deep holes in it. The resulting flow of turpentine was then ladled into barrels. According to Johann David Schoepf, a German traveler in the 1780s, "One man can readily care for 3000 boxes, and that number is generally assigned one negro, the negroes doing the most of this work. At the best and warmest season one negro can easily fill 15–20 barrels of turpentine a day."

After about three years the flow of turpentine ceased, and the pine trees collapsed. During the winter months slaves gathered up "great quantities of this *Light-wood*," which they cut up and burned in kilns to make tar and pitch. To keep the fires burning, slaves tended the kilns "Night and Day," a process that might take up to forty hours. "It sometimes happens," Brickell recorded, "through ill management, and especially in too dry Weather, that these kilns are blown up as if a train of Gunpowder had been laid under them by which accident their *Negroes* have been very much burnt or scalded." Negroes, Brickell admitted, performed the colony's "hard labour."

The cultivation of tobacco also required diligence. Tobacco involved a tedious process of cultivating, topping, worming, suckering, and curing. Such work demanded painstaking attention from slaves and masters.

The number of slave craftsmen in the black population was small, but slave artisans formed an essential part of the colony's skilled labor. Field hands composed approximately 90 percent of the slave population, domestics 4 percent, watermen 1 percent, and artisans 5 percent. In 1711 John Urmston, an Anglican missionary, described the "great number of slaves who understand most handycrafts. . . ." John Brickell declared in 1737: "There are several Blacks born here that can Read and Write, others that are bred to Trades, and prove good Artists." Upon assuming the royal governorship in 1765, William Tryon commented at length on slavery. In the maritime counties, Tryon reported, planters held "from fifty to 250 Slaves. A Plantation with Seventy Slaves on it, is esteemed a good property. When a man marries his Daughters he never talks of the fortune in Money but 20 30 or 40 slaves. . . ." While blacks were employed chiefly "in the Woods & Field, Sowing, and attending and gathering in the Corn," the governor observed, they also made "Barrels, Hoops, Staves, Shingles, Rails, Posts and Pails, all which they do to admiration. . . ." Black carpenters, wheelwrights, coopers, butchers, tanners, shoemakers, sailors, and pilots abounded in the Carolina economy.

Despite the hard work performed by blacks, masters frequently groused about Negro labor. In 1797 the Reverend Charles Pettigrew, writing his "Last Advice . . . to His Sons," spoke candidly about slavery. "To manage *negroes* without the exercise of too much passion," he admitted, "is next to an impossibility. . . . I would therefore put you on your guard, lest their provocations should on some occasions transport you beyond the limits of decency and Christian morality." Pettigrew continued: "They are slaves for life. They are not stimulated to care and industry as white people are, who labor for themselves. They do not feel *themselves* interested in what they do, for arbitrary masters and mistresses. . . ."

Stranded in Edenton because Negroes had shut down the ferry service, Johann David Schoepf complained about the work habits of whites as well as blacks. "No people can be so greedy after holidays," he decided, "as the whites and blacks here, and none with less reason, for at no time do they work so as to need a long rest. It is difficult to say which are the best creatures, the whites here or their blacks, or which have been formed by the others; but in either case the example is bad. The white men are all the time complaining that the blacks will not work, and they themselves do nothing."

Nonetheless, black labor was undeniably productive and profitable for masters. Charles Pettigrew, although he thought it "disagreeable to leave everything to the management of careless negroes," experimented with un-supervised Negro labor. Overseers, he believed, required as much oversight as blacks. Pettigrew discovered that without overseers the "negroes at the Lake plantation have commonly done better by themselves with a little direction than with such overseers as we have had." Two Virginians visiting the Moravian town of Salem in 1772 were amazed to find that the community had only two Negroes. What surprised them was "that white people had done so much work."

The conditions under which blacks labored hardly encouraged them to work at peak efficiency. In colonial North Carolina blacks were ill-fed, ill-housed, and ill-clothed. Johann David Schoepf noted: "The keep of a negro here does not come to a great figure, since the daily ration is but a quart of maize, and rarely a little meat or salted fish. Only those negroes kept for house-service are better cared for." Once a year slaves received "a suit of coarse wollen cloth, two rough shirts, and a pair of shoes." Planters with the largest slaveholdings, said Schoepf, kept blacks "the worst, let them run naked mostly or in rags, and accustom them as much as possible to hunger, but exact of them steady work." In 1781, near the end of the Revolutionary War, a Continental officer was appalled by the condition of slaves in Virginia and North Carolina. "Their Negro's tho' at this Season of the year [late November] are almost Naked in General," he declared. "Some of them Quite as Naked as they were born Have Come into our Camp to look for peices [sic] of Old Clothes.—I don't Know how they Reconcile this treatment of their Slaves with their Liberal Principles of Hospitality."

Rising at daybreak, slaves in the tobacco regions often went without breakfast. Blacks built a fire next to the fields in which they labored and at noon ate "homminy and salt" and sometimes "a little fat, skimmed milk, rusty bacon, or salt herring to relish homminy, or hoecake." When the slaves returned from the fields in the evening, they were expected to strip tobacco leaves before preparing a second meal. Each slave received one blanket for bed and covering and slept on a bench or the ground.

Working conditions in the low country showed a similar severity. In 1777 Elkanah Watson "observed a larger collection of negroes, seated upon rice straw, making a miserable meal upon boiled rice and pure water. It is truly astonishing, how the slave can sustain life with this wretched pittance, and even appear in good health and condition, compelled to labor from dawn to night, through the long summer days, under the scorching rays of the intense sun. . . ."

Masters in the Albemarle region treated their slaves just as negligently. In 1770 a slave approached Penelope Dawson, daughter of royal governor Gabriel Johnston and owner of three plantations, "with a grievous complaint of being starved, & . . . he was sure the Negroes would all leave the plantation if there was not an alteration made. . . ." Dawson blamed the overseer but admitted that with corn scarce, slaves were living "much harder than ever." Wheat, however, was more plentiful, she confessed. Two years later slaves still beseeched Dawson about pitiless conditions. Two slaves told her "they work very hard & are willing to continue so to do & live upon dry bread would they ever please the overseer, but . . . he breaks them just as much without a fault as with one." The overseer had brutally beaten one of the two slaves, Jack, with a hoe and had threatened him further with one hundred lashes. Jack ran. Refusing to go back, the two slaves said the overseer had nine fine cows that made plenty of butter and cheese, yet he allowed the Negroes no milk. Dawson, an absentee plantation owner who kept her residence near Edenton, finally determined that a new overseer must be hired.

To supplement the meager provisions furnished by masters, slaves cultivated their own gardens, hunted, and fished. John Brickell noted that Negroes ate numerous types of wild game and fish that whites eschewed. Blacks esteemed opossums "very much," as well as bats, turtles, owls, and other fowl. But Brickell found such fare ill-tasting and "very hard of Digesting." Janet Schaw recorded: "The Negroes are the only people that seem to pay any attention to the various uses that wild vegetables may be put to. . . . The allowance for a Negro is a quart of Indian corn p^r day, . . . a little piece of land which they cultivate much better than their Master. There they rear hogs and poultry, sow calabashes, etc. and are better provided for in every thing than the poorer white people with us."

Not only did slaves improve their diet by cultivating their own plots, but they also sold any surplus for needed clothing or personal articles. Slaves marketed rice, corn, potatoes, and even tobacco. In the case of tobacco, however, the General Assembly in 1774 prohibited slaves from growing tobacco for their "own benefit" in Bute, Chatham, Edgecombe, Granville, Halifax, Northampton, Orange, and Wake counties. Brickell asserted that blacks used the earned money to "buy Hats, and other Necessaries for themselves, as *Linnen, Bracelets, Ribbons*, and several other Toys for their Wives and Mistresses."

Brickell's observation suggests the ways in which blacks struggled to provide for their families. In the eighteenth century, the imbalance in the number of male and female slaves was wide enough that in the colony's eastern region as many as 39 percent of the slaves could not form marriages on their plantations. Percentages ranged as high as 62 in western counties. Although slaves probably found spouses on other plantations, the competition for wives could be fierce. Brickell said black males were "Jealously inclined, and fight most desperately amongst themselves when they Rival each other, which they commonly do."

Brickell stated further that slave marriages were "generally performed amongst themselves, there being very little ceremony used upon that Head; for the Man makes the Woman a Present, such as a *Brass Ring* or some other Toy, which if she accepts of, becomes his Wife. . . ." Slave marriages were precarious, however. "It frequently happens," Brickell related, "when these Women have no Children by the first Husband, after being a Year or two cohabiting together, the Planters oblige them to take a second, third, fourth, fifth or more Husbands or Bedfellows, a fruitful Woman amongst them being very much valued by the Planters, and a numerous Issue esteemed the greatest Riches in this Country."

A child's status followed that of the mother, so letting a female slave form a marriage with a slave from another plantation could be to a master's advantage. It also extended the slave community and kinship patterns beyond the immediate plantation. Women tended to have their first children before the age of nineteen. Naming patterns among slaves showed strong family ties, with slaves named for fathers, grandfathers, aunts, and uncles.

Slave women rarely received preferential treatment. Their labor was considered as valuable as men's, and the colony levied a tax on masters for female slaves, whereas white women were not taxable. Black women wore "a coarse Kind of Cloth wrapped around their Waists unless they are very small," Ebenezer Hazard observed in Edenton in 1777. He also "Saw a Number of negro Children of both Sexes, stark naked . . . ; they have never been clothed yet. . . ." A British traveler during the 1780s declared: "The female slaves fare, labour, and repose, just in the same manner; even when they breed, which is generally every two or three years, they seldom lose more than a week's work thereby, either in the delivery, or suckling the child."

The property value of slaves remained uppermost in the minds of masters. When Richard Bennehan of Orange County listed thirty-one slaves for tax purposes in August 1778, he also noted their names, ages, and approximate value. For example, Arthur was listed as being between thirty-five and forty years of age and worth £400. Bennehan had purchased Arthur, the slave's wife Phebe ("a Small Wench" about twenty-five years of age), and their daughter Lucy (about three years old) in July 1777, for £250. In the tax listing Phebe was valued at £350. Esther was described as "a Wench about 50 years Old done Breeding"; Bennehan estimated her worth at £250. Nanny (£200) was characterized as "about 30 Sickly & Infirm[;] never had a child." Two infants, each termed "a Sucking child," were not assigned a monetary value. Aggy, on the other hand, was valued at £350; she was about thirty, "Supposed to be done Breeding," and her youngest child was about ten or eleven. In all Bennehan owned 7 males aged sixteen or older, 10 males under the age of thirteen or fourteen, 7 females aged twenty and over, and 7 females under the age of ten or eleven.

Any change in the planter family's life cycle usually affected slave families. Marriage, death, or migration posed the greatest threat to a slave family's stability. Older children and unmarried young adults were especially vulnerable to sale. Occasionally, masters sold slaves to keep black families together. In 1769 Edward Stabler and Richard Bennehan arranged the sale of a "Negro Boy" at £40 so that "he will be with his Relations." Two years later another Bennehan slave, Jack, asked a local planter to buy him because he feared Bennehan might "send him to some other part of the Country to be sold. . . ."

Unfortunately, the trade in African flesh did not accommodate the needs of slave families in most instances. The slave trade was most active during court weeks (usually quarterly) and the first day of each year, when slaves were hired out to other masters, ordinarily for a year. According to one account, Negroes were "driven in from [the] country like swine for market." Observing a slave auction in Wilmington, Johann David Schoepf reported: "A whole family, man, wife, and 3 children were hired out at 70 Pd. a year; and others singly, at 25, 30, 35 Pd., according to age, strength, capability, and usefulness." In the 1780s slaves sold for £120 to £180, or roughly five to six times their annual hire. Artisans brought a higher price, ranging as high as £250.

Slaveholders often tried to sell recalcitrant or sickly bondsmen. A New Bern slave owner in 1752 confessed he would have sold a "wench before this but for a sore on her leg; doctor says its noways bad. . . ." When the court met the following week, he hoped "to sell her as the Country People will be in

Town." During the auctions, Schoepf mused, the Negroes themselves contradicted "everything good that is said about them. . . ." They complained "of their age, longstanding misery or sickness" and warned purchasers not to sell "themselves in buying them . . . because they [the slaves] know well that the dearer their cost, the more work will be required of them."

The sale of black women especially offended Schoepf's sense of propriety. "If negresses are put up," he said, "scandalous and indecent questions and jests are permitted." Elkanah Watson, however, witnessed the ultimate family tragedy at Wilmington in 1778: "A wench clung to a little daughter, and implored, with the most agonizing supplication, that they might not be separated." The slaves were sold to different masters.

Blacks had few ways to defend the integrity of familial institutions, improve unconscionable living conditions, or resist the cruelties of an arbitrary master. Yet, blacks were not passive beings who stoically accepted punishment and benevolence with equanimity. Instead, they sought to carve out larger areas of freedom in their lives, undermine slaveholders' discipline, and develop a community life within the slave quarters.

Resistance to slavery took many forms. Malingering, insolence, carelessness, and dilatory behavior all artfully disguised patterns of slave discontent. Through such methods slaves could define the limits of their work, the hours they labored, and when and how they conducted their assigned duties. The task system in the low country almost certainly grew out of tensions between masters' expectations and slaves' unwillingness to perform merciless labor. Under the task system, slaves could quit work after completing so many assignments, for example, hoeing a specific number of rows. Thereafter slaves were free to tend their own gardens and livestock, fish, hunt, rest, or take care of their own families and homes. Slaves also had Sundays and Christmas to themselves.

The task system, the growing presence of Africans in the colonial population as the slave trade expanded, and the concentration of slaves in large units provided a basis for black autonomy and the survival of African culture. In the 1770s perhaps one-third of the slaves in North Carolina were of African origin. Language, religion, work patterns, naming of children, and much else reflected that African heritage. Recalling visits to Somerset Place, Josiah Collins's plantation on the shore of Lake Scuppernong in the Albemarle region, Dr. Edward Warren described the old "Guinea negroes" who had been imported from Africa before the turn of the nineteenth century. Those Africans retained many of the ideas and traditions of their

North Carolina slaves of the nineteenth century engaged in a colorful Christmastime celebration known as Jonkonnu, or "John Koonering." The custom is believed to have originated in the Caribbean island of Jamaica and to have spread to North Carolina sometime prior to 1824. North Carolina was virtually the only state in North America in which the ceremony flourished. This engraving depicts slaves giving a Jonkonnu performance in the Cape Fear region. From *Ladies' Home Journal* 9 (December 1891): 5.

native land. Dr. Warren detailed how "they still had faith in evil genii, charms, philters, metempsychosis, etc., and they habitually indulged in an infinitude of cabalistic rites and ceremonies, in which the gizzards of chickens, the livers of dogs, the heads of snakes and the tails of lizards played a mysterious but very conspicuous part."

Dr. Warren also observed a Christmas celebration known as "John Koonering." A slave leader, dressed in a costume of rags, animal skins, horns, and bells and accompanied by other slaves playing musical instruments or "gumba boxes," performed songs and dances for the master, who paid for the entertainment with coins. Warren claimed that in Egypt he had seen an "absolutely identical" performance by black Muslims.

Similarly, Janet Schaw witnessed a funeral with African overtones. "[T]he Negroes assembled to perform their part of the funeral rites," she recorded, "which they did by running, jumping, crying and various exercises. They are a noble troop, the best in all the country. . . ."

Other African carry-overs mystified whites. Conjurers or obeah men held great influence within the slave community. Skilled in the use of roots and herbs for medicinal purposes, obeah men could also make various poisons or manufacture antidotes. In the slave quarters obeah men healed the sick, comforted the sad, interpreted the unknown, and avenged the wronged. The 1779 trial of Bristoe, a Johnston County slave, revealed the conjurer's role in the black community. For the slave Jacob, Bristoe prepared a concoction "to make his master sell him." To a slave woman he gave a potion of milk to prevent her having children. For another slave who wanted his master to buy his wife, Bristoe poured brandy in a hole in the ground and gave the supplicant a root to chew. Befuddled, the court ordered thirty lashes for Bristoe.

Herbal medicines and poisons could constitute a form of slave rebelliousness. In 1780 the Johnston County court tried the slave Jenny for poisoning her master, Needham Bryan. Though she denied the charges, she was found guilty and burned at the stake. Another slave conjurer, Will, was brought before a Dobbs County court in 1769. Will was accused of making "some Liquid thing to drink" by which device he had sexual relations with a white woman "at different times." He threatened to kill her if she revealed the dalliance, but in time she gave birth to a mulatto child. According to one witness, Will had boasted that with his knowledge of herbs and roots "he could lye with the best of the Women" in the county.

Other acts of aggression or violence toward slaveholders brought swift and certain retribution. The Halifax County court in 1785 found the slave Peter guilty of murdering John Miller and Sarah Gold. He was hanged, his head cut off and placed on a pole, and his body burned. A Granville County slave charged with murder was burned at the stake in 1773. Five of Henry Ormond's slaves conspired to kill him in 1770. First they attempted to strangle the Beaufort County planter as he slept. When that failed, he begged "earnestly" for his life but was told he "must die." His "house wench, told him it was in vain, that as he had no mercy on them, he could expect none himself." They thereupon suffocated him between two feather beds. According to the *Virginia Gazette*, "The slaves have been tried, two wenches executed, and one burnt at a stake, one made his escape, and is not yet taken, the other who made the confession is saved."

Such frontal assaults on the institution of slavery, however, were relatively rare. Indirect measures not only were more common but also more successful. Perhaps the most prevalent form of resistance to slavery was theft. Slaveholders bemoaned the "indolence, thievery, and untruth" of their bondsmen, according to Johann David Schoepf. Janet Schaw described one planter's problems with slaves who "tore up his fences, carried off what they could eat and destroyed the rest." Schaw asserted: "They steal whatever they can come at and even intercept the cows and milk them. They are indeed the constant plague of their tyrants, whose severity or mildness is equally regarded by them in these Matters."

Slaves stole to keep alive and supplement the inadequate provisions supplied by masters. Moravians journeying up the northwest branch of the Cape Fear River in 1762 kept a vigil for stealthy slaves: "We slept at night under a tent made of blankets, the Brethren taking turns watching the boats, on account of the negroes, not indeed ours, for they were tired enough to sleep after the day's work, but those on all sides, who at night go about in small canoes, stealing where they can. Our watchfulness prevented them from annoying us." In Bertie County in 1793 Negro Sam was hanged for breaking into a smokehouse, stealing "a parcel of meat," and "presenting a gun" at a militia captain. Moravians blamed a runaway slave, who in 1767 had been at large for two years, for the chronic theft of food at Bethania and Bethabara.

Reports of slave criminality, however, can mislead and confuse. Blacks faced so many restraints that any transgression against white prerogatives could be construed as a crime. Bound for life, underfed, poorly clothed and housed, blacks expropriated food and other necessary items denied them by white society. Blacks could not retain or control the fruits of their labor, keep their family intact, or choose where and how they lived. In response to such privations, slaves often absconded. When slaves fled—"stole themselves"—the entire white community mobilized to capture the fugitives and restore slaveholders' pilfered human property.

Runaway slaves, more than most species of black discontent, alarmed white Carolinians because runaways imperiled whites' security and portended the possibility of revolt. As early as the 1680s blacks fled south to St. Augustine, Florida. Near the turn of the eighteenth century Thomas Pollock,

CRAVEN, *August* 1, 1777.

RUN AWAY

FROM the Subscriber in *May* last, a dark Mulatto Man Slave called BEN, a lusty well made Fellow, about 50 Years of Age, has had one of his Thighs broke, so that one Leg is much smaller than the other, his Knee is stiff, which causes him to halt very much in his Walk, is well known on *Pamplico* River, as he formerly belonged to one Mr. *Warwick*, of that Place. I have Reason to believe he is now lurking about that Neighbourhood, as some Applications have been made for the Purchase of him.

I will give a Reward of *Twenty Dollars* to any Person who apprehends the said Runaway, and delivers him at my House; or *Ten Dollars* to whoever secures him in any public Jail in this State, so that I get him again.

WILLIAM BRYAN.

N. B. The Gentleman who applied in my Absence to purchase *Ben*, not leaving his Name, obliges me to give an Answer to his Application in this public Manner: I will take 200 L. Proc. for him, and not less.
W. B.

CRAVEN, *August* 1, 1777.

RUN AWAY

FROM the Subscriber, living on *Clubfoot's* Creek, the 15th of *April* last, a Negro Slave named SAM, formerly the Property of *Henry Chew*, deceased, a stout well made Fellow, of a yellowish Complection, speaks with a hoarse Voice, and is near six Feet high; had on when he went away a homespun Coat the Colour of Nankeen, and homespun Check Shirt and Trousers. He is a Cooper by Trade, and perhaps may attempt to get to *Virginia* or *Maryland*, as he has Sisters and Brothers there. Whoever apprehends the said Slave, and brings him to me, if taken in this State shall have *Twenty Dollars*, and if out thereof *Thirty Dollars*.

LOVICK JONES.

CRAVEN, *August* 1, 1777.

RUN AWAY

FROM the Subscriber, living at the Head of *Clubfoot's* Creek, the 22d of *April* last, a Mulatto Slave named BEN, about 5 Feet 8 Inches high, has lost the little Toe off his right Foot, and has been seen about *Slocomb's* Creek. Whoever apprehends the said Fellow, and brings him to me, shall have *Twenty Dollars* if taken in this State, and *Thirty Dollars* if out thereof.
RICHARD LOVETT.

Runaway slaves represented a particularly vexing problem for slaveholders, who frequently resorted to newspapers to advertise offers of rewards for the return of their human property. These advertisements are for the return of slaves to their owners in Craven County. From *North Carolina Gazette* (New Bern), August 8, 1777.

a large landowner disquieted by the defection of two of his slaves, explained the dangers posed by runaways: "I must use my indeavors to have them catched iff possible least they should gather to a greater head and doe mischiefe on this shore which I have greatt reasons to suspect." If he did not apprehend the truants, more of his Negroes "might runaway and indanger" the colony.

During the eighteenth century North Carolina had a reputation as a haven for slave fugitives. The breakup of slave families in Virginia as white Virginians moved south into North Carolina inevitably compelled slaves left behind to try to reunite families. Of the recorded instances of slaves fleeing from Virginia before 1775, the number headed for North Carolina far exceeded the number headed for other destinations. Slave artisans from Virginia often melted into the Carolina economy by passing as free. For example, John Tayloe's Billy, aged thirty, in 1768 fled to North Carolina, where he "Travelled without much interruption" with a pass, likely forged. Billy, a violinist, was by principal occupation a ship's carpenter.

Fugitive slaves from Virginia and North Carolina turned the Great Dismal Swamp into a sanctuary. The swamp was an ideal hideout. According to a 1780s traveler, runaways were "perfectly safe, and with the greatest facility elude the most diligent search of their pursuers." Blacks had lived there "for twelve, twenty, or thirty years and upwards, subsisting themselves . . . upon corn, hogs, and fowls. . . ." The runaways cultivated small plots of land that were not subject to flooding but "perfectly impenetrable to any of the inhabitants of the country around. . . ." In 1777, during the Revolutionary War, another observer reported that the Dismal Swamp "was infested by concealed royalists, and runaway negroes, who could not be approached with safety. They often attacked travellers, and had recently murdered a Mr. Williams." One man was confronted by "fourteen naked negroes, armed with poles, [who] presented themselves in the attitude of hostility, across the road." The man escaped without injury.

Bands of runaways also harassed New Hanover County. In 1767 the county court ordered the sheriff to raise a posse of thirty men to pursue "upwards of Twenty run away Slaves in abody Arm'd. . . ." The court instructed the sheriff "to shoot Kill and destroy" all runaways who refused to surrender. In July 1788, Wilmington authorities recovered tobacco, beef, and other commodities stolen from a warehouse in town. The contraband had been concealed at Barnets [Barnards] Creek. "This place appeared to have been long a camp or asylum for runaway negroes," a Wilmington newspaper reported, "and probably was generally the repository for the goods which have been stolen in this town for some time past, by them and their confederates." The camp included more than an acre of cleared ground planted with corn; tools; cooking utensils; and other evidence of a permanent settlement.

The reasons why slaves fled were complex. Some desired freedom no matter what the risk. Urban areas in particular seemed to offer the opportunity for escape. Will Cathcart asked James Iredell in 1772 to watch for the "Negro wench Rose," who had "made an elopment." Cathcart believed she was headed for Edenton. Charles Pettigrew regretted that he had allowed the slave Pompey to visit Edenton. When Pompey defected, Pettigrew feared the slave had returned to town, where so many bondsmen found it easy to live anonymously or leave North Carolina. Other slaves sought to reunite families or simply could tolerate brutal treatment no longer. The slave Dick, hired out by the Blount family, ran off because "of very hard usage." Similarly, a "negro wench" sold by Thomas Blount tried to return "to where She was Raised" and to "call for her Husband. . . ."

Before the Revolution, Africans comprised perhaps half of the runaways. Shocked and bewildered by their enslavement, Africans defected at the earliest opportunity. They were the least acculturated slaves, still bearing the marks and scars of African rituals. Few could speak English. A runaway from Wilmington in 1775 was described as "a new Negro Fellow, by name Quamino . . . [who] has a Scar above his right Eye, his Teeth are filed, and [he] is marked with his Country Marks; had on when he went away, a Collar about his Neck with two prongs, marked G.P., and an iron on each Leg." A group of "Five newly imported Slaves" ran off from New Bern, though they were "incapable of uttering a word of *English*." The sheriff of Craven County left a remarkable glimpse of African runaways in the New Bern jail in 1767:

Two New Negro Men, the one named Joe, about 45 years of age, . . . much wrinkled in the face, speaks bad English. The other is a young fellow, . . . speaks better English than Joe, who he says is his father, has a large scar on the fleshy part of his left arm. . . . They have nothing with them but an old Negro cloth jacket, and an old blue sailors jacket without sleeves. Also . . . a Negro named Jack, about 23 years of age, . . . of a thin visage, blear eyed, . . . has six rings of his country marks around his neck, his ears full of holes.

Besides capture by whites, slave runaways faced additional dangers. John Brickell commented in the 1730s: "The *Negroes* sometimes make use of . . . Advantages in the Woods, where they will stay for Months together before they can be found out by their Masters, or any other Person; and great Numbers of them would act after the same manner (which would be detrimental to the Planters) were they not so much afraid of the *Indians*, who have such a natural aversion to the *Blacks*, that they commonly shoot them when ever they find them in the Woods or solitary parts of the country." Indians helped track down runaways and, according to Brickell, put blacks, when captured, through "the most exquisite Torments." Among the Cherokees a certain class of braves held the distinctive title "slave catcher."

At the height of the Stamp Act crises in 1765–1766, Revolutionary dissent and black unrest coincided to create an explosive situation in Charles Town. In what whites characterized as "thoughtless imitation" of white political protest, blacks began chanting "Liberty." The flight of numerous slaves to the swamps, however, could not be dismissed so easily. Whites feared a "dangerous Conspiracy and Insurrection." To quash black resistance, the South Carolina governor invited the Catawba Indians "to come down and hunt the Negroes. . . ." The runaways surrendered rather than "expose themselves to the attack of an Enemy so dreaded. . . ." When the Revolutionary crisis broke in Georgia in 1776, South Carolina and Georgia Whigs cold-bloodedly considered sending Creek Indians to Tybee Island to search for and kill runaway slaves who had taken refuge there.

For runaway slaves, then, the prospects of achieving permanent freedom were minimal. Far greater were the risks of capture, mutilation, whipping, irons and chains, or death. Yet slaves continued to flee. In general runaway slaves were disproportionately young adults between twenty and thirty-five years of age. Male field hands made up the vast majority of absentees. Artisans ran off in numbers roughly commensurate with their proportion of the overall slave population. The two groups most likely to flee were Africans and watermen. The latter knew the province's geography and had the best means of escape. Interestingly, a high incidence of Africans existed among watermen. Africans tended to flee in groups, but two-thirds of the runaways absconded alone. Finally, the most popular time for flight was harvest (September–November), followed by spring planting (February–April). Those seasons demanded the most intense labor and generally offered favorable conditions for escape. Thus, slaves chose shrewdly when to run.

Slave rebelliousness had a spiritual as well as secular side. Despite initial misgivings on the part of Carolina slaveholders about converting Africans, Christianity made slow but certain inroads into the slave community.

From early on, Anglican missionaries attempted to instruct slaves in the tenets of Christianity, but they confronted an apathetic, often hostile, class of slaveholders as well as a cultural chasm between Africans and Europeans.

In 1709 James Adams, an Anglican cleric, complained that planters would not permit the baptism of their slaves because of a "false notion that a Christian slave is by law free." Another Anglican minister in 1719 declared that Negroes in North Carolina were "sensible and civil and . . . inclined to Christianity and . . . would be converted, baptized, and saved, if their masters were not so wicked as they are, and did not oppose their conversion, baptism, and salvation, so much as they do." In 1730 the Crown finally instructed royal governor George Burrington "to find out the best means to facilitate & encourage the conversion of Negroes and Indians to the Christian religion."

The Associates of Dr. Bray, first established in 1723/24 and then recognized in 1729/30, helped spread Anglicanism to the peripheries of the British Empire. The Bray Associates concentrated on the conversion and education of blacks in the North American colonies. The associates opened only five schools—in Philadelphia, 1758; New York and Williamsburg, 1760; Newport, Rhode Island, 1762; and Fredericksburg, Virginia, 1765—but they made notable efforts in Edenton, Wilmington, and Bath.

Besides the opposition of slaveholders, blacks' lack of facility with the English language also proved a serious obstacle. Anglican clergy despaired about blacks' peculiar language, "a wild confused medley of Negro and corrupt English," which was largely unintelligible to all but those accustomed to hearing it. Slaves could repeat words, but they did not necessarily understand them. Writing to the Society for the Propagation of the Gospel in 1760, the Reverend James Reed summarized the frustrations of Anglican clergymen: "the greatest part of the negroes in the whole country, may to[o] justly be accounted heathens[;] 'tis impossible for ministers in such extensive counties, to instruct them in the principles of the Christian religion & their masters will not take the least pains to do it themselves. I baptize all those whose masters become sureties for them, but never baptize any negro infants or Children upon any other terms."

As ignorant of African religions as Africans were of Anglicanism, missionaries decried the native beliefs of slaves. Slaves from Guinea, for instance, were said to be "strongly prepossessed in favour of superstition and Idolatry."

The "unhappy prejudices of the people" and the resistance of planters, many of whom were unchurched themselves, impeded the missionaries' work. Terming the colony profoundly "poor and ignorant," the Reverend Daniel Earl of Edenton said that planters refused to "spare their Negroes from their Service at the Age that they [the Negroes] are susceptible of Erudition. . . ."

A few clerics, nonetheless, succeeded in their mission. Charles Cupples informed the Society for the Propagation of the Gospel in 1768 that in Bute County he had "baptized 382 children, 51 of which were negro children[;] the engagements for some were made by their Masters and Mistresses, and others had God fathers and God mothers of their own color as having been formerly baptized. . . ." In the late 1760s the Reverend John Barnett realized considerable success preaching to slaves in Brunswick and Northampton counties. A "great number of Negroes always attend with great seeming devotion," he asserted, "Of them I have baptized twelve Adults and eighteen of the Children. Several among them can read and having promised me to take pains to instruct such of their fellow Slaves as are desirous to learn I have given them many of the [Bray] Associates books." Through such networks within the black community, Christianity spread among slaves.

In 1768 Barnett asked the Bray Associates for a "parcel" of books to distribute to "Upwards of 150 Slaves" who had requested them. The following year the Associates sent him 215 books, which he dispensed "among those Negroes who can read a little; always giving preference to those who formerly composed part of my Black Congregations."

While Quakers and Presbyterians also made efforts to provide religious instruction for blacks and to teach them to read and write, conversion more frequently occurred through the oral transmission of culture. The Great Awakening of the 1730s and 1740s occasioned the first burst of religious enthusiasm that brought many slaves to Christianity. Evangelists such as George Whitefield exhorted blacks as well as whites to accept Christ. The equalitarian implications of the revivalists' message disconcerted many whites who feared that conversion of slaves would lead to insurrection. In South Carolina, Hugh Bryan, a follower of Whitefield, predicted the fall of Charles Town in 1741–1742. Slaves, he argued, would be God's instrument to punish Carolina's godless gentry. On his plantation, Bryan organized great assemblies of Negroes, who heard evangelical Protestantism's emotional message of equality, guilt, suffering, and ecstatic release.

Baptists and Methodists proved the most successful in conveying this message to blacks. Both denominations conducted services in a democratic atmosphere. Members called each other brothers and sisters, emphasized fellowship, and shunned the rank and deference of the Anglican Church. In its fledgling years the Methodists even espoused abolitionism. John Wesley, the founder of Methodism, denounced slavery as an evil institution, and Methodist preachers were instructed to approach Negroes and whites on a basis of religious equality. Between 1782 and 1790 the number of Methodists in North Carolina grew to more than 8,000 whites and nearly 1,800 blacks. In 1785 Tar Heel Methodists even considered forcing slaveholders to manumit their slaves as a condition of membership.

Before the War of 1812, Negroes—slave and free—made up about one-third of the Methodists in North Carolina. By the early nineteenth century separate African churches had been established in Wilmington, New Bern, Fayetteville, and Edenton. Henry Evans, a free black shoemaker, is credited with starting the Methodist Church in Fayetteville during the 1790s.

The Methodists' antislavery message, however, failed to persuade slaveholders. Itinerant preacher Francis Asbury chastised masters who refused to allow their slaves to attend services, and near the New River in 1802 he lamented: "It was not agreeable to me to see nearly a hundred slaves standing outside and peeping in at the door, whilst the house was half empty: they were not worthy to come in because they were black!"

Baptist fellowship proved just as insidious as the Methodists' audacious support of abolitionism. The Baptists permitted slaves to participate fully in worship. Writing from Brunswick Town in 1766, Anglican minister John Barnett found the Baptists' religious equality shocking: "New light baptists are very numerous in the southern parts of this parish—The most illiterate among them are their Teachers[;] even Negroes speak in their Meetings." Whereas Anglicans and Presbyterians insisted on an educated clergy, Baptists accepted preachers—black and white—who were moved by the spirit. A "poor African" expressed the Baptist position best when he observed, "I perceive . . . that there are many *learned* fools." In Virginia at least two biracial Baptist congregations chose blacks as their preachers in the 1780s and 1790s.

The Baptists inculcated slaves with strict Calvinistic values. Testimonies, baptism, and disciplining of whites and blacks took place in common. When black members moved, they received letters of dismissal from their congregation so as to be placed in another Baptist church.

Especially sensitive to the plight of slave families, Baptists proscribed adultery among blacks as vigorously as that among whites. In 1792 the

Sandy Creek Baptist Association in Franklin County "excommunicated" the slaves Hester and Isam "for living in the sin of Adultery." To stabilize slave marriages, one Baptist church announced in 1778 that "the marriage of servants . . . before God" was legitimate despite legal prohibitions. Any master who broke the marriage of slaves could be expelled from membership. Slaveholders were also instructed to permit slaves to attend worship. Another Baptist association determined that slaveholders had a "moral obligation" to keep slave families together, even if it meant "some inconvenience." In the end, however, even the Baptists could not assure the fidelity of slave marriages. When one Baptist congregation insisted that "no member of color . . . cohabit with any person as a wife or husband until they have . . . made mutual vows of constancy," it also acknowledged that "removal" as well as "death" could bring an abrupt end to the marriage.

Ultimately, evangelical Protestantism was the catalyst for the conversion of the entire South—black as well as white. The Second Great Awakening of 1801 to 1805 inspired great social and religious gatherings. People prayed, sang, shouted, and cried together. The experience loosened the slaves' bonds as revivalism challenged the region's social, racial, and religious hierarchy. But within the white community spiritual equality fostered tensions. Slaveholders became increasingly uneasy about the interracial revivals. Indeed, religious egalitarianism promoted slave unrest.

As early as the 1760s slaveholders grumbled that Negroes had "grown so much worse" from imbibing New Light Baptist teachings. Notices for runaway slaves in the 1760s and 1770s mentioned black Baptists who "pretend[ed] to be very religious" and Negro preachers who claimed "to know something of religious matters. . . ." On the eve of the War for Independence, as whites prepared to make a political revolution, the seeds of a spiritual revolution within the black community had already been sown.

III

The Revolution and Its Aftermath

The white movement for independence from Great Britain spawned deep tensions within colonial society. While the conflict between Whigs and Loyalists has received considerable attention, the story of how blacks influenced military and political decisions and took advantage of the revolutionary situation remains less familiar. Blacks fought for both sides, provided significant manpower to the British and American armies, and initiated steps to achieve their freedom. Such aggressive behavior by blacks shook southern society to its foundations. When the war ended, tensions between the races did not subside quickly. Instead, postwar adjustment to black agitation for freedom proved almost as unsettling and dangerous as the war.

Even before the war started, British authorities and Revolutionary leaders recognized how vulnerable to military attack the South would be with its large slave population. In 1773 one British observer commented: "The Southern Provinces may be entirely thrown out of the Question, not only as being thinly peopled & enervated, But from the great Majority of Negroes intermixed, which exposes them to immediate ruin whenever we detach a small Corps to support an Insurrection." Southern revolutionaries shared the same view. Late in 1774 James Madison, beginning his political career in Orange County, Virginia, reported an alarming incident: "If America & Britain should come to a hostile rupture I am afraid an Insurrection among the slaves may and will be promoted. In one of our Counties lately a few of those unhappy wretches met together and chose a leader who was to conduct them when English troops should arrive— which they foolishly thought would be very soon and that by revolting to them they should be rewarded with their freedom." This incipient slave rebellion was quelled, but it portended future crises.

Despite the evidence of such black aspirations for freedom, revolutionaries continued to accuse the British of fomenting a social upheaval.

Joseph Hewes, a North Carolina delegate to the Continental Congress, asserted in the summer of 1775 that the British intended "to let loose Indians on our Frontiers, [and] to raise the Negroes against us. . . ." Reviewing the causes of the Revolution in June 1776, James Iredell castigated Britain's "diabolical purpose of exciting our own Domestics (Domestics they forced on us) to cut our throats, and involve Men, Women and Children in one universal Massacre. . . ."

In 1774 the North Carolina Provincial Congress took the dramatic step of barring the importation of slaves "from any part of the world." On two occasions the Wilmington Committee of Safety ordered Negroes from the West Indies to be reshipped. Since newly imported slaves tended to run off, Carolina slaveholders hoped to avoid compounding an already unstable situation with troublesome newcomers.

By the spring of 1775 rumors of an imminent slave revolt enveloped the South. Writing from Edenton in May, Robert Smith declared: "We have to add to our misfortunes a report that the Negroes mean to take advantage of the times, which there is too much reason in some places to believe is the case. . . ." A guard of eight men had patrolled the town each night for the past two weeks. In the country, Smith said, "the same precaution is taking, every watch has a Capt. and all are well armed. . . ."

Meanwhile, in Wilmington the revolutionaries disarmed all the blacks in June 1775, to keep the "Negroes in order." Patrols monitored the town each evening, enforcing a 9 o'clock curfew. The committee of safety ordered all citizens, including "apprentices or servants," to take an oath of allegiance to the Revolutionary regime. In particular the Wilmington Whigs denounced royal governor Josiah Martin for "collecting men, provisions, warlike stores of every kind, spiriting up the back counties, & perhaps the Slaves. . . ."

The revolutionaries charged that John Collet, the British commander at Fort Johnston, "had given Encouragement to Negroes to Elope from their Masters & they promised to protect them." Janet Schaw, a Loyalist observer, scoffed at the revolutionaries' provocative claims. The revolutionaries, she insisted, had spread the story that the British had promised "every Negro that would murder his Master and family that he should have his Master's plantation. This last Artifice they may pay for, as the Negroes have got it amongst them and believe it to be true. Tis ten to one they may try the experiment. . . ."

The fears of Carolina slaveholders were not groundless. Governor Martin refused to rule out the idea of arming slaves. In June 1775, he wrote the Earl of Dartmouth: "Although Virginia and Maryland are both very populous, the Whites are greatly outnumbered by the Negroes, at least in the former; a circumstance that would facilitate exceedingly the Reduction of those Colonies who are very sensible of their Weakness arising from it." Then, an even more incriminating Martin letter fell into the hands of the Whigs. The royal governor denied that he had ever advocated a slave revolt except in the case of "the actual and declared rebellion of the King's subjects, and the failure of all other means to maintain the King's Government." The very circumstances Martin outlined had in fact transpired, for he was forced to flee New Bern and take refuge on a British ship off Cape Fear.

As Patriots, Tories, and Crown officials leveled charges and counter-charges against each other, slave leaders attentively watched the unfolding events of the Revolution. In every southern colony from Maryland to Georgia, slaves evaluated their chances for freedom and threatened revolt. Moreover, an effective oral network kept blacks informed. John Adams, learning about slave unrest in Georgia from congressional delegates in Philadelphia, acknowledged: "The negroes have a wonderful art of communicating intelligence among themselves; it will run several hundreds of miles in a week or fortnight."

Word of British intentions had clearly infiltrated Pitt County, where slaves planned to rise up in July 1775. The Pitt County Safety Committee discovered the plot just before the insurrection was to start. The committee ordered out patrollers with instructions to "shoot one or any number of Negroes who are armed and doth not willingly surrender their arms" and any party of four or more Negroes "who are off their Masters Plantations, and will not submit." The insurrection, originating in Beaufort County, was termed "a deep laid Horrid Tragick Plan laid for destroying the inhabitants of this province without respect of persons, age or sex." A posse of one hundred men apprehended the "suspected heads" of the plot and jailed more than forty blacks. A white sea captain and "Merrick, a negro man slave who formerly Belonged to Major Clark a Pilot at Okacock but now to Capt Nath Blinn of Bath Town," were identified as the leaders of the plot. Five Negroes were whipped, several of whom received "80 lashes each" and had their ears cropped.

The revolt was to commence on July 8 with slaves' destroying "the family where they lived" and then proceeding "from House to House (Burning as they went) until they arrived in Back Country where they were to be received with open arms by a number of Persons there appointed and armed by Government for their Protection, and as a further reward they were to be settled in a free government of their own." In "disarming the Negroes" the patrollers discovered "considerable ammunition." Janet Schaw's "hypothesis"—"that the Negroes will revolt"—had come true.

In Virginia royal governor John Murray, Earl of Dunmore, tried to capitalize on the restive slaves' hopes for liberty. When royal marines raided a printing office in Norfolk in September 1775, cheering blacks joined them. Dunmore conducted raids along the rivers and waterways surrounding Norfolk, plundering plantations and seizing Negroes. Then, on November 7, 1775, aboard the *William* in Norfolk harbor, Dunmore issued a shattering proclamation: "all indented servants, Negroes, or others (appertaining to Rebels,) [are] free, that are able and willing to bear arms, they joining His Majesty's Troops, as soon as may be, for the more speedily reducing the Colony to a proper sense of their duty, to His Majesty's crown and dignity." The Whigs' worst fears had been realized.

Reaction to Dunmore's declaration in the black communities was electric. Slaves rushed to Norfolk to fight for the British. The slave Charles defected, his master speculated, because he intended to join "lord Dunmore . . . from a determined resolution to get liberty. . . ." Three blacks boarded what they believed to be a British vessel and were "undeceived" only after they openly admitted "their resolution to spend the last drop of *their blood* in Lord *Dunmore*'s service."

The Virginia governor dubbed his recruits "Lord Dunmore's Ethiopian Regiment." Across the chest of each black was emblazoned "Liberty to Slaves." In the winter of 1775–1776, Dunmore had approximately 2,000 men under his command, one-half of whom were black. North Carolina dispatched to Norfolk Robert Howe, his Continental troops, and minutemen from Edenton. The Battle of Great Bridge near Norfolk in December 1775 quieted immediate fears of a servile insurrection in northeastern North Carolina. Nonetheless, North Carolina troops encountered a "guard of about 30 men, chiefly negroes," at one skirmish. According to a participant, "We killed one, burnt another in the house, and took two prisoners (all black). . . ." North Carolina Whigs believed the defeat of the "Negroes and Tories" thwarted "an avowed Intention to seduce the Slaves of that part of the Colony of Virginia, and the lower Parts of this Province, to revolt from their Masters."

Patriot claims that slave unrest had been quashed proved premature. The slaves' defection to the British continued unabated in 1776. Richard Bennehan, preparing to march to Cross Creek to subdue "Scotch men," that is, Loyalists, in February 1776, cautioned a business associate: "it is said negroes have some thoughts of Freedom. Pray make Scrub Sleep in the house every night & that the overseer keep in Tom." In April 1776, William Hooper declared to a friend: "The negroes are deserting from the Sea Coast to Gov' Martin. Three of mine were intercepted on their way and are now in Goal." Hooper said blacks had "burnt" one of his houses, and he expected to hear at any time his "property in Wilmington and at the Sound are in flames."

In May 1776, the colony's Fourth Provincial Congress appointed a committee "to enquire of ways and means the most probably to prevent the desertion of slaves." The committee recommended that all slaveholders "on the south side of Cape Fear River . . . remove such male slaves as are capable of bearing arms, or otherwise assisting the enemy, into the country, remote from the Sea. . . ."

The committee was responding to the flight of blacks to the British fleet, which dropped anchor off Cape Fear in early 1776. Capt. George Martin, under the command of Sir Henry Clinton, organized the Negroes into a company of Black Pioneers, support troops to relieve British soldiers of such onerous duties as building fortifications, laundering clothes, cooking, and managing the horses and wagons. The Negro unit furnished the British with valuable intelligence on the roads and waterways of North Carolina, South Carolina, and Georgia. For example, Morris knew the road as far as Cross Creek "and above that the road from Virg' to Charlestown." Thomas Payne had worked on the Wilmington ferry and knew the road as far northward as New Bern and as far southward as Georgia.

Not just the slaves of Whigs fled. A Loyalist lieutenant lost his slave London, a baker, who "joined the Kings Troops at Cape Fear in North Carolina, and inrolled in a Company of Black Pioneers . . . by which service the said Slave became intitled to his Freedom. . . ." John Provey, a free black, enlisted with the British in June 1776. Provey was a native of North Carolina who left "all his Property behind him" when he became a Black Pioneer. Serving "until the End of the War," Provey listed among his losses a "small dwelling House," two horses, a small field of Indian corn and potatoes, a dozen fowl, a dozen ducks, and a bed and household furniture.

The admiralty muster rolls of ships stationed off Cape Fear in 1776 frequently listed names of Negroes who "deserted from the Rebels" or "fled for Protection." The HMS *Scorpion* reported thirty-six defectors on March 3, 1776. Of this number at least eleven and probably twelve were women. Fifteen members of the group, including one woman, joined Sir Peter Parker's fleet on May 21 for service in the Royal Navy.

When the British offensive in the South stalled with the revolutionaries' victory at Charles Town in June 1776, the withdrawal of the royal fleet temporarily ended the defection of slaves along the coast. Ever resourceful, blacks swallowed their impatience and awaited more propitious opportunities to strike for freedom. Meanwhile, Revolutionary leaders, realizing the potential reservoir of manpower blacks represented to both sides, considered ways of employing black sinew and muscle.

Early in the Revolutionary conflict the Continental Congress and certain officers in the army decided against using slaves and free blacks. But after Dunmore's proclamation, Gen. George Washington moved to enlist free blacks to forestall their joining the British. After black soldiers performed bravely at Bunker Hill and in other opening battles, Congress reversed its decision to bar black troops. However, southern states, especially South Carolina, resisted efforts to arm Negroes. Only Maryland authorized slave enlistments and included free blacks in the draft, but many free blacks joined the army or navy in Virginia, North Carolina, Massachusetts, Delaware, and Connecticut. Perhaps as many as three-fourths of Rhode Island's Continental troops included slaves who had been offered freedom for their service. In some cases slaves served as substitutes for their masters.

Although plans for organized black regiments ultimately failed, hundreds of Negroes bore arms for the Patriots. At White Plains, New York, in August 1778, a "return of all the negroes in the several Regiments" (755 blacks scattered among fourteen brigades) revealed the presence of fifty-eight Negroes in the North Carolina Continental Line. Most of them were probably free blacks. One exception to this pattern was Ned Griffen, "a man of mixed blood," who won his freedom by substituting for his master. William Kitchen, a soldier in the North Carolina Brigade, deserted shortly before the Battle of Guilford Courthouse in 1781. To avoid returning to service, Kitchen promised freedom to his slave Ned Griffen if the latter went in his place. At the end of the war, however, when Griffen was discharged, Kitchen reneged on his pledge and sold Griffen to a slave owner in Edgecombe County. Griffen petitioned the General Assembly, which in 1784 freed him "forever hereafter."

Although white and black soldiers suffered the same privations of military life, blacks were more likely to perform menial labor or to practice specific skills. Black military laborers built fortifications, crafted weapons, made munitions, cleared roads, and shoed horses. Others served as spies, guides, musicians, or servants to white officers. David Burnet was a "war soldier in Blount's Company, and his waiter sometime"; Burnet enlisted in the Fifth Regiment in 1776 but probably died at Valley Forge in 1778. David Ivey joined the Tenth Regiment in 1777, lived through Valley Forge, and served first as a drummer and then wagoner before his discharge in 1783. Undoubtedly, North Carolina's most famous black soldier was John Chavis. Originally an indentured servant for a Halifax attorney, Chavis enlisted in the Fifth Virginia Regiment in 1778 and served for three years. He later gained fame as a Presbyterian minister and teacher of both black and white pupils in Raleigh. In 1832 he wrote Senator Willie P. Mangum: "Tell them that if I am Black I am free born American & a revolutionary soldier & therefore ought not be thrown intirely out of the scale of notice."

North Carolina blacks also served in the naval forces. The slave James of Perquimans County made "Several Voyages from This State & Virginia" during the war. Twice the British captured him, but he "Embraced the Earliest Opportunity in Making his Escape to Return to this Country." Because he had served on an "American Armed Vessel," the county court granted him his freedom.

The Revolutionary regime often impressed slaves into service. Under the North Carolina confiscation acts of 1777 and 1779, the Whigs seized the property of Loyalists, including slaves. A 1780 law admitted that such seizures often occurred with "violence and barbarity" and under "pretence." Confiscated slaves had been sent "to distant parts"; others were sold "in violation of law and justice." Some of the confiscated blacks were put to work at the ironworks in Chatham County for the "public" benefit. When masters chose to hire out slaves to "the public service," the bondsmen sometimes used the opportunity to escape. John Walker of Wilmington lent five slaves to the deputy quartermaster to convey public stores from town at the approach of the British in 1781. The slaves completed the work but never returned to Walker.

To raise white troops for the Continental Line, the North Carolina legislature in 1780 offered "one prime slave between the age of fifteen and thirty years" to soldiers who signed up for three years. South Carolina proffered even greater inducements—three slaves for three years' service. James Madison deplored the use of slaves as bounties for recruits, arguing that it would be more "consonant to the principles of liberty" to emancipate the blacks and make soldiers of them. To the master class, however, protection of slavery remained a paramount goal of the Revolution. When Georgia and South Carolina slaveholders tried to sue for recovery of their confiscated slaves after the war, the North Carolina legislature swiftly passed laws affirming the titles to Negroes then held by North Carolinians.

In the triangular struggle among Patriots, Tories, and British, however, blacks refused to be mere pawns. They took decisive action to achieve their freedom. Given the Whigs' misgivings about arming them, the limited chances for earning freedom by fighting for the Patriot cause, and the brazen British efforts to encourage defection from masters with pledges of emancipation, land, and perhaps a country of their own, blacks most frequently looked to the king's troops as liberators.

Wherever the British marched, slaves followed. Writing John Hancock in 1777, Gen. Robert Howe fretted about defending the South: "how various and extensive the necessary lines of defence are, how numerous the black Domesticks who would undoubtedly flock in multitudes to the Banners of the Enemy whenever an opportunity offered. . . ." Howe knew from firsthand experience slaves' hidden partisanship. When the British burned Brunswick Town, one rumor held that Howe's slaves had helped torch the village.

Indeed, Dunmore's daring attempt to instigate a slave rebellion became official British policy. In June 1779, Sir Henry Clinton, commander of the British army in America, issued his Phillipsburgh Proclamation, in which he promised "to every NEGRO who shall desert the Rebel Standard, full security to follow within these Lines, any Occupation which he shall think proper." Later Clinton even recommended that the emancipated slaves be settled after the war on lands forfeited by the American rebels.

Blacks, however, did not need the sanction of British generals to flee. As Charles Stedman, Lord Cornwallis's commissary officer, stated in his history of the war, "The negroes in general followed the British army." Cornwallis's invasion of the Carolinas in 1780–1781 produced a mass defection of slaves. Cornwallis employed blacks in various "publick works" to support, maintain, and feed the army. In September 1780, he appointed John Cruden, a Loyalist merchant from Wilmington, "Commissioner of Sequestered Estates" for South Carolina and later North Carolina. Head-quartered in Charles Town, Cruden eventually had responsibility for more than 5,000 blacks on an estimated 400 Whig plantations. To supplement the British army's commissary in the South, Cruden used the runaway slaves to raise provisions on the confiscated plantations. In Charles Town, Cruden utilized Negroes in the Engineer's Department, Quartermater General's Department, Barrack Master's Department, Commissary of Prisoners, Artificers, Drivers, Laborers, and General Hospital (as nurses).

Stedman operated several mills with 120 blacks, a sergeant, one cooper, and four overseers. Cornwallis, meanwhile, let blacks forage for the army as it marched through the Carolinas. To maintain discipline, Cornwallis ordered each regiment or department to mark "all Negroes belonging to the Army" and to flog those not wearing proper insignia. He also enjoined officers "to Execute on the Spot any Negro Who is found quitting the Line of March in search of plunder."

The line between plundering and foraging, however, proved difficult to enforce. At Salisbury in February 1781, Cornwallis denounced "the Excesses Committed by the Troops. . . ." He had received "Great Complaints . . . of Negroes Stragling from the Line of March, plundrg & Using Violence to the Inhabitants. . . ." The British general insisted that "no Negroe . . . be Suffred to Carry Arms on any pretence" and demanded an end to the "Shamefull Marauding" and "Scandalous Crimes." Still, he never ceased using blacks as foragers.

Black Carolinians carefully monitored the progress of the British army to calculate the appropriate moment to revolt or run. A slave plot in Rowan County revealed the internal debate occurring in the black community. Although the exact date of the plot is unknown, the fall and winter of 1780–1781 appear likely because Rowan was directly in the path of Cornwallis's march. Slaves interrogated by court authorities admitted that talk of collecting "powder . . . in order to Kill white people" had begun as early as "harvest" time. One slave had told another not "to be in a hurry to mary" because "War was Coming on" and blacks could then "have [their] choice of the white Girls for wives." This latter assertion, a common theme in all slave revolts, possibly reflected white guilt and fear projected on blacks, whose women whites abused and sexually exploited. The rebel slaves chose a Sunday meeting—probably a religious gathering—as the occasion for collecting weapons and perfecting plans. In the slaves' own words, blacks had to decide "which side" they were for—"the Americans or the British."

The British usually won blacks' allegiance. Rumors kept slaves in a state of readiness. Writing in January 1781, Jean Blair recorded: "The Negroes bring Strange storys. They say people are getting ready to run again and the English are to be in Edenton by Saturday." When Cornwallis approached, she lamented: "All my Brothers Negroes at Booth except two fellows are determined to go to them, even old Affra. W[hitmel] Hill lost twenty in two nights." As Cornwallis pushed northward from Wilmington to Virginia, Blair reported that everybody in Edenton was marching out "to surprise six hundred Negroes who were sent out by L Cornwallis to plunder and get provisions. It is said they have no Arms but what they find in the houses they plunder. When they applyed for arms they were told they had no occasion for any as they were not to go any place where any number of Rebels were collected. It is said there are two thousand of them out in different Partys."

When the British evacuated Wilmington in November 1781, slaves faced a troubling decision. Some chose to escape with the British; others remained with their masters. William Hooper lost three slaves to the British. A fourth, Lavinia, "went on board the fleet . . . and much against her will was forced ashore by some of my friends, and returned to me." Lavinia's brother John, however, resisted British bribes, Hooper said. They offered him everything "to attach him to the service of the British," including clothes, money, and his freedom. John "pretended to acquiesce" but later deserted the redcoats, "stole through the British sentries, and without a pass, accompanied by a wench," traveled seventy miles in pursuit of the Hooper family. John's return gave the family "great joy."

Cornwallis's surrender at Yorktown in October 1781, left the Americans and British with a diplomatic puzzle respecting the disposition of thousands of black refugees. Slaveholders, Revolutionary governors, and American military leaders tried to block the mass evacuation of Negroes from the continent, but to no avail. Perhaps as many as 5,000 blacks sailed with the British from Charles Town late in 1782, their destinations Jamaica, St. Augustine, New York, London, and Halifax, Nova Scotia. Not every black, to be sure, was free. Some slaves accompanied white Loyalists. In other instances, British officers claimed Negroes as their own property. But, as one British general in Charles Town commented, "the slaves are exceeding unwilling to return to hard labour, and severe punishment from their former masters. . . ."

In New York, Sir Guy Carleton, commander in chief of the British army, determined, much to Washington's chagrin, that any Negroes with the British army before November 30, 1782, should be considered free. Despite the provisional peace treaty that prohibited the British from carrying away "any Negroes or other Property," American slaveholders were unable to reclaim their human chattels. Carleton's ruling calmed black anxieties about reenslavement. Boston King, a black Baptist preacher, recalled: "This dreadful rumour [reenslavement] filled us with inexpressible anguish and terror, especially when we saw our old masters, coming from Virginia, North-Carolina, and other parts, and seizing upon their slaves in the streets of New-York, or even dragging them out of their beds." In the end more than 3,000 blacks evacuated New York.

British promises of a black nation for insurgent slaves did not materialize immediately, and even then not every black defector shared in the dream.

Thomas Peters, a slave from the Lower Cape Fear region, joined the British army in 1776 and served as a sergeant in the Black Pioneers. When the British evacuated New York in 1783, Peters accompanied them to Nova Scotia, where he became a leader of disgruntled black Loyalists. The black exiles were disappointed that they did not receive the land grants or fair treatment the British had promised. Acting as a spokesman for more than one hundred black families in Canada, Peters negotiated with British authorities in London. The British agreed to settle some 1,200 black Loyalists in Sierra Leone, grant them their own government and equality as British subjects, and abolish slavery. The black émigrés formed the nucleus of a modern African state that to this day traces part of its heritage to Afro-American Loyalists.

The disruptions of the Revolutionary War left the social arrangements of southern life in serious disarray. Hundreds of bondsmen had been lost to the British. Other slaves earned their freedom or attempted to pass as free. To rebuild their plantations, slaveholders moved quickly to import more blacks. After a four-year tax on imported slaves was repealed in 1790, the Negro population of North Carolina grew faster during the 1790s than in any other decade during the antebellum period. But the South's weakened social structure after the war made the region vulnerable to racial conflict. Free blacks, manumitted legally and illegally, multiplied. Slave unrest persisted, and humanitarian efforts to aid blacks perplexed many whites.

The confusion that dominated North Carolina's race relations in the 1780s and 1790s revealed itself in several ways. Plagued by an epidemic of illegal manumissions, North Carolina was the only state in the South in which emancipation was not a slaveholder's prerogative. The power still resided with the county courts, and laws passed in 1788 and 1796 upheld that provision.

Quakers in particular contributed to the lawmakers' consternation. In 1776 North Carolina Quakers declared that "Keeping our fellow men in Bondage is inconsistent with the Law of righteousness" and further stated "that all the members . . . who hold slaves be earnestly and affectionately advised to Cleanse their Hands of them as soon as they possibly can. . . ." Within the first year of this ruling Friends liberated more than forty slaves. The General Assembly reacted angrily. In 1777 it enacted a law "to prevent domestic Insurrections" and denounced the "evil and pernicious Practice of freeing Slaves in this State, [which] ought at this alarming and critical Time to be guarded against. . . ." Any slaves freed contrary to the law were to be apprehended and auctioned off by county sheriffs.

The Quakers protested vehemently. In a 1778 "Affirmation," Quakers named thirty-three slaves in Perquimans County and thirteen slaves in Pasquotank County who had been manumitted before the 1777 law was passed but who since had been reenslaved. The Quakers termed their arrest "unjust illegal & extrajudicial," "a gross infringement of the civil liberties of divers subjects . . . in positive violation of the Bill of rights" in the state constitution, which prohibited ex post facto laws. Unmoved, the legislature made only one exception in 1778. Those slaves illegally freed who had joined the army before enactment of the 1777 law could remain free. When the Friends petitioned the General Assembly in 1779 to repeal the offending statutes, a legislative committee responded bluntly that "the conduct of the said Quakers in setting their Slaves free, at a time when open and declared Enemies were endeavoring to bring out an Insurrection of the Slaves, was highly criminal and reprehensible. . . ."

Quaker agitation for manumission, nevertheless, continued during the last two decades of the eighteenth century. The Friends introduced numerous bills in the General Assembly calling for an end to the slave trade and the emancipation of all slaves. Quakers surreptitiously manumitted slaves and gave them the "full Benefit of their labour." In 1795 a grand jury in Pasquotank County censured Quakers for imperiling the state. It blamed Quakers for encouraging "the idea of emancipation" among slaves. The "Minds of the Slaves, are not only greatly corrupted and allienated from the Service of Their Masters," the grand jury asserted, ". . . But runaways are protected, harbored, and incouraged by them—Arsons are even committed, without a possibility of discovery." In a 1797 congressional debate Nathaniel Macon declared that he viewed the Quakers as warmakers rather than peacemakers, "as they were continually endeavoring in the Southern States to stir up insurrections amongst the negroes."

Typically, southern whites blamed religious dissenters and outside agitators for slave discontent. They remained purblind to the reality that slaves themselves might be the agents of their own liberation. The years between the Revolution and 1800 proved turbulent as restive blacks at home and abroad tested the boundaries of their enslavement. The great Negro insurrections of the West Indies, especially Saint-Dominque in 1791, set off alarms throughout the South, including North Carolina. Responding to those fears, the General Assembly in 1794 enacted a law that barred the importation of all slaves "by land or water." The law allowed an exception for any slaveholder who, under oath, pledged to use imported slaves only for his "own service." Slaveholders could not import slaves for "sale or traffic." The following year, when French refugees fleeing the racial wars of the Caribbean tried to land thirty or forty of their slaves in Wilmington, the lawmakers tightened restrictions further. In 1795 the General Assembly passed a law prohibiting the importation of slaves over the age of fifteen (the traditional age at which males began service in the militia) from the West Indies "or the French, Dutch or Spanish settlements on the southern coast of America. . . ." North Carolinians feared that the contagion of rebellion might spread from the Caribbean to the mainland.

A report from New Bern in 1792 declared: "The negroes in this town and neighborhood, have stirred a rumour of their having in contemplation to rise against their masters and to procure themselves their liberty; the inhabitants have been alarmed and keep a strict watch to prevent their procuring arms; should it become serious, . . . the worst that could befal[l] us, would be their setting the town on fire. It is very absurd of the blacks, to suppose they could accomplish their views. . . ."

In the summer of 1795 Wilmington was plagued by a "number of runaway Negroes, who in the daytime secrete themselves in the swamps and woods" and at night commit "various depredations on the neighboring plantations." Posses eventually killed five of the renegades, including their leader the "General of the Swamps," and captured and executed four others, but not before the rebel slaves killed one overseer and wounded another. Later that year Wilmington residents barred French refugees, escaping the conflagration in the Caribbean, from landing thirty or forty of their slaves because of fears that the West Indian blacks might incite a revolt. In 1798 Gov. Samuel Ashe issued a proclamation ordering citizens to prevent the landing of any blacks, slave or free, from the West Indies and to observe strictly the trade barrier imposed by the 1795 law.

The same year as the governor's proclamation, Bertie County authorities arrested three black men and charged them with heading a conspiracy of 150 slaves. Evidently, the blacks "did attack, pursue, knock down and lay prostrate the patrollers," but only a horse was injured. Instead of rebellion, the blacks were charged with a high misdemeanor against "the laws and dignity of the state," for which each received thirty-nine lashes and cropped ears.

Perhaps the most striking example of how the Revolution's ideology inspired black hopes of freedom was the case of Quillo, a Granville County slave owned by James Hunt. In April 1794, Quillo was accused of plotting an insurrection. According to slaves who testified, Quillo "intended to give a large treat at Craggs Branch to the black people" during which an "election" would be held for slaves to choose burgesses, justices of the peace, and sheriffs "in order to have equal Justice distributed so that a weak person might collect his debts, as well as a strong one. . . ." After the election Quillo and his associates planned to link up with Negro insurrectionists marching from Person County. The slave legions would then "force their way wherever they choosed, and . . . murder all who stood in their way or opposed them."

Quillo's shadow government of elected representatives, talk of "equal Justice," and apparent attempt to revolt and establish a free colony of blacks plainly disconcerted whites, but a much more serious challenge to the social order occurred in 1802. A slave insurrection scare swept the northeastern counties of North Carolina. In many respects it culminated several decades of social and political conflict. The conspiracy came in the midst of the Second Great Awakening, in which evangelical Protestantism promoted a sense of equal worth and fellowship among blacks and whites. The white backlash against initiatives for emancipation and the reenslavement of scores of freed blacks frustrated slaves' hopes for freedom. Slave unrest during the 1790s heightened tensions between the black and white communities. And finally, North Carolina slaves had a model for revolt closer to home than the West Indies. In 1800 Gabriel Prosser, a blacksmith, had led an unsuccessful slave rebellion in Richmond, Virginia.

The North Carolina plot encompassed primarily those counties through which the Roanoke River flows and those bordering the Albemarle Sound. The waterways allowed the black conspirators to transmit information and pass written messages among literate slaves. Indeed, the conspiracy may have reached all the way into Virginia. Virginia too experienced a slave insurrection scare in the spring of 1802, and the plots may have been linked. In February 1802, former governor William R. Davie of Halifax County warned Gov. Benjamin Williams of a possible plot originating in Southampton County, Virginia—ironically the scene of Nat Turner's bloody rebellion three decades later. Davie reported that a printed circular letter had been found addressed to the "Representative of the Roanoak Company." The letter said that once the "conflagration" began, whites would "acknowledge liberty and equality" and "purchase their lives at any price." Whites must learn that "the breath of liberty is as free for us as for themselves." Davie compared the situation to Saint-Dominque, where "the whole Colony" had been stained by the slaughter of several thousand whites.

No certain evidence of a slave conspiracy was found, however, until June 2, 1802, when patrollers near Colerain in Bertie County discovered a letter that began: "*Captain Frank Sumner is to command* (and then names of the men, and the 10th of June was the time) *you are to get as many men as you can—To Capt. King, Brown, &c.*" The Bertie County court convened on June 10, the day the Negroes were to have risen. Among the justices was United States senator David Stone, whose slave Bob was deeply implicated in the plot. With ruthless dispatch the Bertie court hanged eleven blacks, including Bob, deported six more who offered testimony, and whipped and cropped perhaps two dozen others.

As with most slave insurrection scares, white perceptions of Negro intentions, concerns, and objectives were confused but not necessarily exaggerated. Accumulated tensions, the example of Prosser's revolt, and intolerable grievances and frustrations clearly inflamed slaves. A few conspirators associated the plot with a class revolt, for they anticipated assistance from Tuscarora Indians and "a number of poor people (white which they expected would Join them)." Caesar, one of the "captains" of the cabal, told Moses that he foresaw "a Warm Winter, a dry Spring & a Bloody Summer, & that he expected the Negroes were going to Rise." Dave, another leader ultimately executed, declared he was "very tired & weary" because "the Damn'd White people plagued him so bad they ought all to be killed & shall . . . if he could get a great many to join him." An overseer's whipping of two Negroes at "a logg roling" outraged Peter, who himself had felt the overseer's lash. Peter swore he would kill the overseer and "all the rest." Sam told Harry "that them guns we heard was in Virginia & that the Negroes was then fighting the White people." Dave insisted the conspirators "could get encouragement from Virginia. The head negroes in Virginia lives about Richmond."

Religion also inspirited the conspirators, who used revival meetings and worship services to organize the revolt. In May 1802, the Pasquotank County court tried Dr. Joe, a slave preacher, for conspiring with Tom Copper "to Rebel and make insurrections." Copper was a black guerrilla with a camp hidden in the swamps near Elizabeth City. Copper staged the most daring raid of the rebellion when he attacked the Elizabeth City jail with "six stout negroes, mounted on horseback" to liberate slaves held there on charges of conspiracy. Four of the raiders were captured, but two escaped. Although Dr. Joe was found innocent of any complicity with Copper, the court ordered the preacher not to "Assemble or hold any Meeting, Congregation or other Assembly of Slaves or other people of Colour upon or under any pretence Whatsoever."

Other black insurgents, nevertheless, used religious meetings to prepare for the uprising. A Baptist elder gave his slave Virginia permission "to hold a night Meeting on Monday night," that is, a religious service, at which plans for the revolt were discussed. The slave Moses confessed that "Joe preached with a pistol in his pocket." Another slave had noticed several conspirators "talking low" and "while at preaching saw [a] number of Negroes standing talking two & two during the sermon." The date of the uprising, June 10, 1802, had been chosen to coincide with the quarterly meetings of several Kehukee Baptist associations, when whites would be most vulnerable.

As reconstructed by white interrogators, the blacks had cached guns and ammunition in the swamps and fashioned other weapons such as clubs with nails driven through them. On the night of the revolt the insurgents were to form into companies under their captains, "go to every man's house, set fire to it, kill the men and boys over 6 or 7 years of age; the women over a certain age, both black and white were to share the same fate; the young and handsome of the whites they were to keep for themselves, and the young ones of their own colour were to be spared for waiters."

This white fantasy of Negro sexual aggressiveness contradicted the role black women played in the plot. It seems unlikely that they would have organized meetings and passed messages for the purpose of their own extermination or reenslavement. Guilt-ridden whites imputed to blacks their own secret desires, values, and view of the social order. Thus, in a world turned upside down, blacks became masters, taking white wives, dividing up lands among themselves, and keeping slaves. Even so, it is entirely plausible that rebel slaves hoped to acquire their own lands and create a free society for themselves. Slaves who fled to the British during the Revolution, coaxed by promises of freedom and land, shared a vision compatible with the aims of the 1802 insurrectionists. White hysteria simply failed to distinguish between black longings for liberty and whites' misinterpretation of black motivations. That hysteria generated dissonant responses. As one dispassionate observer noted, some people credited the wildest reports of slave insurgency; others dismissed the most sober evidence.

The fear that gripped eastern North Carolina resulted in the execution of two dozen slaves and the punishment of scores of others. In Martin County alone more than one hundred Negroes were jailed. Only two were hanged, but the others "received a very severe reprimand, and were made sensible to the folly and danger of their attempt; after which every one was chastised, more or less, according to his previous bad or good conduct, and ordered home."

Still, the 1802 slave insurrection scare revealed a strong collective consciousness among blacks. During the quarter century between the outbreak of the Revolution and the turn of the nineteenth century, the political, spiritual, and intellectual revolutions under way made deep and lasting impressions on blacks. Whereas runaway slaves and small bands of insurgents sought to withdraw from society before the Revolution, by 1800 slaves wanted to join society and share in the blessings of American freedom. This revolutionary process caused profound repercussions throughout southern society and intensified conflict between whites and blacks. Though the brutal subjugation of rebellious slaves in 1802 had temporarily turned aside Negro agitation for liberty, whites by no means had extinguished the silent rage for freedom that burned fiercely within the black community.

IV

Nineteenth-Century Slavery

The silent rage for freedom had to burn quietly within black North Carolinians for three more generations. The antebellum period brought suffering before it produced deliverance; before jubilation there were days of deeper despair. For slavery expanded greatly in America between 1800 and 1860, and as it grew it deepened its hold on southern society. In North Carolina the restrictions of the law gripped blacks more tightly as slavery's final crisis—the Civil War—approached.

Changes in the law reduced free black people to a status little different from slavery and made slavery ever more difficult to escape. "Little by little," historian Guion Griffis Johnson has written, "the Legislature stripped the free Negro of his personal liberties." In 1826 legislators passed a law prohibiting any free Negro from entering the state of North Carolina. Nine years later, in 1835, free blacks lost the right to vote, no matter how much property they might own. Other laws passed in the antebellum period denied free black people the right to preach in public, to possess a gun without a special license, to buy or sell liquor, or to attend any public school. Ultimately, in 1861, the General Assembly barred any black person from owning or controlling a slave, thus making it impossible for a free person of color, through hard work and thrift, to purchase freedom for wife, husband, or child.

For the slave, North Carolina's laws became more encompassing. In 1830 the General Assembly passed a law prohibiting anyone from teaching a slave to read or write. At the same time, manumission—already severely restricted in the Tar Heel State—became considerably more difficult. Previously, any master who wished to free one of his slaves had only to convince the county court to make that grant of freedom. The new law required in addition that the master give bond of $500 for aged or meritorious slaves who wanted to remain in the state; all others were compelled to leave North Carolina within ninety days "and never thereafter return."

State courts also granted wide "discretion" to the often violent patrollers, instructing juries not to "examine with the most scrupulous exactness into the size of the instrument, or the force with which it was used" against a slave unlucky enough to fall into the patrol's hands. Even murder did not move the state's jurists to protect the vulnerable slave. In one case the state supreme court declared that "the homicide of a slave may be extenuated by acts, which would not produce a legal provocation if done by a white person." In another well-known case, Chief Justice Thomas Ruffin had the temerity to state the logical principle that underlay the legal oppression of slaves. "The power of the master must be absolute," Ruffin wrote, "to render the submission of the slave perfect." Southern courts shrank from so blatant a denial of human rights, and North Carolina did not follow Ruffin's dictum thoroughly; but the legal position of blacks deteriorated substantially during the antebellum period.

One cause of this deterioration was the intensifying sectional crisis between North and South, but a more direct cause was the resistance and rebelliousness of black people themselves. The bloody uprising led by Nat Turner, who with his followers killed sixty whites in nearby Southampton County, Virginia, in 1831, spread fear and panic throughout white North Carolina. Mounted horsemen sped between towns in the eastern part of the state to confirm or disprove numerous rumors of slave uprisings. But Tar Heel whites, and southern slaveholders generally, were already on edge and fearful because of a vehement and powerful protest against American slavery by one of North Carolina's sons, David Walker.

Walker, born in Wilmington in 1785, was entitled to a birthright of freedom in the newly independent nation. His mother was a free black woman, and thus he also was free, since under the laws of slavery the status of children followed that of the mother. (Such laws guaranteed that the illicit offspring of slave owners became their property as well.) But his father was a slave, and the laws and conventions of a slave society soon became obnoxious to David Walker. Described as "prepossessing" in appearance, "being six feet in height, slender and well-proportioned" with "loose" hair and "dark" complexion, David Walker could not endure life in a slave-holding state. Impelled by his hatred of slavery, he left North Carolina, traveled through other southern states, and by 1827 had become established as a clothier in Boston.

There he composed a thundering attack on slavery known as David Walker's *Appeal*, published in 1829. Writing with the fire and authority of an Old Testament prophet, Walker denounced American slavery and all those, black or white, who supported or tolerated it. Appalled by the cruelty and injustice of slavery, he wrote out of a faith in God's justice and confidently predicted that the Lord would not suffer human bondage to continue much longer. Moreover, he called on all people of color to aspire to full freedom and to give their support to God's plan of deliverance.

Drawing upon biblical and historical comparisons, Walker argued that "we, (coloured people of these United States,) are the most degraded, wretched, and abject set of beings that ever lived since the world began." Any observers "who believe that God is a God of justice, will believe that SLAVERY *is the principal cause*," Walker continued. The slavery imposed by "the *white Christians of America*" was far worse than the bondage that existed in biblical or classical times. Not even the Egyptians "heaped the *insupportable insult* upon the children of Israel, by telling them that they were not of the *human family*." This American Democrats did after growing "fat on our blood and groans."

But God would not allow these wrongs to continue, Walker believed. "God will not suffer us, always to be oppressed. Our sufferings will come to an *end*," he wrote, "in spite of all the Americans this side of *eternity*." "I tell you Americans!" he warned, "that unless you speedily alter your course, *you and your Country are gone!!!!!!* For God Almighty will tear up the very face of the earth!!!" Walker alluded directly to the possibility of slave rebellion and urged slaves to fight like men, but he also prophetically observed that God might bring about "the destruction of the oppressors" in another way, "for not unfrequently will he cause them to rise up one against another, to be split and divided, . . . and to open hostilities with sword in hand."

The *Appeal* also spoke eloquently against schemes of colonization, which enjoyed the support of many prominent white political leaders. David Walker discerned in the speeches of Henry Clay that one goal of the removal of free black people was to enable slaveholders to keep slaves "the more secure in ignorance and wretchedness." "Let no man of us budge one step," Walker counseled other blacks. "America is more our country, than it is the whites—we have enriched it with our *blood and tears*."

Making his own arrangements for distribution of the *Appeal* and using both the mails and cooperative individuals, David Walker succeeded in introducing his publication into many parts of the South, from Richmond to Savannah to New Orleans. In North Carolina copies appeared in

Fayetteville, Wilmington, Chapel Hill, New Bern, and Hillsborough. Predictably, the authorities reacted with fear and alarm, for the truths that Walker spoke could not coexist with the slave system. Within a year David Walker himself was dead, having died suddenly under suspicious circumstances, perhaps a victim of the tightening grasp of the powerful and defensive institution of slavery.

However much the *Appeal* had inspired or heartened North Carolina slaves, they had to live under a system they hated but could not remove. Bereft of power, they had to accommodate themselves to the reality of slavery. For in the American South objective facts militated against successful slave revolt, no matter how stubbornly slaves might resist and work against the system day by day. Of all the slaveholding regions of the Western Hemisphere, the South was the most extensive slave society and the one with the highest ratio of whites to blacks. It lacked impenetrable jungles and high mountain ranges in which rebels could hide securely. Slaves and free black people were constantly under white surveillance, and the organized power of patrols, the state militia, and the federal army were close at hand to suppress any uprising.

Thus, the inescapable tasks of most black North Carolinians were to endure bondage and live with oppression. In a hostile environment that was becoming more restrictive, a growing population of black men and women struggled and persevered. They shouldered slavery's burden and refused to be broken. They resisted innumerable daily wrongs, maintained their self-respect and resentment of injustice, and fashioned lives that encompassed as much as possible the joys of family, love, and hope. Those were not small accomplishments. For people in slavery, they were essential, hard-won victories.

Direct evidence of their success in surviving bondage was the substantial increase of the black population. The number of black people in North Carolina increased from 140,000 in 1800 to 361,522 in 1860. As a percentage of the total population, blacks also increased—from 29.3 percent in 1800 to 36.5 percent on the eve of the Civil War. The total black population would have been substantially larger but for the sale and removal of considerable numbers of men, women, and children to destinations outside North Carolina. Throughout the antebellum period the Cotton Kingdom to the south and west was expanding rapidly, and planters there were eager to buy slave labor. The comparatively stagnant economies of the upper South states, by contrast, had more workers than were actually needed. As a result, there were large interregional transfers of human property.

Between 1810 and 1820, for example, 137,000 slaves were sent from North Carolina and the Chesapeake states to Alabama, Mississippi, and other southwestern regions. This was one, but only one, of the causes of forced separation in slave families.

There were 30,463 free blacks in North Carolina's population in 1860, more than six times the number in 1790. These Tar Heels worked industriously to improve their position and gain all the benefits possible from freedom. The high goals and standards they set for their families often shone brightly through subsequent generations of accomplishment. Some individuals, such as the noted cabinetmaker Thomas Day of Caswell County or the well-known educator John Chavis of Raleigh, achieved wide recognition for their talents. A few amassed considerable property, even including slave property. But most free blacks were forced by the restrictive rules and mores of society to work hard for a living. The largest number were agricultural laborers who might toil in the fields beside slaves, but a sizable proportion lived in towns and followed skilled occupations.

Thomas Day, a free black of Caswell County, achieved renown for his skills as a cabinetmaker during the antebellum years. This rocking chair is an example of Day's craftsmanship. Photograph courtesy North Carolina Museum of History.

Whatever their status, or wherever in the state they lived, black North Carolinians generally performed the hard labor that built wealth. After the Revolution, large planters such as the Reverend Charles Pettigrew, who owned many acres in Washington and Bertie counties, made profits by sending timber, fish, and grains to the sugar plantations of the West Indies. Slaves grew the grain, felled the timber, and caught the fish that produced these profits. In later decades, although North Carolina never participated fully in the short-staple cotton boom, centers of cotton production arose in several eastern counties, notably Edgecombe. Rice plantations flourished in the southeastern corner of the state in Brunswick and New Hanover counties. In the 1850s, tobacco production grew rapidly in a line of counties along the North Carolina-Virginia border.

Slave labor was the basis of these prosperous operations. In fact, most opportunities for wealth in North Carolina required agricultural labor, whether one planted a staple crop or engaged in mixed farming and live-stock raising, as was the case with Paul Cameron, the state's largest slave owner. Thus, slaves were a vital asset. Even in mountain counties or in towns and urban areas, affluent whites prized slave property as an ever popular form of investment and as a source of labor that could be compelled to perform whatever tasks were necessary.

The nature of many of North Carolina's crops ensured that slaves' work would be hard. Cotton was a demanding, labor-intensive crop. After the seeds were planted in hills, constant attention was required to "chop" weeds out of the growing plants with a hoe. Because weeds were relentless without pesticides and sapped the vigor of the cotton plant, slaves spent many hours in hot, humid weather "chopping cotton." Then from late summer to fall, beginning in August and continuing into November, slaves picked cotton by hand, stooping down over each plant. As many as six pickings routinely took place because the cotton bolls did not ripen all at once, but gradually. Each picking required the back-breaking labor of plucking cotton out of the boll and stuffing it in a sack—usually until well over 100 pounds was collected.

Tobacco may have been even more demanding. Indeed, white farmers later called it the "thirteen month" crop because the many tasks in its production often were not completed before the next year's crop had begun to grow. First the tiny seeds were planted in beds and then trans-planted as young plants to the field. As tobacco plants grew, the slaves had to work constantly to "sucker" them and remove worms. They pinched off, or "suckered," the secondary stems or branches to ensure that the main leaves would develop fully. Slaves who missed the voracious worms were sure to encounter their master's wrath. Finally, when the leaves had matured, large and golden, slaves would begin to pick and pack the leaves carefully. As with cotton, more than one pass through the field was required to gather the gradually maturing crop.

Rice also had a reputation in the South as a difficult, arduous crop. Its cultivation required long hours of labor, with the workers bent over in flooded, swampy, and mosquito-infested fields. Slaves on rice plantations often worked under the "task system," which allowed each laborer to spend his time as he saw fit once the day's task was completed. Thus, slaves who grew rice often had the opportunity—rare among the enslaved—to control part of their time. Nevertheless, growing rice was never popular with free laborers (and proved difficult to reestablish after emancipation).

Even with mixed farming there was heavy labor to perform, and the nature of slavery made agricultural labor harder and far more unremitting than it was for free farmers. Most slave owners tried to get as much work as possible out of their slave labor force. Everyone except infants and the infirm had tasks to perform. Joe High, a former slave from Zebulon, North Carolina, remembered that as a young slave child he "kept chickens out of the garden" and "fanned flies off the table." Other young children toted water to the field workers, collected kindling for fires, or cleaned up the yard. Elderly slaves who lacked the strength to work in the field prepared food or did small tasks by hand. From the able-bodied much more was demanded.

Louisa Adams, who had been a slave in the town of Rockingham, recalled a schedule that was universal: "They waked us time the chicken crowed, and we went to work just as soon as we could see how to make a lick with a hoe." Field work continued until darkness fell, a routine known as working "from sun to sun." At the Warren County plantation on which Henry Bobbitt lived, slaves "worked seven days a week, from sunup to sundown six days, and from seven till three or four on a Sunday." Often slaves carried a light breakfast of cornbread or ashcake (cornmeal baked in the ashes of the fireplace) with them to their work and paused briefly to eat lunch in the fields.

After working all day, slaves had other tasks to perform at night before they could go to sleep. Generally the men had to feed, water, and tend to the livestock on the plantation or repair farming tools. The women usually had assignments related to the making of clothes. Jane Arrington of Nash County recalled that on her plantation there was "a task of cotton to be picked [removing the seeds] and spun" at night. "This was two ounces of cotton" for each slave, she reported. Little time remained for leisure after the evening meal was prepared and these tasks completed.

On some plantations work went on with little regard for weather. Sarah Gudger, who as a slave had lived near Asheville, recalled that her owner would "send us niggers out in any kind of weather, rain or snow, it never matter. . . . Many the time we come in with our clothes stuck to our poor old cold bodies, but 'twarn't no use to try to get'em dry. If the Old Boss or de Old Missie see us they yell: 'Get on out of here you black thing, and get your work out of the way.'" Sarah Gudger added that "we knowed to get," for the penalty of disobedience was "the lash."

Slave women labored in the fields beside men, for their gender brought them no exemption from heavy work. Slave owners generally expected women to pick fewer pounds of cotton or hoe fewer rows of corn, but the labor nevertheless was heavy and almost never done by white women. One former slave, Susan High of Wake County, reported that for her owner women had even "cleared land by rollin' logs into piles and pilin' brush in the new grounds."

Slave women joined their male counterparts in performing strenuous labor in the fields of their owners. This engraving depicts antebellum slave women picking cotton. Engraving from the files of the Office of Archives and History.

Compared to those heavy tasks, the work of house servants might seem highly desirable, and former slaves who had worked in the owner's house appreciated the fact that their physical labors had been lighter. But there were distinct disadvantages to house work as well. The house servants were always on call—at any time of day or night they might be ordered to perform some task. Moreover, house slaves had little privacy or time away from whites and were cut off from much of the regular contact with the fellow blacks on the plantation. These were substantial prices to pay for the advantages of house work.

Popular legends about slavery often suggest that there was a gulf between privileged house servants and common field slaves, with the former regarding themselves as far superior to the latter. But basic statistics and the tenor of the slave narratives suggest that social distinctions within the slave community were rather modest. Perhaps on Paul Cameron's vast plantations, where roughly one thousand slaves lived, it was possible for a small percentage of slaves to specialize in housework, associate only with other house servants, and become a class apart. But most slaveholdings in North Carolina were very different in scale. The typical slave owner in North Carolina in 1860 owned only one slave. Fifty-three percent of the state's slave owners held only five or fewer slaves, and in the total population of slaves a modest 2.6 percent lived on plantations with fifty or more slaves. These were not conditions in which rigid class distinctions among the slaves were likely to develop. Moreover, many house servants from small plantations reported that they also worked in the fields at busy times such as the harvest season.

What were the physical conditions of life for North Carolina's slaves? Housing was rudimentary, little more than minimal shelter. The slave cabins that have survived to the present were the most substantial and well built in existence during the slavery era. Most slaves got by with much less. Almost universally former slaves described small "log houses with stick an'

Slave cabins typically were crudely contructed log houses with dirt floors and window openings covered only with shutters. The structures offered minimum protection against the elements and frequently were dark, smoky, and crowded. Engraving from the files of the Office of Archives and History.

dirt chimneys." These cabins had dirt floors and window openings covered only with shutters; many former slaves recalled that the logs were poorly chinked and that the wind blew through cracks in the walls on cold winter days. Slave cabins were dark, smoky, and crowded, and the wattle-and-daub chimneys were a fire hazard. If the sticks in the chimney caught on fire, someone had to push the structure away from the house quickly before it too was in flames.

The slaves' food was monotonous, uninteresting, and possibly nutritionally deficient, although it appears that most masters tried to supply sufficient quantities of food. Southern slave owners generally distributed cornmeal and fat pork to their slaves each week, along with molasses and possibly a small amount of coffee. It was up to the slaves, if they were permitted, to supplement and improve on this diet. To make their dull diet more palatable, slaves invented kush, a spicy alternative to simple cornbread. "Kush was cornmeal, onions, red pepper, salt and grease, that is if we had any grease." The added flavor in kush caused former slaves to remember it fondly.

Far more important, nutritionally, were the efforts slaves made to improve their diet by hunting or fishing. "My old daddy partly raised his children on game," reported Louisa Adams. "He caught rabbits, coons, an' possums. He would work all day and hunt at night." Many masters allowed slaves to tend a garden patch, which they had to cultivate at night after their regular work was done. Greens from the garden and sweet potatoes or other vegetables provided vitamins that were invaluable in the slaves' diet. But not all slaves received adequate nutrition, and not all were well fed.

The slaves' clothes were rough and inadequate. Men usually had only two trousers and two or three shirts to last the year; women had a similar number of dresses in dull colors. These garments often were made from osnaburg (commonly called "nigger cloth"), a heavy coarse cotton of the kind used today in feed sacks or drapes. Children, both male and female, frequently wore only a shirt until they were substantially grown. "I went as naked as your hand," said Mattie Curtis of Orange County, "till I was fourteen years old. I was naked like that when my nature come to me. Marse Whitfield ain't carin', but after that mammy told him that I had to have clothes."

Though their bodies often were cold, former slaves complained most in later years about shoes—both the absence of shoes and the poor quality of those they were given. "We got one pair of shoes a year," said Louisa Adams, reporting the typical practice. "When they wore out we went barefooted. Sometimes we tied them up with strings, and they were so ragged the tracks looked like bird tracks, where we walked in the road." Even though slaves' shoes were poorly made, or very stiff and uncomfortable if sturdy, it was much worse to be without them. "My brother wore his shoes out," Louisa Adams recalled, "and had none all through winter. His feet cracked open and bled so bad you could track him by the blood."

Although slaves were valuable property, that fact was no guarantee that they would receive good physical treatment. Their physical benefits were meager, and their treatment reflected the fact that they were a despised and oppressed race. It is true that a few, fortunate slaves had a master they could sincerely call "a good man," but most whites had limited concern for people they regarded as inferior. A few masters purposely underfed their slaves and encouraged them to steal from neighboring plantations rather than incur the expense of providing an adequate diet. Most were not as greedy as that, but it nonetheless was true that the white community looked down on blacks and assumed they neither needed nor deserved the level of care that would be considered essential among whites.

Almost universally, slaves regarded whipping and physical abuse as the worst part of bondage. A good master was one who whipped relatively little, but virtually all masters on all types of plantations did some whipping. Whites regarded the lash as an essential instrument of labor control and discipline. They relied on whippings to punish individual slaves who were disobedient and to frighten and intimidate the much larger number who merely witnessed a whipping. Thus, beatings strengthened authority and supported plantation order.

But to the slaves, whippings were cruel and unjust, something they hated and remembered with feelings of pain or outrage. Viney Baker of Durham County, formerly a slave, later recalled that during her bondage "They used to tie me to a tree and beat me till the blood run down my back. I don't remember nothin' that I done, I just remember the whuppin's. Some of the rest was beat worser than I was too, and I use to scream that I was sure dyin'." Clay Bobbitt carried through his life a large scar above the elbow where his master had "whupped me with a cowhide." He acknowledged that most of his whippings came "cause I won't obey his orders," but he denied that that fact lent any justification to beatings.

Willis Cozart, who grew up in Person County, recalled seeing "niggers beat till the blood run, an' I've seen plenty more with big scars. . . . A moderate whuppin' was thirty-nine or forty lashes an' a real whuppin' was an even hundred." He added, "Most folks can't stand a real whuppin'." Usually the master or overseer administered the whippings, but some former slaves testified that they had had a mistress who "liked to see slaves beat almost to death." In addition to the master or mistress, patrollers were a danger to the slaves, for patrollers freely whipped any slaves they caught off their owner's plantation at night. "If you were out without a pass," said Andrew Boone of Wake County, "they would sure git you. . . . If you was out of place, they would wear you out."

Some slaves were "bucked" before they were whipped. The master "would tie their hands together and then put their hands down over the knees, then take a stick and stick it 'tween their hands [elbows] and knees." Immobilized in this position, the slave could offer no resistance to a beating.

Even pregnant women were not safe from whippings. Lucy Brown's mother told her that "before the babies was borned they tied the mammy down on her face if they had to whup her to keep from ruinin' the baby." Sometimes the master or overseer dug a shallow hole in the ground to hold the pregnant woman's abdomen, and then he whipped her back.

Andrew Boone described other aspects of the cruelty of beatings:

They whupped me with the cat o' nine tails. It had nine lashes on it. Some of the slaves was whupped with a cabin paddle. They had forty holes in 'em and when you was buckled to a barrel they hit your naked flesh with the paddle, and every where there was a hole in the paddle it drawed a blister. When the whuppin' with the paddle was over, they took the cat o' nine tails and busted the blisters. By this time the blood sometimes would be runnin' down their heels. Then the next thing was a wash in salt water. . . .

Other former slaves gave similar descriptions, saying that vinegar or water with peppers in it was used to wash off the torn flesh on a slave's back. They also told of greasing other slaves' backs to help them recover from the pain of a whipping.

Although beatings sometimes ended in death, they were not the only form of physical abuse that slaves feared. Caroline Richardson, whose owner had lived in Johnston County, remembered seeing slaves "with clipped ears"—slaves who had had part of their ears cut off as punishment. Slaves who repeatedly rebelled by running away sometimes had a toe cut off or the Achilles tendon severed to keep them from running again. John C. Bectom, from Fayetteville, shared a bed with a slave who "was wearing a ball and chain as a punishment for running away." Bectom recalled, too, that "The cuff had imbedded in his leg, it was swollen so."

As great as the pain of physical abuse was the enduring inner suffering caused by the forced separations of slave families. As persons, enslaved men and women felt emotions of love, loneliness, and loss, but as property to their masters, slaves represented an investment or asset to be used. An owner could put one of his slaves "in his pocket"—sell him, and thus turn him into money—at any time. In the 1820s and 1830s North Carolinians, whose economy was relatively stagnant, sold thousands of slaves to new owners in Alabama and Mississippi, where boom times were under way.

In other ways it proved useful to whites to dispose of slave property. Fathers gave slaves away to their daughters as wedding presents. Courts sometimes ordered the sale of slaves to settle an estate or divided slave families in order to give the different portions of an inheritance the prescribed dollar value. To be sure, there were white people who honored the sanctity of slave families; but southern society in general did no such thing, and circumstances often overrode good intentions.

Tar Heel former slaves remembered slave traders, who drove manacled slaves along the roads, and auction blocks, where slaves were sold to the highest bidder. As a little boy, W. L. Bost repeatedly saw slaves chained together in groups of four or five as speculators drove them through his town. "The poor critters nearly froze to death," he recalled, because they were being moved in December, so that they could be sold or hired out at the beginning of January. Cornelia Andrews, a former slave from Johnston County, had heard that "one day at Smithfield" three hundred slaves were auctioned off. Whether or not that number was correct, sales were common events. "They sold slaves jus' like people sell hosses now," observed Andrew Boone. "I saw a lot of slaves sold on the auction block. They would strip 'em stark naked. A nigger scarred up or whaled and welted up was considered a bad nigger and did not bring much. If his body was not scarred, he brought a good price."

To family members, the pain from these sales lasted through life. Recalling sales to a speculator, Sarah Gudger exclaimed, "Oh that was a terrible time" and described how "the tears roll[ed] down [one woman's] cheeks, cause maybe it [was] her son or husband and she knows he never see them again." Viney Baker lost her mother through a sale. "One night I lay down on de straw mattress with my mammy, and the next mornin' I woked up and she was gone. When I asked about her I finds that a speculator comed there the night before and wanted to buy a woman. They had come and got my mammy without wakin' me up." Losing her mother was so traumatic that in later years Viney Baker felt "glad somehow that I was asleep," since that saved her from seeing her mother being taken away.

Sales and the disruption of families testified to the enormous control that slaveholders exercised over the lives of black people. That control was some-thing that slave owners prized and sought to make more encompassing.

Negro Girl for Sale.

I shall proceed to sell at the Courthouse door in Lexington on the 13th of May next—it being Teusday of May Court—one likely Negro Woman, twenty years of age, belonging to the estate of Richard Owen deceased. Said girl is a good field hand or house servant. Terms made known on day of sale. JOHN WILSON, Executor.

may 2 402t

IMPORTANT SALES IN
WARREN COUNTY.

On Monday, the 24th of January next, we will sell to the highest bidder, at the residence of the late Gen. M. T. Hawkins, all of the perishable property: consisting of a large and valuable stock of thorough-bred horses, six jacks, nine jennetts and thirteen mules; a large stock of cattle, hogs and sheep, a large quantity of fat pork, corn, wheat, cotton, fodder, oats, shucks and straw, wagons, carts, plantation utensils, &c. There will be hired, at the same time and place, 80 or 100 negroes---among them are several valuable mechanics.

Also, on the 1st day of February next, at the Baker plantation, all of the stock of mules, cattle and hogs; a quantity of fat pork; crop of corn, fodder, and shucks; wagons, carts, and plantation utensils.

Terms made known on the days of sale.

S. G. WARD, \
JNO. WATSON, } Executors.

December 24th, 1858.

Printed at the *News* office, Warrenton, N C

Slave owners occasionally advertised for the sale of slaves. Such sales disrupted slave families and caused lifelong pain and suffering for the victims of the practice. Shown above are advertisements for the sale of slaves in connection with the settlement of North Carolina estates by their respective executors. TOP: advertisement from *Lexington and Yadkin Flag* (Lexington), May 9, 1856; BOTTOM: broadside from the Thomas M. Pittman Papers, State Archives, Office of Archives and History.

It was not enough to dictate the behavior, movements, or even future of black people; slaveholders also wanted to control their thoughts. To dominate the minds of their chattels, masters attempted to regulate the information and ideas to which their slaves had access.

Although some slaves learned to read from the white children, masters generally followed the law, which after 1830 prohibited the education of slaves. Because knowledge was power, masters wanted their slaves to have none of it. "Lord, you better not be caught with a book in your hand," recalled Louisa Adams. "If you did, you were sold. They didn't allow that." Similarly, they did not allow slaves to be exposed to potentially subversive information or hear the wrong kind of preaching.

All meetings of slaves, even for religious purposes, were supposed to be supervised, and ministers were expected to support the system of slavery. Lizzie Baker, who grew up in Duplin County, reported that her parents were taken with the master's family "to the white folks' church. They said the preachers told them they had to obey their missus and master." That was the message heard in white churches. Obedience was the essence of religion whites gave to the slaves.

But in the testimony of former slaves can be found abundant evidence that such religion was not the only kind of faith they had or practiced. After telling about the "white folks'" religion, Lizzie Baker described secret prayer meetings arranged by the slaves, who continued to meet and pray even after patrollers found them and beat them. In assemblies of their own the slaves could seek deliverance and voice their longing for justice. Emma Blalock, who had been a slave in Wake County, remembered "prayer meetings around at the slave houses" and described a common method for trying to maintain secrecy: "We turned down pots on the inside of the house at the door to keep master and missus from hearing the singing and praying." This practice probably derived from West African ceremonies and rituals involving pots, and although it may not have dampened the slaves' voices, it indicates the independence of their outlook and the influence of African elements in their culture.

Despite the power marshaled against them, despite the manifold efforts of whites to control them, black people maintained their mental independence and nourished a resistant spirit. They suffered the wrongs of slavery, but it did not break them. They were denied many of the valuable things of life, but they did not falter in their belief in themselves or in the meaning of justice. Knowing they were wronged, the slaves resented their mistreatment, condemned its perpetrators, and relied on each other for comfort and support. They had a solidarity among themselves, an identification with each other, that helped them endure the experience of bondage.

Slaves regarded whites as their oppressors. Certain individuals, to be sure, might treat slaves with more feeling or decency than the ordinary master, but the entire system was wrong, and blacks never forgot that central fact. "I think slavery was an injustice, not right," said John C. Bectom. He voiced the universal opinion, which Clay Bobbitt, a former slave from Warren County, repeated with more acerbity. Discussing the whippings that he had suffered, Bobbitt denounced the injustice of slavery by declaring that his owner "ain't whupped me for nothin' 'cept that I is a nigger."

As they toiled and labored in the fields, the slaves well knew that the fruits of their effort went primarily to the benefit of their owners. Black workers ate cornbread and fat pork, whereas white owners enjoyed white biscuits and tasty hams. Some slaves were permitted to raise collards at night in a garden patch, but their regular work during the day produced an abundance of vegetables for the master's table. Slaves lived crowded into rude cabins, whereas their owners lived in spacious, comfortable homes. The basic purpose of slavery was exploitation, and the slaves knew it.

Andrew Boone acknowledged that he had received little formal education, but, he said, "they learned us to count. They learned us to count this way. 'Ought is an ought, and a figure is a figure, all for the white man and nothin' for the nigger.'" Countless other slaves would have agreed with him that "niggers make the cotton and corn and the white folks get the money."

Because they felt intense resentment over slavery's injustice and abuse, blacks lived with few illusions about white character or white motives. Even children were taught by their parents or aunts and uncles to be suspicious of whites. "Gifts" from the master were probably nothing more

The Boyette Slave House in Johnston County is a rare and unaltered reminder of the era of slavery in North Carolina. The small, one-room structure of hewn planks once housed the slaves of the Boyette family. The cabin features a largely intact stick-and-mud chimney, a rare holdover from medieval building methods customarily employed only in connection with slave quarters. Photograph from the files of the Office of Archives and History.

than the clothes or rations that were slated for distribution anyway. Medical care represented not kindness but the owner's desire to protect his valuable investment. Slaves believed that the whites always had their own interests at heart and that these were diametrically opposed to the interests of black people. Experience had instilled this belief, and few incidents in the slaves' lives ever challenged its validity.

Moreover, the resentment felt by blacks, as well as whites' determination to dominate, came out in daily events of plantation life. A woman named Fanny Cannady described a violent confrontation that exposed all the bitter emotions and passions produced by slavery. Only a child at the end of the Civil War, Fanny nevertheless remembered one event clearly: the murder by her master of a proud and defiant slave named Leonard Allen, which occurred during the Civil War.

Fanny's master had two sons, who enrolled in the Confederate army. The master was proud of his sons' patriotism, but the slaves had their own opinion of Confederate soldiers and the goal for which they fought. When one son came home on furlough, "struttin' 'round the yard showin' off" his uniform, Leonard Allen turned to another slave and said, under his breath, "Look at that God damn soldier. He fightin' to keep us niggers from bein' free."

Noticing that some comment had been made, Fanny's master walked up to Leonard and demanded to know what he had said. Without hesitation the defiant slave repeated his comment, unaltered, to the master, who became almost apoplectic with rage. His face, said Fanny, "begun to swell. It turned so red that the blood near about bust out." Then the master turned to Fanny's father and ordered him to run to the house and bring back his shotgun.

Before long, Fanny's father returned, bearing the shotgun, and with him came the master's wife, Miss Sally. Knowing her husband's character and fearing the worst, Miss Sally was already upset. "The tears was streamin' down her face," remembered Fanny. "She run up to Marse Jordan and caught his arm," but he "flung her off," took the gun, "leveled it on Leonard and told him to pull his shirt open." Although Fanny was frightened, she remembered with admiration Leonard's manner, as he "opened his shirt and stood there big as a black giant sneering at Old Marse."

Again Miss Sally interposed herself, running between the gun and Leonard. Her husband ordered Fanny's father to pull her away, but none of the slaves moved toward her. Then "Old Marse let down the gun," but not to reconsider his actions. He "reached over and slapped Miss Sally down, then picked up the gun and shot a hole in Leonard's chest big as your fist." Fanny was "so scared" that she ran and hid for hours in the stable loft, but then and ever after she remembered, with powerful emotions, the sight of "Leonard layin' on the ground with that bloody hole in his chest and that sneer on his black mouth."

Leonard hated slavery and exploitation as the other slaves did, and he had given up his life to make a dramatic statement of his profound resentment. Fanny respected him for that, just as she respected the simple decency of her mistress and hated the viciousness of her master. In their hearts, most slaves longed to make the kind of declaration that Leonard Allen paid for with his life.

Slaves recognized differences of character among whites: Fanny and her mother, for example, stayed with Miss Sally and helped her until she died. But the foundation of their outlook was knowledge of their oppression by whites. The slaves felt a bond with each other as the objects of white cruelty and contempt, and they identified with each other as people sharing a common burden and common culture. They all were subject to sale, separation from their family members, whipping, overwork, and mistreatment. They all hoped in secret for freedom and justice. They all resisted when they could. The awareness of their distinct racial and cultural identity never left them.

Charlie Crump, who knew slavery on a small farm near the border of present-day Chatham and Lee counties, told an interviewer that he had been able to get along with white folks, but he let his anger at white people show. "I'll tell you," he said, "I'd rather be a nigger any day than to be like my old white folks was." With unusual honesty and boldness, Thomas Hall, a former slave from Orange County, described what many blacks had learned from their long, bitter experience with whites: "There are a few white men who are [all right], but the pressure is such from your white friends that you will be compelled to talk against us and give us the cold shoulder when you are around them, even if your heart is right towards us. . . . The white folks have been and are now and always will be against the Negro."

Oppression drew the slaves together, and knowledge of their African origins strengthened the bonds between them. They felt the differences between their cultural background and that of the whites in a number of ways. Dance was an area of clear difference, for even the whites admired and marveled at the athleticism and energy of black movement in dance. Religion was another; in addition to their emphasis on justice rather than obedience, many slaves expected a greater amount of ecstatic experience in their religion than was common among whites. Belief in supernatural forces, including ghosts and haunts, was widespread among rural whites and blacks. But here, too, black culture exhibited specifically African roots, especially in regard to conjuration. Many slaves believed that a "hand" or bag containing certain magical items could work a spell or protect and deliver them from the master's wrath.

Thus, psychologically and functionally, slavery held together two fundamentally opposed and antagonistic groups. Weighed down, but not broken, by slavery's wrongs, black people naturally resisted their enslavement in every way practical. They rejected and rebelled against their treatment whenever they could and resisted slavery at each step in the daily routine of labor.

Complaints were rife among owners about the grudging, inefficient labor of slaves. The evidence from white and black sources indicates that masters could force slaves to work long hours at tiring tasks, but they could not compel slaves to give all their effort or do the best possible job. There was no incentive for a slave to do so, and no owner could supervise closely during every minute of the day. This day-to-day resistance to slavery's demands cost the slave owners something in profit and return on their investment. More importantly, it protected the slaves from demands that were too onerous and a pace that could not be sustained.

To protect their health and provide food for their hungry stomachs, slaves "stole" from the master without apology or guilt. "When we got hungry and could find a pig, a calf or a chicken," recalled one man, "no matter who it had belonged to, it then belonged to us." Such appropriation of goods that their labor had produced—goods to which they would never have access—did not seem wrong to the slaves. Rather, it lessened an injustice they knew they would continue to suffer.

One former slave, Kitty Hill of Pittsboro, remembered a song that was well known among whites and enjoyed by the blacks:

Some folks say that a nigger won't steal	Run nigger run
I caught two in my corn field	Pateroller catch you
One had a bushel, one had a peck	Run nigger run
And one had roasting ears	Like you did the other day.
Strung 'round his neck.	

The popularity of this song suggests that "stealing" was common, for the whites expected it. As a black woman, Kitty applauded those who filled their empty stomachs. She also cheered for blacks in their contests with patrollers. Sometimes the result was "patrollers catching niggers and whipping them," but at other times blacks "outrun the patrollers and got away."

Some slaves rejected being treated in the cruel and degrading ways that were typical of slavery and openly defied white authority. Much of this defiance was directed against whipping. From a strong inner pride, or from desperation, slaves occasionally put the master on notice that they would not tolerate being beaten. Martha Adeline Hinton, who had been a slave in Wake County, recalled that her father "worked hard every day, and done as near right as he knowed how to do in everything," but one day "his master got mad and hit him with a long switch." Martha's father then made a decision. He told the master that "he was working best he could for him and that he was not going to take a whippin'." Fortunately for Martha's father, the master walked off "and that was the last of it . . . he never tried to whip him again."

Essex Henry, who was born into slavery near Raleigh, likewise testified that "there was a few spirited slaves that wo[uld]n't be whipped." His uncle was one of those defiant slaves, and he escaped whippings for some time. But he could not avoid conflicts with the master, and thus "he finally was sold for this." More unfortunate was Essex Henry's grandmother. One day "the overseer tried to whip her and he can't, so he hollers for Mr. Jake [the master]. Mr. Jake comes and he can't, so he hauls off and kicks granny, mashing her stomach in." A few days later, as a result of her injuries and the absence of medical attention, Essex Henry's grandmother died.

Another bold but dangerous form of resistance was flight. The slave who ran away had crossed a significant line. Escape from the South was difficult and perilous, and the runaway who was recaptured knew to expect severe physical punishment or sale away from his plantation and family. Nevertheless, despite all the dangers, some slaves accomplished their escape. Their numbers were not large, but almost every slave had heard of an individual who refused to accept a life in continuing bondage.

One slave who successfully fled to the North was Harriet Jacobs. Born in Edenton in 1815, by her early teenage years she had become the target of her master's sexual harassment. With the help of both black and white neighbors, Jacobs went into hiding in her grandmother's home. Finally, about 1842 she escaped to the North. There she became an active reformer

Harriet Jacobs, (1815–1897) was born into slavery but escaped to the North. Drawing by Rev. Edna Hathaway Lawrence, the pastor of the Kadesh A.M.E. Zion Church, Edenton. Used by permission of Historic Edenton.

and abolitionist. In 1861 she published a pseudonymous slave narrative, *Incidents in the Life of a Slave Girl, Written by Herself* (ed. by L. Maria Child). Probably the only slave narrative to speak with unflinching candor about sexual oppression as well as racial brutality, *Incidents* remains unique among nineteenth-century American autobiographies.

Much more common was running away from the plantation but not from the immediate neighborhood. The slave who ran away into the woods remained close enough to his family and friends to receive their aid. At night he could sneak back to the vicinity of the plantation and pick up food or clothing. Although his days were spent in hiding, every day away from the plantation deprived the master of his labor and thus increased the possibility of winning some adjustment of his grievances. A former slave named Joe High recalled that his brother ran away. Eventually "young master sent him word to come on back home; he won't going to whip him, and he come back." Similarly, Martha Hinton's independent father ran off one time to foil plans to sell him. He stayed away for two weeks, during which time his master reconsidered and altered his plans.

Inevitably, however, there were many times when a slave could not change his lot, even through courageous resistance. During such times religion offered both consolation and support for the independent spirit from which resistance sprang. Religion affirmed the slaves as human beings and confirmed their belief in values hostile to the power and control of whites. It comforted them in defeat and encouraged them to struggle on toward ultimate victory.

Accordingly, the slaves refused to abandon religion and defeated white attempts to suppress it. "The white folks feared for niggers to get any religion," said W. L. Bost of Newton, "but I reckon something inside just told us about God and that there was a better place hereafter. We would sneak off and have prayer meeting. Sometimes the patrollers catch us and

```
TWENTY DOLLARS REWARD.
RANAWAY FROM THE SUBSCRIBER ON THE
4th inst., a negro boy named LOVELESS. Said boy
goes by the name of LOVE. he is about 18 years of
age. medium height, dark complected, spare built, stoops
when walking, and a little bow-legged. He was hired to
me by Washington Pridgeon, guardian for the minor heirs of
Mrs. Jintz Pridgeon, on South River, where he is supposed
to be lurking.
   I will give the above reward of TWENTY DOLLARS
for his delivery to me, or confinement in any Jail in this
State so that I can get him again.
                              JAMES M. LEWIS.
Brunswick county, N. C., Jan. 11th, 1858        20-3m*
```

Slaves occasionally asserted their resistance to authority by running away from the plantations on which they resided. North Carolina's newspapers of the antebellum era are replete with advertisements for the return of runaways. The example reproduced here is from the *Wilmington Journal* of February 12, 1858.

beat us good, but that didn't keep us from trying." If the patrol broke up one meeting, the slaves simply held another. To avoid capture, they often posted lookouts, who could raise an alarm, or fast runners, who could lure the whites away from the common meeting place. Then they continued to worship and pray.

North Carolina's slaves were basically a religious people, and many firmly believed that one day God would deliver them from bondage. They saw themselves as a people of faith—the Lord's people, just as the Israelites had been Jehovah's people in biblical times. The Israelites had kept the covenant, and God had delivered them from bondage. His ways were just. Therefore, many slaves believed that He would not forget those who suffered under American slavery. Despite slavery's hold on American history, many slaves truly seemed to expect that divine intervention would effect a great change in human affairs. Thus, they were not surprised when emancipation finally came; it was the unfolding of God's plan. "I thank the will of God for setting us free," said Hannah Crasson, who had been a slave near Garner, North Carolina. "He got into Abraham Lincoln and the Yankees." In this interpretation, God put human instrumentalities to work, and the ensuing war resulted, at last, in freedom. Unquestionably, the Civil War ushered in a new era in black history.

V

War, Emancipation, and Reconstruction

In 1860 Abraham Lincoln of Illinois won the nation's election for president. Lincoln had promised not to disturb slavery in the southern states, but he firmly opposed any extension to new territory of an institution that he regarded as "wrong." Many slaveholders saw Lincoln's election as a dire threat. Rather than tolerate his inauguration, seven states of the deep South seceded from the Union and formed their own government, the Confederate States of America. On April 12, 1861, Confederate artillery fired on Fort Sumter in Charleston harbor, beginning the bloodiest war in America's history. North Carolina and three other states of the upper South then joined the Confederacy. The future of slavery and the Union hinged on the outcome of war.

To many slaves the Civil War represented the unfolding of God's plan, a divine purpose to end the great evil of human bondage. In this view men and women were neither controllers nor makers of history but merely the agents of a higher plan and power. Before four years of carnage and destruction ended, other Americans had come to share the slaves' opinion, for the Civil War proved to be a maelstrom that engulfed a suffering people and mocked their leaders' efforts to control events.

Abraham Lincoln agreed with Shakespeare that "There is a divinity that shapes our ends, rough-hew them how we will." Sounding chastened rather than victorious on the occasion of his second inauguration, Lincoln solemnly reviewed the war's cause and its unexpected course:

All knew that [slavery] was, somehow, the cause of the war. . . . Neither party expected for the war, the magnitude, or the duration, which it has already attained. Neither anticipated that the *cause* of the conflict might cease with, or even before, the conflict itself should cease. Each looked for an easier triumph, and a result less fundamental and astounding. . . . The Almighty has His own purposes.

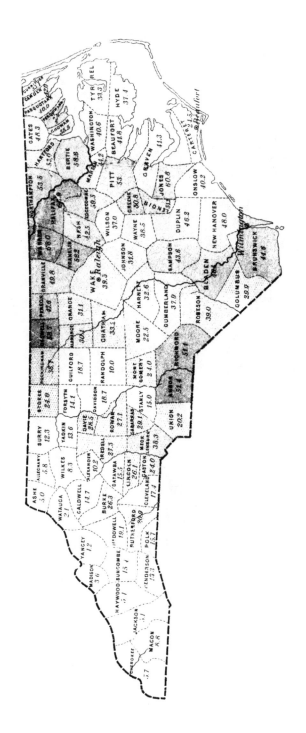

This 1860 federal census map of North Carolina indicates the percentage of slaves in each county's total population. From the map collection, Southern Historical Collection, Wilson Library, University of North Carolina at Chapel Hill.

The war had brought to Lincoln—and the nation—much that was neither expected nor desired, and its conclusion ushered in a period of turbulent competition and violence that would define the meaning of freedom.

For North Carolina's slaves the Civil War brought great joy but also sorrow, momentous excitement but also suffering, new opportunities but also dangerous risks. It was a watershed event in the history of America's black people, but it was more complex and threatening than the over-simplified history of popular legend suggests. The Civil War destroyed slavery and brought jubilation, but it also brought dangers and difficult choices in the uncertain new world of freedom. For black Tar Heels, these years of upheaval were packed with excitement, hopes, fears, challenges, opportunities, and ultimately disappointment.

As the war began, the slaves observed many changes in their owners. Initially, many white Southerners were overly optimistic, even boastful, about their chances. Hannah Crasson recalled that her owner proclaimed that the Confederates "could eat breakfast at home, go and whip the North, and be back for dinner." He was sadly mistaken. Crasson recalled that "It was four long years before he come back to dinner. The table was sure set a long time for him. A lot of the white folks said there wouldn't be much war, they could whip them so easy. Many of them never did come back to dinner."

Crasson's owners, like other whites, tried to control the flow of information that reached the slaves. But it proved impossible to keep the truth from them. An entire society was mobilizing for a war that demanded all of its resources, and because the war affected all Southerners so deeply, important developments could not be kept secret. "There were stories of fights and freedom," recalled Mary Anderson, who had been a slave in Wake County. "The news went from plantation to plantation, and while the slaves acted natural and some even more polite than usual, they prayed for freedom." Since the truth could not be hidden, whites tried to misrepresent it. Hannah Crasson's mistress "told us the Yankees were going to kill every nigger in the South." These tales made Crasson, a child at the time, cling to her mother when Yankee troops arrived, but they had less effect on adults.

Before two years had passed, the scope of the war became so great that it threatened slavery itself. To strengthen the Union's position and deprive the Confederacy of vital human resources, Lincoln issued his Emancipation Proclamation, which punished rebellious states by promising freedom to

As one result of President Abraham Lincoln's Emancipation Proclamation, freed slaves began entering Federal lines near New Bern early in 1863. Engraving from *Harper's Weekly*, VII (February 21, 1863), 116.

their slaves. Confederate leaders and the Southern press denounced Lincoln's act, thereby giving added substance to the slaves' hopes. "Of course the niggers knew what all the fighting was about," said W. L. Bost, "but they didn't dare say anything. The man who owned the slaves was too mad as it was, and if the niggers say anything they get shot right then and there."

Despite their hunger for freedom, many slaves had to labor to help the Confederacy. Some owners who went to war took body servants with them or sent slaves to the front with their sons. Those who stayed behind raised food to support the Southern cause as often as they grew cotton or tobacco to enrich their masters. Striving to make efficient use of its human resources, the Confederate government sometimes impressed slave labor and used the slaves to build fortifications or move munitions and other war materiel.

Carefully and circumspectly, however, other slaves could act. Approximately seven thousand black North Carolinians took advantage of their proximity to the lines of battle and fled from Confederate territory to enlist and fight, in four black regiments, for the Union cause. More than ten thousand others in eastern North Carolina slipped away from their owners and traveled to New Bern and other coastal areas controlled by Union forces.

There they experienced the first fruits of freedom in refugee communities such as James City (near New Bern) and on Roanoke Island.

Still more slaves—those whose owners had fled from exposed portions of Confederate eastern North Carolina—gained large amounts of control over their lives. As Union victory neared and the position of overseers became increasingly untenable, those blacks remained slaves in name but in practice set clear limits to white domination of plantation life. At Somerset, the estate of Josiah Collins III on Lake Phelps, the slaves were in virtual control. Collins's desperate overseer reported that he was trying "Evry skiam [scheme] to keep them hear [here]." He gave "hogs and Cattle to Each family [and] by those meanes I have kept them on the lake." But "I can not say a worde," he complained, when the slaves took property or did as they pleased. There was, he concluded, "no Dependance in no nigro when the weard fredom is given."

For most of North Carolina's slaves, freedom did not come until the war ended or Federal troops marched onto their plantation. Those who encountered the "blue bellies" had cause both to rejoice and to be circumspect. Delighted though the slaves were to be free, they had good reason to approach the Union troops with caution. Most Federal soldiers were not abolitionists, and many were straight-out racists. Moreover, the men of Sherman's army were hardened veterans who had fought in numerous bloody campaigns and endured a great deal of suffering. Their mission, as

Edwin G. Champney, a native of Boston, an artist, and a member of the Fifth Massachusetts Volunteer Regiment, arrived in eastern North Carolina in October 1862, and saw service at several locations there during the ensuing eight months. While in North Carolina, Champney compiled a sketchbook of sixty pen-and-ink drawings of various subjects. Two of Champney's works are shown here. They depict two unidentified African Americans he apparently encountered during his eight-month-long sojourn in eastern North Carolina. Photographs from the files of the Office of Archives and History.

they marched from Atlanta to the sea and then north into the Carolinas, was to wreak destruction on the South, and they proved adept at their task. Foraging as they went, Federal troops destroyed property and seized anything that could benefit a tired and hungry soldier.

Kitty Hill, whose owner had brought her from Virginia to North Carolina near the end of the war, remembered that "Horses, cows and chickens just didn't have no chance if a Yankee laid his eyes on them. A Yankee was poison to a yard full of fowls. They killed turkeys, chickens, and geese" and slaughtered hogs or cows for portions of the meat that they could carry with them. With distaste, Elbert Hunter, who lived near Raleigh, remembered the soldiers "shootin" chickens and pigs and everything. I've seen them cut the hams off a live pig or ox and go off leaving the animal groaning. The master had them killed then, but it was awful."

Sarah Debro of Orange County remembered Yankee horsemen "jumping over the palings, 'trompling' down the rose bushes and messing up the flower beds. They stomped all over the houses, in the kitchen, pantries, smoke house, and everywhere." The behavior of some soldiers was more threatening to Sarah personally, for she "had to keep fighting off them Yankee men." On Louisa Adams's plantation the soldiers "went in the smoke house and emptied every barrel of molasses right in the floor and scattered the cracklings on the floor."

Mary Anderson told a typical story about her encounter with soldiers in Wake County. The Yankees announced to the slaves that they were free, urged them to celebrate, and then "busted the door to the smoke house and got all the hams. They went to the icehouse and got several barrels of brandy, and [had] such a time. The Negroes and Yankees were cooking and eating together. Master and missus sat on the porch. . . ." Where Sarah Augustus had worked as a slave, near Fayetteville, the soldiers raided the smokehouse and then "told us we were all free. The Negroes begun visiting each other in the cabins and became so excited they began to shout and pray."

Although the newly liberated slaves on Mary Anderson's plantation joined in the soldiers' celebration, many others felt some unease around the Federals. Not only did the soldiers rob from the slaves' few possessions and destroy food and livestock the black people would need but they also put them in a difficult position with the very white people whose influence over them was likely to continue. Long after the victorious army had moved on, the freed slaves would be living among southern whites, and they knew it. Therefore, they rejoiced over the coming of freedom and sang and celebrated. "We was glad to be free even though we had good white folks," recalled Elbert Hunter of Wake County. But they usually did not betray the whites' secrets, such as where valuables were hidden, and they soon began to plan how best to live with whites in a changed world.

The first critical decision that black people made in freedom was whether to stay on with their former master or leave the plantation and look for work elsewhere. Sometimes circumstances made the choice easy. Henry Bobbitt's master in Warren County "walked the floor and cussed Sherman for taking his niggers away." The work had been hard and the pleasures few on that plantation, and the slave owner's attitude did not promise much for the future. Accordingly, "All of the niggers left, of course," Bobbitt noted, "and me, I walked clean to Raleigh to find out if I was really free."

Lucy Ann Dunn, on the other hand, remembered that her family in Neuse, North Carolina, had always had "plenty" to eat and decent clothes, and when the war ended, her owner called the slaves together and made a speech. He reminded them that "he ain't had to sell none of us, that he ain't whipped none of us bad, that nobody has ever run away from him yet." Then he invited his former slaves to stay on and work for him for wages. "Well, we stayed two years," Lucy reported.

She was fortunate that her owner had announced the coming of freedom and forthrightly outlined to the former slaves their options. Where the Federal army had not arrived, or where the Freedmen's Bureau remained a distant influence, many owners tried to delay news of emancipation and hold onto their slaves as long as possible. A native-born official of the Freedmen's Bureau in the Piedmont concluded, after an investigation, that "there is a tendency on the part of *Some of* the citizens to keep every thing they can from the knowledge of the Freedmen that pertains to their welfare." Another means of retaining control over the former slaves was to gain control of their children, and the Freedmen's Bureau had to counter this as well. "The County Courts of . . . New Hanover, Brunswick and Robeson," reported one official, "pursued the plan of taking colored children away from their parents, and binding them as apprentices to their former Masters . . . without regard to whether the parents can support the children or not."

A few wise planters offered their former slaves tools, a hog, or other livestock if they decided to stay with them in freedom. Most former slaves based their decision on the reputation of various whites. The mother of Georgianna Foster, who lived on a plantation twelve miles from Raleigh, "said livin' at master's was hard and when they set us free we left as quick as we could and went to Mr. Bob Perry's plantation. . . . He was a good man and give us all a chance." W. L. Bost recalled that soon after freedom his mother moved the family to the land of "old Solomon Hall . . . a good man if there ever was one." The evidence for this white landowner's goodness was clear: "He freed all of his slaves about two years before emancipation."

Choosing an employer was a vitally important decision for black families, but black people as a whole also had critical decisions to make. They were free, at last, but their new position in society was unclear. Black North Carolinians wanted to have a voice in all discussions about their future role, and they moved quickly to claim their rights as American citizens. The nation's political process moved more slowly and more uncertainly than black Tar Heels were prepared to move during the period known as Reconstruction. The Congress and President Andrew Johnson disagreed about how to bring the southern states back into the Union and how to define the place of the former slaves. Nearly three years passed before black men gained the right to vote, and the outcome of Reconstruction remained uncertain until 1877. But all through this period black people in North Carolina fought for their political and civil rights, pressing diplomatically but persistently for an equal citizenship that they viewed as part of their American birthright.

Throughout this process blacks demonstrated determination, idealism, and a patient realism about their situation. Although they had been denied education through generations of slavery, they quickly chose able leaders to work for their interests. These leaders displayed a shrewd appreciation of realities facing black people, such as the persistence of white power in all areas of life. They pressed for black rights and simultaneously appealed for white cooperation. To establish a new position for the freedpeople involved substantial risk, but blacks worked for progress without vindictiveness, offering to their former masters the hand of brotherhood.

In the fall of 1865 there assembled in Raleigh a convention of blacks numbering 117 delegates and representing roughly half of the counties of the state. Most of the delegates were former slaves, although their number included some antebellum free Negroes. A substantial portion were veterans of the Union army, such as A. H. Galloway of Fayetteville, one of the organizers of the assembly; many, such as James H. Harris of Raleigh, were self-educated; most had skilled occupations—carpenter, teacher, minister, barber—that brought them into contact with a broad range of blacks and whites. They wanted to act for Tar Heel blacks and were somewhat uncomfortable about the presence of a few delegates born in North Carolina but educated in the North and only recently returned.

Meeting "to express the sentiments of the Freedmen" while a white convention across town revised the state constitution, the black delegates drafted an address and sent it to the latter body, as well as to the legislature that would follow. Their address was both a strong and a carefully worded document. With faultless courtesy it requested a hearing and "kind consideration" from the legislators, and its essence was a "moral appeal to the hearts and consciences of the people of our State." But it also revealed honestly the attitudes of blacks toward slavery and their aspirations for the future.

Referring to the recent war, these black leaders admitted that "it was impossible for us to be indifferent spectators." The struggle, after all, had involved the "precious boon of freedom," and many northern blacks had fought on the Union side, while most slaves in North Carolina had "been obliged" to aid the Confederacy in many ways, from raising food to building fortifications. Calling on whites to acknowledge that North Carolina's slaves had remained "obedient" through the war, "calmly waiting upon Providence," they nevertheless asked, "Do you blame us that we have, meantime, prayed for the freedom of our race?"

This frankness entailed no desire for conflict, however. The black delegates noted their birth "upon the same soil" as the state's whites and the "intimacy of relationship" that had existed under slavery. With respect for "the kindly ties which have so long united us," they declared: "We have formed attachments for the white race which must be as enduring as life." Moreover, the black leaders candidly admitted that they could not "long expect the presence of government agents, or of the troops" to protect their interests; their future treatment depended, ultimately, upon the white majority of North Carolina.

To all those whites who displayed "a just and humane disposition towards their former slaves" the delegates offered thanks. But there were widespread and serious problems. "Many planters," the blacks declared, were concealing the news of freedom or had driven black families off the land they had tilled for years. Others were refusing fair wages or even employment to women with dependent children. "Is it just or Christian," asked the convention's address, "thus to thrust out upon the cold world helpless families to perish?" Protective legislation clearly was needed.

Looking to the future, these blacks acknowledged that their conduct would affect their place in society, but they asked the white lawmakers for help. "We desire education for our children," they declared, and they asked for legal protection of the black family, aid for orphans, and support for the reunification of families broken up by slavery. In addition, "we most earnestly desire to have the disabilities under which we formerly labored removed, and to have all the oppressive laws which make unjust discriminations on account of race or color wiped from the statutes of the State."

This address closed with a statement of love for North Carolina and its people, but its courteous words had made clear that Tar Heel blacks wanted justice and equal rights. No specific reference was made to voting, but surely denial of the suffrage would have to pass away with other "unjust discriminations" based on race. As an "intelligent negro" told Whitelaw Reid, a northern journalist, "We ain't noways safe, 'long as dem people makes de laws we's got to be governed by. We's got to hab a voice in de 'pintin' of de law-makers." Obtaining that voice depended upon the course of politics in the South and the nation.

Almost immediately the whites in the constitutional convention signaled their hostility to black advancement and sternly warned against "the assertion of impracticable claims for social and political rights." The state's white leaders were, very generally, opposed to any major improvements in blacks' status, including the right to sit on juries or give testimony. White hostility manifested itself throughout the state in disputes about wages, additional examples of what the Freedmen's Bureau called "injustice" to laborers, and violence against blacks. The Freedmen's Bureau recorded hundreds of assaults on blacks, often by prominent white people. In Charlotte a white magistrate struck a black man in public with a club, and in New Hanover County three experienced county officeholders faced charges for beating, shooting, or whipping blacks. On scores of plantations whites resisted with force the new roles that free blacks began to claim.

Knowing that progress would not be easy, blacks were undeterred. On the Fourth of July, 1865, they marched through Raleigh carrying banners that read "Equal Rights before the law: the only equality we ask." In several cities they met in Equal Rights leagues, and upon adjournment the Freedmen's Convention resolved itself into the North Carolina Equal Rights League to work for "repeal of all laws . . . that make distinctions on account of color." Free blacks were ready to reach out for every opportunity that freedom offered.

For two more years the opportunities that developed were close to home and unconnected with politics. Under President Johnson's plan of Reconstruction, southern state governments remained in the hands of whites, and blacks had no right to vote or hold office. The legislature gave freed people only "the same privileges . . . as . . . were conferred on . . . free persons of color prior to the ordinance of emancipation." This meant that blacks still could not testify against whites, serve on juries, enter into contracts worth ten dollars or more on their own, or even keep a gun without a special license. Under Jonathan Worth, who won election as governor of North Carolina under Johnson's Reconstruction program, the prospect of any improvement through government policies was bleak. Determined to avoid any federal intervention on behalf of the freedpeople, Worth felt that even "the Com[mon] School fund had better be discouraged, and thus avoid the question as to educating negroes."

In the meantime, however, a changed status for black people as laborers and citizens was beginning to emerge through daily struggle. One of the most important and contested areas of life concerned employment. Although emancipation had been decreed, its benefits were not automatic or self-executing. Especially in regard to plantation labor, white southerners seemed determined to continue the old practices of slavery. Unaccustomed to free labor and well versed in defending slave labor, most planters asserted that freed Negroes would never work. Coercion had made the system of slavery work, and coercion would be necessary after emancipation, they declared. Whitelaw Reid encountered what was obviously the prevailing view among southern whites when he heard one in New Bern declare that "the poor, shiftless creatures will never be able to support themselves in freedom." Another northern journalist, Sidney Andrews, "everywhere" encountered "the complaint that the free negro will not work." As Reid summed up the situation: "Nothing could overcome this rooted idea, that the negro was worthless, except under the lash."

Accordingly, the aim of most white landowners was to restore as much of the slave regime as possible. Beatings and whippings were common until the Freedmen's Bureau intervened, much to the consternation of former slave owners. Deprived of the whip, they sought to employ every other form of discipline that was familiar to them. The overseer who worked for Thomas Ruffin, former justice of the state supreme court, revealed the spirit of his approach to farm management plainly. He was driving off uncooperative laborers, he reported, "and what is left [kn]ow very well that [they] have got to work slave fashion or they can't stay."

Working "slave fashion" meant working virtually as slaves. The actions of Paul Cameron, one of the largest slave owners in the state, were representative of white landowners generally. Trying to adjust to freedom, Cameron approached his former slaves in 1865 with a proposed labor contract. But the terms of this contract mocked the idea of free labor. In return for a share of the crops, his former slaves were to continue to work, in gangs of laborers, under Cameron or his agent, who would direct the "whole business of the farm." Every laborer would have to "promise to be perfectly respectable in language and deportment to the proprietor," who could approve or reject any preacher whom the workers desired to hear. All sales "of any species of property, by the Negroes" were subject to Cameron's regulation. The plantation was not to have visitors, and no nonreligious assembly on Sunday would be permitted.

This contract was unacceptable to the black people on Paul Cameron's land, and similar contracts were unpopular elsewhere. Freed from slavery, black people wanted to realize some of the benefits of freedom in their everyday work. They wanted to escape the close supervision and total control of overseers and drivers. They wanted to have their own piece of land to own or rent, or if that proved impossible, at least a piece of land they could work on shares as a family unit. In this way they could live independently and make their own decisions about each day's chores. To gain those benefits, black people throughout the state refused to sign slavelike labor contracts. By holding out for a greater degree of autonomy and self-direction in the conditions of work, they grasped a larger portion of freedom. It was far from a full portion, but it was substantially more than the former slave owners had wanted to grant them.

Another area in which blacks could seize some benefits of freedom immediately was education. Through the Freedmen's Bureau and the efforts of charitable and religious organizations from the North, schools began to open all over North Carolina. These schools were hastily organized affairs, often dependent upon a variety of cast-off books as texts, but they proved immediately and immensely popular. Black people knew that education was important because under slavery the law had rigidly denied it to them. Now that they were free, they leaped at the chance to learn.

One teacher walked into his little schoolhouse to find three hundred black people assembled for a lesson. "I never knew anything like the craving the[y]. . . have to learn," he said. Old people came to night schools after a day of work, fired by "eagerness and youthful enthusiasm." Blacks who did not have free schools in their neighborhood dug into their meager financial resources to support subscription schools. In one school run by the Freedmen's Bureau there were "*representatives of four generations* in a direct line. . . a child of six years, her mother, grandmother, and great grand-mother, the latter being more than seventy-five years of age." The desire for education was powerful and universal.

One of the first benefits of freedom enjoyed by former slaves was the pursuit of an education. Through the efforts of the Freedmen's Bureau and various northern charitable and religious organizations, schools for the former bondsmen began to open throughout North Carolina. A typical "Freedmen's School" is shown here. Engraving from J. T. Towbridge, *The South: A Tour of Its Battle-Fields and Ruined Cities, A Journey through the Desolated States, and Talks with the People* (Hartford, Conn.: L Stebbins, 1866), facing 338.

In a third area—religion—freedom meant that the existing rules had changed. For generations blacks had faced discrimination in the white Christian churches. The preaching they had heard there condoned slavery and invariably said less about loving one's neighbor than about obeying the master and mistress. Not surprisingly, then, black people, having attained their freedom, poured into churches controlled by blacks and into denominations such as the Baptists, who favored independent, locally controlled congregations. The Methodist Episcopal Church, South, declared a group of blacks in Raleigh, had split with its northern wing "for the purpose of perpetuating Slavery" and had "taught rebellion." "Compelled to liston to her ministers till the coming of the Fedaral Army," these blacks explained, "now we Desiar. . . to worship God according to the dictates of our consciences." The secret church of the days of slavery came out into the open as blacks worshiped in their own congregations.

Much energy and enormous amounts of hope went into the search for family members from whom Tar Heel blacks had become separated during slavery. One man, who ended up in Illinois after the Civil War, journeyed back to Roxboro, North Carolina, and surprised parents whom he had not seen in years. They were overjoyed; the father "had a few days previously remarked that he did not want to die without seeing his son once more." The son recalled that he "could not find language to express my feelings. I did not know before I came home whether my parents were dead or alive." Mattie Curtis of Orange County recalled that her parents "tried to find their fourteen oldest chilluns what was sold away, but they never did find but three of them." For other families, whose members lived on different but nearby plantations, the task of reunion was easier but still satisfying. "When we was freed," recalled Betty Cofer, who had been born in 1856 in Forsyth County, "Pappy come to get Ma and me." Bringing the family unit back together was certainly an important gain.

But to secure other dimensions of freedom, black people needed political rights and power, and these were slower in coming and involved risks and dangers of their own. As national politics evolved, Tar Heel blacks gained the rights of political participation. Hoping to make freedom real, they exercised these rights and committed themselves to the rigors of competition in the political arena. The competition, which was vigorous, brought first success, and then violence and disappointment. But again, black people took the opportunities that freedom offered.

The door to political opportunity began to open when the northern-controlled Congress reacted unfavorably to President Andrew Johnson's attempt at Reconstruction. Johnson had pardoned many prominent Confederates, who promptly reappeared in political offices. The white governments that he had constituted in the South passed many laws—some harsher than North Carolina's—that discriminated against the newly freed black people. Outbreaks of racial violence were disturbingly frequent. These developments caused deep concern in the North. Although northerners were not committed to full equality for black people, they assumed that victory, after four years of costly warfare, would produce changes in the South that were more substantial than the ones they saw. Despite the North's victory, it appeared to most of the northern public that unchastened rebels were having things their way. A misguided president was losing the peace.

Accordingly, a majority in the northern Congress intervened in the Reconstruction process and began to draft new conditions that southern states would have to meet in order to rejoin the Union. Andrew Johnson fought the Congress at every step and encouraged white leaders in the South to be intransigent. The split between Congress and president deepened until, early in 1868, the House impeached Johnson, and the

Senate nearly removed him from office. In the meantime, Congress had redesigned the Reconstruction process. Under Congress's plan, the southern states were required to form new governments and to extend to black men the right to vote and participate fully in politics. For a few years northern lawyers also barred the highest-ranking former Confederate officials from political activity.

Congress's actions were significant, though not revolutionary. A few legislators had proposed the confiscation and redistribution of land—"forty acres and a mule"—to blacks. The former slaves desperately wanted such a measure, for in an agricultural society the possession of land would have given them the means to economic independence. But Congress never came close to enacting that proposal, and it moved quickly to wind up the business of the Freedmen's Bureau and leave southern affairs to southerners. Black southerners now were part of the decision-making process, but they could count on no guarantees. Whites were in the majority in most southern states, and they formed a majority of almost two-to-one in North Carolina. Progress for blacks depended on how much support they could gain and how well they could fare in a political competition that was likely to be intense.

Although blacks were aware of the risks, they did not shy away from the attempt to cooperate with whites and make things better. In North Carolina, for a time, the prospects were encouraging. When the new constitutional convention assembled in 1868, the Republican Party showed that it was learning how to organize. This new party, containing both blacks and whites, won 107 of the 120 seats in the convention; fifteen of the delegates were black people. The convention proceeded to write a dramatically more democratic constitution for North Carolina. It guaranteed manhood suffrage, abolished the state's high property qualifications for holding office, provided for the election of judges to terms of eight years, and revamped local government. The county courts, through which an appointed, wealthy elite had for generations controlled local affairs, were scrapped. In their place, the convention created an elected government, consisting of five commissioners, for each county.

The convention also committed the state to a modern system of tax-supported public schools. There was enormous white opposition to the idea of integrated public schools, and Republicans fought only for an expanded school system that would serve whites and blacks separately. James W. Hood, a black leader from Cumberland County, successfully opposed placing in the constitution any reference to separate schools, but he had his own reasons for accepting the practice of racial separation. "I do not believe that it is good for our children," he said, "to eat and drink daily the sentiment that they are naturally inferior to the whites, which they do in three-fourths of all the schools where they have white teachers." It was understood that black and white children would learn separately, but the state constitution now called for public education for all.

Shortly after the convention adjourned, Republicans swept to power in the first elections for the new government. Voters in 1868 elected the Republican William W. Holden as governor, chose the Republican candidate in all but one congressional district, and put Republicans in more than two-thirds of the seats in the legislature.

Among the legislators were twenty black men—three state senators and seventeen representatives. Some of these individuals—including A. H. Galloway, Isham Sweat, and James H. Harris—had been active in the Freedmen's Convention of 1865. All of them came from the east, usually from counties in which blacks formed the majority, and they reflected the diversity within the black population. Most had been slaves, but at least five were free men before the war. Four were mulattoes. They counted among their number Union army veterans, at least three ministers, and one attorney.

James H. Harris was probably the most prominent black official of the day. Born in Granville County in 1832, he had been apprenticed to an upholsterer in Warren County, where he opened his own business after his employer went bankrupt. Probably a free man, Harris was described as a dark-skinned mulatto in 1851. He moved to Ohio and traveled in the United States, Canada, and West Africa before accepting a commission in Indiana to raise the Twenty-eighth Regiment of U.S. Colored Troops. After the war he returned to North Carolina, where he worked for the Freedmen's Bureau and helped to organize the Union League, an organization allied with the Republican Party, in the state. As president of the state Equal Rights League, he had succeeded in obtaining a charter for the organization even before he was elected to the legislature.

Republicans also dominated the elections for county governments, putting into office a new kind of official. In New Hanover County, for example, the Democrats, or Conservatives, as they were then known, nominated for the county commission five men who sat previously on the county court, wealthy men who had owned considerable property and slaves. The Republicans defeated them with nominees who owned far less property, including one African American. Instead of planters, slave owners, lawyers, and physicians, the people holding power were plain farmers, mechanics, blacksmiths, and artisans, and some of these new officials were black.

Black people did not dominate or control the new political system—their numbers were too few for that—and when blacks gained office their proportion among officeholders was usually less than the percentage of blacks in the total population. But their presence in politics at all was a stunning change. In Edgecombe County, for example, two of the five county commissioners were black, and the former slaveholders in that wealthy county, which had led the state in cotton production, surely noted the change.

Because black people formed the majority in sixteen counties in eastern North Carolina, the Republican Party was strong in that part of the state. Republicans also had a strong power base in the mountainous west, where there were few black voters but many strong Unionists and foes of secession. The key to future political control of the state was the Piedmont, where blacks were a not-insignificant minority. If the Republicans could forge a biracial coalition of black voters with 30, 40, or 50 percent of the white voters, they could win in that region and statewide.

Black and white voters began to join together in support of the Republican Party in Piedmont North Carolina, carrying a majority of the counties in the 1868 elections. Most whites in the Piedmont had not been slave owners but small farmers, and they had suffered acutely during the Civil War. With husbands and sons away in the armies, many families had struggled to survive and had known real hunger. For them the war had brought primarily death, destruction, and impoverishment, and many blamed those results on the group of leaders who had long been in charge. One man who wrote to Governor Holden denounced the "unhung rebels" in the Democratic Party and said: "I do not want such men to dictate and domineer over me and my friend[s] as has [been the case] for the last 8 or 10 years." Joining with black voters, these whites decided it was time for a change.

With Republicans in office, black Tar Heels could expect local judges and constables to treat them with a reasonable degree of fairness and respect and not side automatically with the former slaveholders. Black Republicans and white Republicans as well were enthusiastic for expansion and better funding of the public school system. This issue excited the strongest interest among black representatives and senators in the legislature. They joined white Republicans in passing a law that established a school term of four

Beginning in 1868 African American men were elected members of the North Carolina General Assembly for the first time. Throughout the Reconstruction period blacks served in a variety of state and local offices. Shown here are members of the 1874 North Carolina House of Representatives, fourteen of whom were African American. Photograph from Appleton Oaksmith Papers, Southern Historical Collection, Wilson Library, University of North Carolina at Chapel Hill; reproduced by permission.

months and guaranteed each child a minimum of sixteen months of schooling. Going beyond this, the black legislators pushed, unsuccessfully, for a bill to allow localities to tax themselves further for the support of schools. A majority of them opposed separate schools for each race, and, though they were unsuccessful on that issue, they prevailed in having James W. Hood, a black minister and educator, appointed assistant to the superintendent of public education.

The Republicans also improved and opened state-operated charitable institutions, such as the lunatic asylum, to people of both races. To revive the economy of the state, Republicans put their faith in railroad development, which was tremendously popular in that day among all parties. They promised generous support to many schemes to link isolated communities with new miles of track. Black legislators tried, without success, to require equal treatment in transportation and public actions and fought vigilantly at all times for equality before the law. They were supporters of reform as well, and were interested in women's suffrage, temperance, and the ten-hour workday. All these measures improved either the welfare or the prospects of black North Carolinians.

But the new Republican regime faced political challenges that would have been substantial under the best of circumstances. New programs, such as those proposed for improved public education, cost money, and the state's wealth had been devastated by the war. Moreover, in previous years a tax on slaves had produced a large portion of all tax revenues, but with property in slaves abolished, the tax burden fell much more fully on land and weighed heavily on small landowners as well as large planters. Many of the railroad proposals were overly optimistic or poorly planned, and some of the railroad promoters were plainly corrupt. To get their way, they bribed some of the legislators, who in many cases found themselves in economic straits because of discrimination against them as Republicans.

Recovering from their defeat, the Democrats were beginning to fight back. A prominent white Republican state senator, John W. Stephens of Caswell, who later was murdered, admitted that "I have not means to buy what I actually kneed for the support of my family." Black Republicans received offers of "the most *tempting* considerations . . . to come out and curse the [Republican] party." One man who refused such an offer found that "My life has been freely threatened, and once attempted." He also described the economic pressure to which black Tar Heels, who owned little or no land and had only their labor to sell, were especially vulnerable:

"[There is] a general conspiracy among the landowners of this section to starve me and my family out and to kill or drive me from the country."

Between 1868 and 1872 opposition to the biracial Republican Party often took the form of violence, and at the center of the violence was the Ku Klux Klan. "When we pushed our rights," recalled a black man named Squire Dowd, the Ku Klux Klan became active. W. L. Bost accurately recalled their costumes: "They wear long gowns, touch the ground. . . . Some time they put sticks in the top of the tall thing they wear and then put an extra head up there with scary eyes and great big mouth." Their acts were plain in the memory of Mandy Coverson, who had lived in Union County. "They done a heap of beatin' and chasin' folks out of the country," she said, and she suspected that the contest for political power "was mostly the cause of it."

The Ku Klux Klan, a secret terrorist organization created to intimidate African Americans and other minorities, made its appearance in North Carolina in 1868. Its members donned masks and robes and engaged in nighttime raids designed to discourage its victims from participating in political activities. The Klan particularly sought to blunt the political gains achieved by the Republican Party after 1868. Shown at left is a Klansman clad in typical regalia; at right is an authentic KKK mask created about 1870 by an actual member of the Klan who resided in Person County. The mask, made of cloth and trimmed in red and black ribbon, features a mustache, beard, and side-whiskers fashioned of rabbit fur. Photograph at left from the Barden Photograph Collection in the custody of the State Archives; at right from the North Carolina Museum of History.

Centered in the Piedmont, the Ku Klux Klan had as its leaders the old elite of Democratic officeholders who had been driven from power by the Republican revolution. Determined to regain power, these former leaders employed the Klan for political purposes. Although the Klan sometimes terrorized blacks as a means of controlling their labor or making them act once again in a subservient, slavelike manner, it sought most of all to damage the Republican coalition. Because the party's margin of victory had been narrow in the Piedmont, violence there had the clear potential to reverse the Republicans' gains. By frightening some voters into staying away from the polls or by inducing some whites to return to the Democratic Party for reasons including race, the Ku Klux Klan could tip the electoral balance.

Accordingly, Klansmen launched a campaign of terror throughout the Piedmont. Among the most famous victims were white Republican leader John W. Stephens, who was stabbed to death in the Caswell County courthouse, and a well-known black Republican, Wyatt Outlaw, whose body was found one morning hanging from a tree outside the Alamance County Courthouse. But hundreds of others suffered beatings, whippings, and shootings. There were between one hundred and two hundred whippings in Rutherford County alone, and far more in Alamance, Caswell, Chatham, Cleveland, Gaston, Guilford, Lincoln, Mecklenburg, Montgomery, Moore, Orange, and Randolph counties combined. Dozens of school-houses where black people were learning to read burned to the ground. Scores of farmers could "not sle[ep] in their houses any time" during months of Ku Klux Klan night-riding.

African American residents of North Carolina's Piedmont counties were especially vulnerable to intimidation by the Ku Klux Klan in the tumult-uous 1870–1871 period. Caswell Holt of Graham (Alamance County), a victim of Klan violence, was forced to flee the county. Photograph of Holt (1912) courtesy Southern Historical Collection.

Essie Harris, who worked a farm in Chatham County for an elderly white man and the man's sister, had his cabin window broken in late one night by Klansmen, who immediately began to shoot at him. For nearly ninety minutes the night riders fired into his house. "The shot just rained like rain," Harris recalled. Although the elderly white employer and his sister both ventured from their home to plead, "Gentlemen, . . . let this nigger alone. . . . He is a hard-working nigger, and don't bother anybody," the Klan forced them back inside. Before his ordeal was over, Harris wounded one of his attackers, but he was shot "almost to pieces" and severely frightened. "I thought my wife and children were all dead," Harris said. "I did not expect anything else."

Daniel Jordan, a black man in Alamance County, experienced the most common type of Klan violence. In the dark of night ten Klansmen suddenly broke into his house, frightened his child, and chased him outside into the surrounding woods. Soon they caught him and gave him a thorough whipping—forty or fifty blows with switches. Places where blacks met to discuss politics, either in the Republican Party or through the Union League, came under attack. More than one black church building was burned down because the Klan opposed the organizing that it assumed was taking place there.

In Cleveland County a black man seized an ax and killed two or three of his attackers. Kitty Hill recalled that another man near Pittsboro waited until the Klansmen broke a hole through his door and then "blammed down on them with a gun and shot one of their eyes out." But these acts of resistance did not stop the Ku Klux Klan from committing murders and beatings that terrorized many people. After the Klan's campaign in Cleveland County, a white Republican estimated that of "some three or four hundred colored voters," not "twenty-five of them would dare to vote the republican ticket now." "And," he added, "I do not think that in Rutherford [County] the colored men would dare to vote at this time." Essie Harris stated after he recovered from his wounds that "I do not expect to vote anymore. It is not worth while for a man to vote and run the risk of his life."

Thus, the Klan's reign of terror was effective. Added to vigorous Democratic appeals against taxes, railroad corruption, and racial change, the campaign of violence turned the tide against the Republican Party. In 1870 the Democrats regained control of the legislature, and in 1871 they impeached Governor Holden and removed him from office. Four years later Democrats called for a new constitutional convention. "The Issue," declared the *Alamance Gleaner*, was "Shall the [convention] . . . be controlled by white men or by the negroes of the State." "You are not in favor of negro equality," the paper argued. "Then leave the party that advocates it. You owe it to yourself, and your children, . . . to your race, and your country."

Although Republicans fought back and actually won a plurality of votes statewide, the Democrats carried more counties for the convention and narrowly controlled its membership. This convention drew up amendments that would roll back many of the most important changes of Reconstruction. It proposed giving to the General Assembly "full power by statute to modify, change, or abrogate" the system of elective county government that had come into being in 1868. The argument in support of this sweeping restriction of democracy was racial: in eastern counties in which blacks were in the majority, whites must control the government. One Democratic broadside charged that black majorities caused "White Slavery in North Carolina—Degradation Worse Than Death" and called on white voters to "Help Your Eastern Brethren By Voting For the Constitutional Amendment." The convention also proposed amendments prohibiting intermarriage and integrated schools.

The 1876 campaign was a heated and vigorous one, with popular Democrat Zebulon B. Vance running for governor against Republican Thomas Settle. Amid strong racist appeals Vance won, and the constitutional amendments were adopted. Promptly the legislature abolished the elective system of county governments and put appointed officials—usually white and Democratic—back in control. Reconstruction had been overthrown, or, as Democratic propaganda alleged, the state had been "redeemed" from the horrors of Negro rule.

What did this mean for black North Carolinians? It was, of course, a profoundly depressing denouement for a period that had begun in high hopes. Although black North Carolinians had not yet lost their political or civil rights under the Constitution, the tide had turned against them in a region where racial prejudice had a long history. They still could vote and hold office, if elected, but it was certain that their power would be slight, probably inadequate even to block discriminatory measures that might be proposed against them. The political rights that they enjoyed had little effect under the circumstances.

Economically, black people had gained freedom without gaining a foothold on the path to economic security. Predominantly agriculturalists, they lacked land of their own. As sharecroppers, they had to divide their crops with a landowner and go into debt each year to a furnishing merchant, who advanced them needed supplies as a loan against the harvest. Required to grow cotton, southern sharecroppers increasingly found that the price of cotton—and their welfare—was declining. It was possible for some individuals to make progress and improve their position, but the situation for black people as a whole was bleak and inhospitable.

The most tangible benefits of emancipation had proven to be personal gains. Black people now could worship in their own churches and hear the gospel preached by their own ministers. They could work each day under their own supervision, instead of under the obtrusive control of an overseer or owner. They could live together in family units, knowing that in freedom no white landowner could buy their wives and children and send them away. These were precious gains, important steps up from slavery, but they fell far short of the equal chance that black Americans desired.

The failure of Reconstruction was manifest in 1877. After a disputed election, the Republican Party compromised with the white South, abandoning interference in southern affairs in return for the election of Rutherford B. Hayes as president. In disappointment, black people from many parts of the South began to move west and out of the region. Known as "Exodusters," those emigrants hoped to find more opportunity in areas such as Oklahoma or Kansas. It is estimated that several thousand black people left eastern North Carolina at that time to seek a new life in Kansas and Indiana. Those who stayed knew that the road ahead would not be easy.

An unusually large number of African Americans departed the South after 1877. Many set out for areas such as Kansas, Oklahoma, or Indiana. Several thousand black people are estimated to have left eastern North Carolina in pursuit of better economic opportunities. Shown in this engraving are black North Carolina emigrants waiting at a railroad station. From *Frank Leslie's Illustrated Newspaper*, February 15, 1890.

Looking back from the 1930s on the era of emancipation and Reconstruction, former slaves identified the weakness of their position and spoke eloquently of the joy and the despair they had experienced. "Slavery was a bad thing," affirmed Raleigh's Patsy Mitchner, who remembered that the "slaves prayed for freedom." But "freedom of the kind we got with nothin' to live on was bad. Two snakes full of poison. . . . Their names was slavery and freedom. The snake called slavery lay with his head pointed south and the snake called freedom lay with his head pointed north. Both bit the nigger, and they was both bad."

Thomas Hall, who had been a slave in Orange County, explained more fully his thoughts based on a lifetime of experience: "Lincoln got the praise for freeing us, but did he do it? He give us freedom without giving us any chance to live to ourselves, and we still had to depend on the southern white man for work, food, and clothing, and he held us through our necessity and want in a state of servitude but little better than slavery. . . . The Yankees helped free us," Hall concluded, "but they let us be put back in slavery again." For most black people, as for Thomas Hall, the road up from slavery was hard. Nevertheless, in the years between Reconstruction and the turn of the twentieth century, thousands of black North Carolinians labored to rise on that road.

VI

Progress and Repression

The period from 1877 to 1900 was a complex time for black North Carolinians. It was a time of growth and progress in many ways, as black people earned a living, reared their children, pursued the benefits of education, and strove to better themselves individually and collectively. In another sense it was a time of vitality and change, as diversity became a notable characteristic of the black community. Free to follow a variety of paths, blacks became businessmen as well as farmers, urban dwellers as well as rural folk, and men and women of high culture as well as untutored simplicity. Yet, these were also years of retrogression and ultimate disappointment, as racism eroded the legal foundations of civil and political rights for black Americans.

With the benefit of hindsight, historians have focused on the crushing reverses and new forms of oppression that wrote the conclusion of this chapter of history. In 1896 the Supreme Court of the United States, in the *Plessy v. Ferguson* decision, decreed that "separate but equal" facilities (which in fact were never equal and always discriminatory) did not violate the constitutional rights of black citizens. During the decade of the 1890s, one southern state after another passed laws or constitutional amendments depriving black citizens of their right to vote. A vicious white-supremacy campaign in 1898 launched this process in North Carolina, and the adoption of a constitutional amendment in 1900 completed it. Immediately, new "Jim Crow" laws began to appear on the books of state and local governments, requiring segregation and discrimination in one area of life after another.

These years were the "nadir" period, "the lowest point in the quest for equal rights," according to black historian Rayford Logan. "Second-class citizenship for Negroes," Logan explained, "was accepted by Presidents, the Supreme Court, Congress, organized labor, the General Federation of

Women's Clubs—indeed by the vast majority of Americans, North and South, and by the 'leader' of the Negro race [Booker T. Washington]." Logan saw an iron curtain of bigotry descending on black Americans with scarcely a contrary movement or protest.

Unquestionably, Rayford Logan's judgment was well founded. Yet, to view the period only in this way is to read history backward and to ignore the way people experienced the years from 1877 to 1900. In the 1880s no one, white or black, knew what would happen in 1900. In the years before disfranchisement black North Carolinians had work to do, goals to reach, and progress to make. They set about performing those tasks. Rather than worrying about the future, they labored to make things better in the present.

The record of those years reveals obstacles and problems, but it also contains substantial evidence of optimism and purpose. With slavery behind them, black people wanted to improve their condition and grasp freedom's opportunities. Their individual and joint efforts often focused on progress or the betterment of the race. Knowing that the white majority was not yet willing to give them an equal chance, blacks worked to gain ground and be ready for the day when equality would be theirs. Many pursued goals of betterment with a sense of mission.

Before the imposition of segregation and disfranchisement, there were three themes to black experience after 1877: organization, uplift, and increasing diversity. At both the state and local levels, blacks formed many groups, large and small, for pleasure, self-improvement, and mutual support. After the regimentation of slavery, this organizing impulse allowed black people to express themselves and determine their own goals. Through all their activities, secular and religious, ran a strong strain of racial uplift— the self-improvement and advancement of a once-enslaved race. And, as the black community grew and progressed, unprecedented diversity emerged among its members, whose varied talents and tastes produced a wide range of social classes and life-styles.

Association with others has always brought pleasure and benefits for Americans, whose tendency to join together in groups is sometimes seen as an identifying national characteristic. Naturally, then, the impulse to organize and associate had a strong attraction for black North Carolinians. For generations slave owners and the law had tightly restricted their mobility and communication with each other. One of the blessings of freedom for blacks was the opportunity it afforded to come together.

Black clubs, lodges, and societies also provided their members with chances to speak, to lead, and to develop their abilities.

In North Carolina's cities and towns—Raleigh, Charlotte, Wilmington, and smaller communities—it was easier for people to come together, and consequently clubs flourished there, although they were never absent from the rural counties. The *Charlotte Messenger*, a black newspaper edited and published by William C. Smith, regularly reported the activities of numerous lodges and social groups through the 1880s. Their meetings and parties were as important a part of the black community's social life as wedding celebrations. In February 1887, the *Messenger* listed six "social societies among colored people" in Charlotte: the Winona, the Oriole, the Young Men's Pleasure Club, the Young Ladies' Pleasure Club, the Young Ladies' Independent Club, and the Married Ladies' Social Tea.

In addition to these purely social organizations, black people formed a variety of fraternal, service-oriented, or benevolent organizations. Volunteer fire companies were a necessity in urban areas before municipalities provided fire protection, and considerable pride and élan attached to membership in those groups. When the *Charlotte Messenger* praised one company of firemen in 1882, it aroused a protest from another company whose members, equally deserving, had not been mentioned. A larger number of black men belonged to the Royal Knights of King David or to the United Order of True Reformers, lodges that were active throughout the state—as was a similar organization for women, the Household of Ruth. To those one must add the Masons, the Odd Fellows, the Good Templars, and the Sons of Ham, all popular organizations that had a wide and loyal membership.

As historian Raymond Gavins has pointed out, many of these organizations worked in close cooperation with the black churches. "Business, educational, political, and religious leaders," Gavins writes, "eyed the orders as agencies of character building and self-help." The membership of churches and lodges often overlapped considerably, and lodge members frequently assembled in church-owned halls for their meetings. "The Masons," Gavins observes, "promoted solidarity, thrift, mutual aid, and Christian morality right beside the Baptist State Convention."

Black community life came together in the churches, lodges, and fraternal organizations, all of which functioned as promoters of individual character and group progress. Economically, the associations that members formed were valuable, as the emerging class of artisans, businessmen, and professionals learned to identify and work with each other. From some of the urban organizations—notably burial societies, whose members regularly paid a small fee to defray the funeral costs of any member—evolved insurance companies that became important businesses and sources of employment.

The churches had their own organizations, such as the Baptist Women's Home Mission Convention or the African Methodist Episcopal Zion Woman's Home and Foreign Missionary Society. Between one-third and one-half of all black North Carolinians during this period belonged to churches, with the number and percentage of communicants steadily rising. The Baptists and the AME Zion churches were dominant, accounting for more than 80 percent of all black church members, but substantial numbers of blacks belonged to the African Methodist Episcopal Church, the Colored Methodist Episcopal Church, and the Presbyterian Church, with a sprinkling of individuals in other denominations.

In the era between 1877 and 1900, churches played an important role in the community life of North Carolina's black people. Between one-third and one-half of all black North Carolinians belonged to churches during the period. New Bern's Ebenezer Presbyterian Church, a black congregation, is shown here. Engraving from L. C. Vass, *History of the Presbyterian Church in New Bern, N.C.* . . . (Richmond, Va.: Whittet & Shepperson, Printers, 1886), facing 183.

Charles N. Hunter (ca. 1851–1931), an educator and former slave, along with his brother founded the North Carolina Industrial Association in 1879 as a means of improving the lives of the state's African Americans through emphasis on economic progress rather than political activity. One of Hunter's most ambitious and successful goals was to establish an annual industrial fair to publicize that progress. Photograph from Charles N. Hunter, *Review of Negro Life in North Carolina with My Recollections* (Raleigh: N.p., n.d.), frontispiece.

At the state level, two other organizations achieved considerable notice. The first of these was the North Carolina Industrial Association (NCIA), founded by Charles N. Hunter, an educator and former slave, and his brother, Osborne. The Industrial Association focused on the promotion of economic progress, instead of political activity, among black people. According to its charter, which Charles N. Hunter drafted and secured from the legislature in 1879, the purpose of the NCIA was to "encourage and promote the development of the industrial and educational resources of the colored people of North Carolina," most notably by holding "annually an exhibition of the progress of their industry and education."

Despite initial opposition by blacks who feared that Hunter was subservient to white Democrats, the champions of white supremacy, the Industrial Fair became a success, and the North Carolina Industrial Association grew in numbers and influence. Blacks prepared exhibits designed to show how much their communities had accomplished. Gov. Thomas Jarvis addressed the fair repeatedly during his terms in office (1879–1885), and other prominent white people visited the fair. Some came on their own to observe, whereas others were invited by the black organizers in recognition of their support for measures helpful to the black community.

By the mid-1880s the fair had become, according to historian John H. Haley, "the most popular social event for blacks in North Carolina." From all over the state blacks came to Raleigh to mingle, to compete for distinction, and to enjoy themselves. During the fair prominent black men and women became better acquainted with each other, formed friendships,

The North Carolina Industrial Fair quickly became "the most popular social event for blacks in North Carolina." Prominent white political leaders, notably North Carolina governor Thomas J. Jarvis, frequently attended the annual event, as did their black counterparts from throughout the nation. Shown in this engraving is a large contingent of African Americans passing down Raleigh's Fayetteville Street on its way to the Industrial Fair. From *Frank Leslie's Illustrated Newspaper*, December 6, 1879.

and discussed the status and future of the race. Outstanding black leaders received invitations to address the fair, and by the 1890s the North Carolina Industrial Association had become one of the most inclusive black organizations in the state. "Its rolls," according to Haley, "included almost every prominent black in the state."

The North Carolina State Teachers Association had a similarly distinguished membership. Black political leaders had always shown a great interest in education, a master key to future progress for the race. When the State Colored Education Convention met in Raleigh in 1877, with 140 delegates from forty counties in attendance, it selected former legislator James H. Harris as president. Other prominent politicians played active roles, including former state senator and representative G. W. Price of New Hanover and his colleague George L. Mabson, who became vice-president of the convention. At the fourth annual meeting of the State Teachers Association in 1885, the Executive Committee included two future congressmen—Henry Plummer Cheatham of Plymouth and George Henry White of New Bern. Education was so important to race progress that prominent men from other fields joined black educators to plan improvements.

Through many of the activities mentioned above, and even more strongly in other endeavors, ran a unifying thread: an emphasis on racial self-improvement and uplift. For a race just liberated from slavery, there was much to do in all areas, both to strengthen the race and to protect its position in the future. Consequently, black leaders took naturally to a role as exhorters of progress and cheerleaders for those who climbed higher. The goal of uplift revealed itself clearly in black newspapers, in educational efforts, and in religious leadership.

William C. Smith, for example, began publishing the *Charlotte Messenger* "to promote the moral, intellectual and material standing of our people." Though he did not neglect politics, Smith took very seriously his responsibilities for promoting uplift in all nonpolitical ways. The pages of his paper regularly listed, approvingly, the churches in the black community and lauded special achievements such as the fact that "Clinton Sabbath school runs up to over 175 scholars." Editor Smith printed inspiring sermons on his pages and urged morality and high purpose for leaders and ordinary citizens alike. In 1882 he took Charlotte's young black men to task for showing "too great love for pleasure and too little for learning." Shortly after printing that article, he called for the establishment of a night school for young men in the city.

At all times Smith was an advocate for progress, citing individuals' accomplishments to spur the black community on to new success. When the black people of Tarboro made plans to erect a college, Smith's paper helped publicize the fact and commended their example to others for imitation. In 1886, Smith proudly noted the return to Charlotte of Dr. J. T. Williams, formerly a young schoolteacher, who had earned a medical degree and opened his practice as the first licensed black physician in North Carolina. "Since we have here a colored newspaper, [and] a colored doctor," the *Messenger* proclaimed, "next we want a colored lawyer." A year later Smith praised the blacks of Fayetteville for producing no fewer than seven lawyers to serve the needs of their race. "Patronize our lawyers, doctors, preachers, and teachers," Smith urged in 1888, arguing that such racial solidarity opened a way for youth to advance. He also counseled his readers never to hold each other down because of rivalry or pride.

Progress in education was a special interest of editor Smith. Each year his paper carefully covered the graduation exercises at black schools, including nearby Scotia Seminary for girls and Biddle University, and he vigorously endorsed the opening of new institutions for black people. During the 1880s the AME Zion denomination opened Zion Wesley Institute (later Livingstone College) in Salisbury, and Smith's paper applauded each step in its progress and the efforts of its talented president, the Reverend J. C. Price. In 1882 Zion Wesley Institute had completed one building, had another under construction, and reported thirty students in attendance. It progressed rapidly thereafter, growing in enrollment and graduating nine students from the collegiate and three students from the theological department in 1888. The race needed well-trained leaders, and another reason for Smith's enthusiasm was his firm conviction that "The ministry must be educated."

Knowing that primary education for the masses was as vital as higher education for a cadre of leaders, Smith and other black spokesmen promoted education at all levels. In 1883 the *Messenger* reported with pride that the Colored Graded School in Charlotte had 625 pupils, and a few years later Smith noted that "our new graded school building will be large and well ventilated, each of the eight rooms having fine, large windows." Normal schools also were essential to train greater numbers of teachers for the coming generations. By 1887 there were normal schools for blacks in Salisbury, Plymouth, Franklinton, Fayetteville, and New Bern, and discussion of the need for a state-supported "Normal and Collegiate Institute" for blacks was growing.

The career of the Reverend J. C. Price illustrates the central role of education as a means of uplift for the race. Although he was only twenty-eight years old in 1882, when he became president of Zion Wesley Institute, Price rapidly attained regional and national prominence as a black leader. He traveled widely, raising more than $10,000 for his school in England and returning repeatedly to New England, other parts of the North, and California to interest philanthropists in the work to which he dedicated his life. As he journeyed he spoke frequently about education and racial progress, and his stature as a black leader grew.

From the end of his training in theology to his premature death, from kidney disease, in 1893, Price adhered to a coherent set of ideas about education, uplift, and equality. "The American Negro has a peculiar work," Price declared in an oration on his commencement day, 1881. "Our mission here is providential and peculiar . . . the carrying out of a

At the age of twenty-eight the Reverend J. C. Price (1854–1893) became president of Salisbury's Zion Wesley Institute (later known as Livingstone College) and subsequently rose to national prominence as a zealous campaigner for black self-help and uplift. Throughout his career Price maintained an unswerving faith in the capacity of black Americans to achieve moral, educational, and social progress through character and inner strength. Updated photograph from the *News and Observer* (Raleigh) Negative Collection, in custody of the State Archives.

divine plan," he said. As Price looked to the future, he believed that "The Negro himself . . . is to solve his own problem" through moral and material progress founded upon character and education. Inner strength would be the foundation for social progress.

Emancipation by itself, Price argued, could not give black people equality, for the evil heritage of slavery still worked against them. "We are insulted," he declared, "not because we are black or colored, but because we belonged to [an] enslaved race," and he frankly acknowledged that slavery's "influence still lives in the democratic party." To gain "the full stature of an American citizen," black people would have to develop their potential and realize their destiny. "Legislation has not solved this problem," he noted. "The 14th and 15th amendments and the Constitution itself have not done it. The solution must come through the gradual, but thorough development of his [the Negro's] mental and moral nature." In accord with these beliefs, Price dedicated himself unreservedly to "the Christian enlightenment of a race whose future will determine to a great extent the weal or woe of the republic."

This faith in the capacity of black Americans to secure their rights through moral, educational, and social progress did not prevent Price from denouncing discrimination. When white southerners urged the nation to leave the fate of the Negro in their hands, Price answered that the Negro was "willing and ready to live in peace with white brethren under any conditions save those which violate the very essence of his being and imply the surrender of his manhood and God-given rights." Compromise was possible, he continued, but any "compromise that reverses the Declaration of Independence, nullifies the national constitution, and is contrary to the genius of this republic, ought not to be asked of any race living under the stars and stripes; and if asked, ought never to be granted." Countering white propaganda about the political power of blacks, Price asserted that "The Negro is not seeking supremacy through the ballot, he is not after power, but protection—not control, but rights." And he flatly denied that "to give the Negro a free ballot where he is the majority, means mismanagement and financial ruin to the country or district in which he resides."

In 1887, in a speech at Charleston, South Carolina, Price proved his ability to defend black interests while favorably impressing white observers. Attuned to the racial thinking so popular among whites at the end of the nineteenth century, Price praised "mind power" as the key to Anglo-Saxon success and then documented several examples of impressive mind power among black leaders. After praising the progress of blacks in Georgia, who owned 800,000 acres and $10 million worth of property, he ridiculed the idea of colonization. No one had a better claim as Americans than black people. "Why not," he asked, "send back home the Pilgrims' descendents?" Because prejudice derived from the association of blacks with "a degraded condition," neither removal nor amalgamation was necessary to solve the race problem. Prejudice would disappear, Price argued, as ignorance changed into intelligence, vice into virtue, and poverty into wealth. It was God's plan, he believed, for blacks to civilize and educate themselves in America and ultimately assist in the civilization of Africa. Impressed by his ability, confidence, and power, the Charleston *News and Courier* praised Price as "evidently a deep thinker" and a speaker of "undoubted eloquence [and] beautiful imagery."

Price's ability, industry, and busy speaking schedule resulted in substantial progress for Livingstone College (so named in 1887) and increasing renown for him individually. Offered the post of United States minister to Liberia, Price declined in order to remain true to his mission and to answer those who said, "We can't spare him." In 1890 he became president of a new, national organization, the Afro-American League, which had been founded by New York editor T. Thomas Fortune to defend the rights of black people in the nation. Although the League did not endure, its selection of Price reflected his growing eminence outside the state. It seems very likely that Price would have enjoyed national prominence if his health had remained strong.

James Walker Hood (1831–1918), a northern bishop in the African Methodist Episcopal Zion Church, came to North Carolina in 1864 to work as a missionary among the state's freedmen. He subsequently represented Cumberland County in the state Constitutional Convention of 1868 and from 1868 to 1870 was assistant superintendent of public instruction. He was ordained a bishop of the AME Zion Church in 1872. From its founding until his death, Bishop Hood was chairman of the board of trustees of Livingstone College. Photograph from Carter G. Woodson, *The History of the Negro Church* (Washington, D.C.: Associated Publishers, 1921), 236.

Another religious leader who distinguished himself was James W. Hood, bishop of the AME Zion Church. The church, in Hood's view, was the essential institution for blacks because it "opened the way for the development of the race in a material and intellectual sense." Without "a moral as well as a literal training," Hood declared on another occasion, "we are more likely to have educated rascals than useful citizens." But as a religious leader, Hood gave the strongest support to education and uplift. "I think our first great need is education," said Hood, who had served as assistant to the superintendent of public instruction. Hood also declared that "No matter what the pursuit, education is necessary to make it safe and profitable."

Directing himself to black audiences, Hood could call upon the members of his race to "work out their own salvation" and to progress by paying "strict attention to our habits." He opposed the playing of "cards and other games" on the ground that "We have too much important work on our hands." But Hood also could demand fair treatment from whites. "Take away the hedge, and give the black man an open field," he challenged whites in one public address, "and he [the Negro] will everywhere exhibit qualities of the first order."

As many of the examples cited above suggest, black Tar Heels were becoming a more diverse group in freedom. North Carolina remained a rural state, and the great majority of black people still lived on the land. Because southern agriculture was in a depressed condition and sharecropping was prevalent, many black farmers struggled to stay out of debt or make even slight progress. Yet, even in the rural economy, diversity was appearing as some blacks made progress. At the first Negro State Fair, in 1879, black political leader James E. O'Hara, a northerner who settled in eastern North Carolina, gave an accounting of agricultural success. Praising individuals' "accumulation of wealth," O'Hara declared that black farmers owned "in the county of Halifax over 13,000 acres of land; in the county of Warren over 8,000 acres of land, and in each of the counties of Nash, Wilson, Edgecombe, Wake, Franklin, Granville, Craven, Northampton, Wayne, and thousands of acres."

Moreover, as the black population had grown, a small but increasing proportion had located in the cities and towns, in which rural workers moved into other pursuits and became storekeepers, businessmen, laborers, artisans, or professionals. A black middle class of somewhat more affluent, educated, and aspiring families appeared. Urban amusements and urban life-styles had a natural attraction for these middle-class blacks as they sought to balance work and play. Softball leagues, for example, generated great enthusiasm in towns and cities during the 1890s, and black North Carolinians organized their own teams, which competed within and between cities, to the delight of loyal fans. Reports of dances, balls, and parties claimed space in black newspapers, and articles such as "Marriages in

As the African American population of North Carolina expanded after the Civil War, blacks increasingly left behind their traditional roles as agricultural laborers and moved to cities and towns to take up middle-class trades. This engraving shows a black carpenter who resided in the western North Carolina town of Waynesville about 1875. From Edward King, *The Great South* (Hartford, Conn.: American Publishing Company, 1875), 487.

High Life" described a wedding celebration that began in Hillsborough and ended with a reception in Charlotte.

These diverse life-styles were signs of natural and healthy development in the black community, and another, similar phenomenon was the emergence of debate and disagreement. Churches, because they were the center of much of black life, did not remain free of controversy. As they grew, they sometimes divided, forming new congregations that better suited the tastes or goals of their members. At the beginning of 1886, for example, the *Charlotte Messenger* reported the formation of a new AME Zion congregation that some people regarded as "the prohibition church." Churchmen also differed in their views on the importance of advanced education for the clergy. Should a man answer God's call without going to college first? AME Zion leaders differed vigorously over that question in 1886, with some declaring that uneducated ministers were hurting the denomination and others arguing that a way should be left open for the talented but unschooled preacher.

The growing black community was not monolithic, and the diverse interests and abilities of its members appeared in a variety of economic aspirations. In the eastern part of the state, black businessmen attempted to develop the Wilmington, Wrightsville, and Onslow Railroad. The North Carolina Mutual and Provident Association in Durham and the AME Zion Publishing House in Charlotte emerged as two of the most substantial black businesses. Notable black entrepreneurs included Richard B. Fitzgerald, who manufactured bricks in Durham; John H. Williamson, the editor and publisher of the Raleigh *Gazette*; and Warren C. Coleman of Concord. Coleman built up a very successful mercantile business as a wholesaler and retailer of "groceries, provisions, confectionaries, notions, hay, lumber," and other commodities. Eventually he launched a black-owned and black-operated textile mill, which succumbed, like many other firms, to the depression of the 1890s. Black businesses, though small, were growing and reflecting the diversity and progress of a recently enslaved race.

Despite the outstanding energy and talent of individuals, the future of black people as a whole would depend on the amount of opportunity permitted by the political and economic system. Thus, politics remained a vitally important area of life, one in which blacks won some victories before disfranchisement. Through the 1880s blacks in North Carolina were alert, vigilant, and sometimes combative in politics, resisting attempts to restrict their rights or damage their interests. In the 1890s they joined in a major political revolt, aiding the new Populist Party in a bipartisan, biracial effort

Beginning with a modest combination barbershop and cake and candy store and branching into real estate, a mercantile establishment, and ultimately the Coleman Manufacturing Company, the nation's first black-owned and -operated textile mill, Warren Clay Coleman (1849–1904) of Concord was one of the South's most successful black entrepreneurs. Photograph from J. K. Rouse, *The Noble Experiment of Warren C. Coleman* (Charlotte: Crabtree Press, 1972), frontispiece.

to alleviate agricultural distress, democratize government, and challenge the privileges of industrial wealth in the state. But this effort eventually was overwhelmed by the white supremacy campaign that brought the nineteenth century to a close. Defeat, disfranchisement, and the new, legally mandated discrimination of the Jim Crow system eventually reduced three and a half decades of life in freedom to a nadir.

Much about the political situation of the 1880s was discouraging. At the end of Reconstruction the Democrats had seized control of the state, returned local government to the hands of appointed officials, and prohibited both interracial marriage and integrated schools. These measures stripped blacks of local political power, at least in the several counties in which they formed a large majority, and signaled an intent by the ascendant Democrats to impose further discriminatory measures. But for a time, fear of renewed federal supervision restrained the Democrats from overt assaults on black citizenship. Moreover, black men still possessed the franchise and exercised their right to vote in large numbers. Although the Democrats were in control, black support kept the Republican Party fairly competitive statewide.

Most black leaders had substantial complaints against the Republicans. Because black voters had no alternative, they stayed with the Republican Party, but they resented the way the party treated them. Republicans relied upon the votes of black people but offered black leaders few nominations for office, even to minor positions. In an editorial entitled, "Colored Men in Office," the *Charlotte Messenger* declared in 1882 that "the colored man has had nothing like justice in this particular." Five or six years before, whites had argued that black Republicans lacked education, but now, the paper observed, there was no change in practice, even though two or three hundred blacks had graduated from colleges during that time. Later that year the *Messenger* demanded that blacks receive some spaces on the ticket, since they furnished four-fifths of Mecklenburg County's Republican votes. In 1886 the editor advised blacks to "cast your vote for no man who will not agree to give us colored men on juries." "Access to the jury box," he argued, will be worth more than "a ballot that counts only one way."

But in some urban wards and in several eastern counties, black residents were a majority, and in those locales political activity by blacks put some of them in office. Black candidates won such offices as register of deeds or solicitor and continued to hold higher offices. In the years from 1877 to 1890, for example, Edgecombe County elected eleven different black men to the state legislature to serve fifteen terms. New Hanover County in the same period elected six black men to the legislature for twelve terms. Statewide during these years, forty-three blacks became state representatives, and eleven became state senators, serving a total of sixty-five and sixteen terms respectively (see Appendix 1).

Outnumbered and facing much hostility, these legislators could not pass many bills, but they could and did speak up for the interests of their race. The same was true of men from the Second Congressional District, the famous "Black Second," which sent to Congress James E. O'Hara of New Bern from 1883 to 1887 and Henry Plummer Cheatham of Vance County from 1889 to 1893. O'Hara and Cheatham would be followed, a few years later (1897–1901), by George H. White of New Bern, who proved to be the last black congressman elected from the South until after the civil rights movement of the 1960s.

During the 1880s black officeholders and spokesmen fought courageously for a fair chance and against efforts to restrict black freedom and opportunity. A clear example of the ability and readiness of blacks to speak out during the 1880s may be found in the issue of lynching. This crime, a spreading form of racial terrorism, was increasing alarmingly, but that fact did not quiet editor William C. Smith, who boldly condemned it. In 1887 Smith's *Charlotte Messenger* charged that "a majority of the white press of the South encourage [lynching]" and declared that *every* participant

In the years between 1872 and 1901 North Carolina's Second Congressional District became known as the "Black Second" because of the frequency with which African Americans were elected from that district. Henry Plummer Cheatham (1857–1935; *left*) and George H. White (1852–1918; *right*) were two of the black men who represented the Black Second during much of that period. Engraving of Cheatham from W. H. Quick, *Negro Stars in All Ages of the World* (Richmond, Va.: S. B. Adkins & Co., second edition, 1898), 211; photograph of White from Josephus Daniels, *Editor in Politics* (Chapel Hill: University of North Carolina Press, 1941), facing 314.

in a lynching ought to "be hung as a murderer." Among blacks, Smith said, "organization is necessary" to stop the crime.

A year later Smith's paper reported that a white man had been lynched by colored men "for an outrage upon a colored woman." When a white paper explained that the white assailant was " 'weak-minded'," an angry Smith shot back, "Don't the *Chronicle* know that any 'negro brute' who attempts such an outrage is " 'weak-minded.'" Then he continued:

If white men are justifiable in lynching a negro for a certain crime, then black men are justifiable in lynching a white man for the same. Colored men have borne these great wrongs very patiently many years. A spirit of retaliation is growing—and who can blame the colored man? Don't we love our women as dearly as the white men love theirs? . . . We advise and urge upon colored men everywhere to see that our women are protected against the vile of our own and low "weak-minded" white men. When one of our ladies is insulted, see that the brute is punished, whether he be black or white.

In 1886 education rose to the top of the agenda for North Carolina's blacks with open discussion of the need for a state-supported black college. The North Carolina State Teachers Association, with the Reverend J. C. Price as president, petitioned the governor for an appropriation of $10,000 to establish a state college for black youth. Such an institution, the association believed, was necessary to provide educational opportunity beyond the level of state-operated or private normal schools and private colleges.

This proposal became unusually controversial after one speaker at the association's convention declared, according to a newspaper report: "if the legislature refuses to provide for us, who can object to our knocking at the doors of the State University at Chapel Hill?" White politicians and newspapers immediately thundered against this threat to white society and the specter of social equality that it ostensibly raised. Defending black rights, the *Charlotte Messenger* countered: "We want no social equality. We want fair opportunities to educate our youth, and we want the State to do its part." Debate over this issue continued into the 1887 legislative session, before which J. C. Price and numerous other black educators testified on one side or the other. This activity resulted in an $8,000 appropriation to be divided among the state-supported normal schools but not to finance a new institution. The *Star of Zion* (Salisbury) called this result "a fair compromise," while other black spokesmen called for more substantial evidence of fair treatment.

Of greater importance for black education generally was the fight against the Dortch Act. In 1883 the Democratic-controlled legislature passed a bill that empowered localities to divide the revenues that supported public education. If as few as ten citizens petitioned, any school district could call for an election on the question of whether white tax revenues should support only white schools and black tax receipts support only black schools. Moreover, if whites called for the election, blacks could not vote, and vice versa. Since black North Carolinians had little property, compared to the white population, this bill threatened the virtual destruction of black public education, which was essential for the progress of the race.

Black leaders of all backgrounds denounced and opposed the Dortch Act. Even the conservative Charles N. Hunter, who usually worked assiduously to maintain cordial relationships with powerful whites, spoke out strongly. He denounced the assumption behind the bill that some must rule while others must be kept in subjugation and ignorance, and he assailed the idea, prevalent among whites, that blacks should be "thankful and satisfied with any miserable pittance which in sheer charity may be doled out to them." What was at stake was a matter of rights. The act was grossly unconstitutional, Hunter declared, and blacks had to fight against it.

Representative James H. Harris joined Hunter by calling the law "wrong and unjust." Another black lawmaker, Noah Newby of Pasquotank County, suggested that many blacks would leave North Carolina "when such an injustice is done them." The *Star of Zion* attacked the Dortch Act as a "monstrous enactment—a disgrace to the State." Black voters began to use their power, where they could, to block changes in school funding. In Tarboro, for example, the black majority defeated a shift to racially based funding, causing the editor of the local white newspaper, the *Tarboro Southerner*, to criticize their "ingratitude."

The North Carolina State Teachers Association also marshaled its opposition to the act, and—in a reversal of white paternalists' tactics—denounced the ingratitude of white people. For more than 250 years, the association pointed out, black people had labored to build up the South. Yet this law allowed a newly arrived white immigrant "who had never dug up a root or planted a flower in this beautiful Southland" to benefit from high-quality schools that were being denied to blacks.

The fight over the Dortch Act had a happy ending. Black opposition led to a series of legal challenges, and in 1886 the state supreme court ruled that the law was unconstitutional. According to the state's constitution— a document written during Reconstruction by black and white Republicans—"there shall be no discrimination in favor of or to the prejudice of either race," the court announced. Although unfriendly white sentiments remained strong, blacks had nullified them on the Dortch Act and successfully defended their rights.

The stakes of politics proved much higher in the 1890s, when the entire direction of southern politics and society came into question. At the root of a massive challenge to Democratic control lay profound economic discontent, not only among black sharecroppers but also among average white farm families. Southern farmers were growing cotton as their main cash crop; indeed, merchants and creditors who advanced the food and supplies that farmers needed usually insisted that the farmers raise cotton. Yet, the price of cotton was steadily falling, from 15 cents a pound in the 1870s to 5 cents a pound or less in the 1890s. Farmers could not survive at those prices, and they resented as well the exactions and privileges available to railroads and corporations. While farmers everywhere were suffering, industries in the much-heralded "New South" were growing and prospering under the protective hand of government.

Tar Heel agriculturalists, who cherished their independence, were losing their land at an alarming rate. In the twenty years between 1880 and 1900, the number of tenants in the state burgeoned from 53,000 to 93,000, and the percentage of farms operated by tenants rose from one-third to 41.4 percent. Black farmers had been suffering for years, and an estimated 47,000 despairing blacks had left the state during the 1880s. In the 1890s white farming families grew desperate as they saw their futures foreclosed. "The money men have closed in on us," one man complained, while another predicted ominously that capitalists "will crush the farmer." "Damn a country," said a third, "where there is nobody prosperous but the bond-holder and the money-lender."

The social and moral basis of society seemed to be changing for the worse. As a farmer named J. A. Wilson put it, "Owing to legislation in favor of monopolies our lands are gradually slipping from the hands of the wealth-producing classes and going into the hands of the few. I do not believe that God ever intended that a few should own the earth, but that each should have a home." Another Tar Heel farmer declared: "The issue confronting the American people today is the liberty of the laboring people, both white and black, an issue of vastly more importance than the enslavement or freedom of the negro ever was."

As this comment suggests, a growing number of white farmers viewed the crisis as more fundamental even than maintaining racial barriers. They were ready to consider cooperation with black voters, if that was a way to remedy their perilous situation. Two events soon made the possibility of biracial cooperation a reality. First, the Democratic Party failed to act on the program of the farmers, expressed through the Farmers' Alliance. The breach with the Democrats began to open in 1890, when Senator Zebulon Vance opposed key parts of the Alliance program. Second, it became evident that farmers' candidates needed the support of black voters in order to win elections. When the Alliance fielded a separate slate of Populist Party candidates in 1892, they took a large number of votes from Democrats but failed to win. Combining Populist support with Republican votes, however, would produce a majority, and it was logical. After all, black Republicans, who were mostly farmers and tenants, suffered from the same problems that troubled the Populists.

To counter such cooperation, the Democrats turned immediately to racial politics. "The success of the Democratic party should not be endangered," warned the *Greensboro Southern Democrat.* "All good citizens," said the paper, would oppose "any" effort to divide white voters on the ground that it might result in "a Republican victory . . . the rule of the Negro." Furnifold M. Simmons, leader of the Democratic Party, warned all party workers in 1892 that success for the Populists threatened to "reman[d] [the state] to the conditions which prevailed during the days of reconstruction." White men had to stand together, the Democrats argued, for white supremacy.

North Carolina Populists were not warm friends of the African American, but they desperately needed to bring about change. Therefore, Populists and Republicans put into practice a tactic called "Fusion." Together Populists and Republicans agreed on a slate of candidates, with some positions being filled by each party. Then they voted for the agreed-upon slate, maintaining their separate party identities but effectively combining their votes. This tactic produced a smashing victory in 1894, when Fusionists won seventy-four seats in the legislature to the Democrats' forty-six. In 1896 the technique of Fusion elected white Republican Daniel L. Russell governor, as 87 percent of eligible black voters went to the polls.

In power, the Populists and white Republican leaders again resisted giving black leaders anything like a fair share of offices or responsibility. But the Fusion victory was a major political upheaval that quickly brought significant improvements for black North Carolinians. The Populists and Republicans agreed on the vital importance of increasing appropriations for the public schools and made education a higher priority. They brought democratic processes back to the selection of local governments, allowing blacks once again—for the first time since Reconstruction was over-thrown—to help elect fair-minded officials. In counties in which the black population was large, some of these officials turned out to be black. The Fusion legislature also shifted the tax burden away from workers and farmers and placed it, to a greater extent than previously, on railroads and wealthy industrial corporations. A new law limited the maximum rate of interest to 6 percent.

The cooperation of white Populists and black Republicans was revolutionizing state politics, destroying Democratic control, and damaging powerful interests loyal to the Democrats. The defeated party struck back

In this derogatory cartoon of Republican governor-elect Daniel L. Russell drawn by Norman E. Jennett of the fiercely Democratic *News and Observer*, Russell's election as governor is characterized as presaging an era of racial permissiveness. Cartoon from *News and Observer*, December 13, 1896.

with its traditional stock-in-trade: racist threats and scare tactics. In 1898 the Democrats relied upon such practices to the greatest degree ever witnessed in North Carolina. According to major Democratic newspapers such as the Raleigh *News and Observer*, the dreaded specter of Negro rule hung over North Carolina, and no white man or woman was safe from insult or humiliation at the hands of ignorant, degraded, half-savage blacks. Democrats charged that Negroes were gaining control of the state and denounced "NEGRO CONGRESSMEN, NEGRO SOLICITORS, NEGRO REVENUE OFFICERS, NEGRO COLLECTORS OF

CUSTOMS, NEGROES in charge of white institutions, NEGROES in charge of white schools," and so on. Claiming that whites would be "forced to social equality" with blacks, Furnifold Simmons called on white voters to assert that "North Carolina is a WHITE MAN'S STATE and WHITE MEN will rule it. . . ."

Not stopping at inflammatory rhetoric, the Democrats mounted a massive program of fraud, intimidation, and violence to assure their victory. Thousands of votes were stolen through ballot-box stuffing or destruction of votes. Red Shirts (typically prosperous, respectable white men devoted to the Democratic Party) appeared throughout the state, mounted and well armed, their clothing helping to call attention to their determination that the Democratic Party would prevail. Numerous Republicans received threats or beatings. In Wilmington a bloody coup d'état occurred in which whites deposed the elected city government, ran out of town the black newspaper editor, Alex L. Manly, who had written a biting editorial on the hypocrisy of lynching, and killed between seven and thirty blacks.

After stealing the 1898 election and regaining control of the legislature, Democrats proceeded to draw up a constitutional amendment that would strip black citizens of their right to vote. This measure was more than a racial proscription, though it certainly embodied and encouraged racial hatreds. It also constituted a potential restructuring of the political system that would remove a large body of dissenting voters from politics and leave powerless those dissenters who remained. The disfranchisement of black North Carolinians would enthrone racism, but in addition it would guarantee the supremacy thereafter of the Democratic Party and the conservative business interests inside it. No longer would insurgent groups such as the Populists have a chance to build a majority.

The Democrats' campaign for this constitutional amendment in 1900 was as vicious and violent as the 1898 campaign. White supremacy clubs and Red Shirts employed threats and intimidation widely. Charles B. Aycock, Democratic candidate for governor, led a propaganda campaign for white supremacy, denouncing whites who opposed the amendment as "public enemies" who deserved the "contempt of all mankind." The tenor of the campaign stood revealed in the words of former congressman and prominent white politician Alfred Moore Waddell of Wilmington. Waddell told a crowd of whites that if they found "the Negro out voting," they should warn him to leave, and "if he refuses, kill him, shoot him down in his tracks."

These provocative cartoons, rendered by N. E. Jennett in 1898, were designed to frighten white voters by portraying the post-1896 political ascendancy of white Populists and black Republicans as a threat to the well-being of white men and women. The 1898 election featured the employment of such race-baiting tactics by the Democratic Party and ushered in a period of political white supremacy. Cartoons from *North Carolinian* (Raleigh), August 25 (*top*), and October 13 (*bottom*), 1898.

With remarkable courage, an estimated 67 percent of black voters risked their lives to vote and defend their rights in 1900. But their efforts were in vain, for the amendment carried. Indeed, fraud had made its passage certain, as the Democrats curiously managed to roll up their "largest and surest majorities . . . in the [N]egro counties and [N]egro districts." Not only had black men lost their right to vote, but opposition movements such as Populism had also lost any realistic chance of succeeding. In future years interest and participation in politics dropped precipitously, for it was clear that the Democrats would win every election. By 1904 there was hardly a black voter in North Carolina.

The success of these white supremacy campaigns cleared the way for discriminatory legislation against black people. The era of Jim Crow arrived in full force in North Carolina and the entire South. With the Supreme Court giving its approval and the North raising no objection to disfranchisement, white lawmakers began to write into the statute books at all levels new requirements of separate, and often grossly inferior, public facilities. Segregation came to envelop black people in every phase of life, from birth to death, stigmatizing them as a despised and inferior race.

Pauli Murray, who overcame discrimination to lead a long life of achievement, nevertheless remembered what it was like to grow up in the Jim Crow world of Durham early in the twentieth century. "The signs," she recalled,

literally screamed at me from every side—on streetcars, over drinking fountains, on doorways: FOR WHITE ONLY, FOR COLORED ONLY, WHITE LADIES, COLORED WOMEN, WHITE, COLORED. If I missed the signs I had only to follow my nose to the dirtiest, smelliest, most neglected accommodations. . . .

Our seedy run-down school told us that if we had any place at all in the scheme of things it was a separate place, marked off, proscribed and unwanted by the white people. We were bottled up and labeled and set aside—sent to the Jim Crow car, the back of the bus, the side door of the theater, the side window of a restaurant. We came to know that whatever we had was always inferior. We came to understand that no matter how neat and clean, how law abiding, submissive and polite, how studious in school, how churchgoing and moral, how scrupulous in paying our bills and taxes we were, it made no essential difference in our place.

It seemed as if there were only two kinds of people in the world—*They* and *We*—*White* and *Colored*. The world revolved on color and variations in color. It pervaded the air I breathed. I learned it in hundreds of ways. I picked it up from grown folks around me. I heard it in the house, on the playground, in the streets, everywhere. The tide of color beat upon me ceaselessly, relentlessly.

No one can measure how much pain white society inflicted through these laws of segregation. They were a constant assault on the worth and dignity of black people and a crime against their humanity. Black leaders abandoned politics and turned their attention to "education, business and industrial progress." They concluded that it was time to "keep quiet and saw wood." Through commerce, if not through politics, they would "hammer away" at prejudice and continue to seek equality. They were deeply discouraged but not despairing; they had lost much, but they retained the will to fight. The continuing fight against discrimination and the quest for equality shaped the agenda for black Tar Heels in the twentieth century.

VII

Black Life in the Age of Jim Crow

From the turn of the twentieth century to the Second World War, North Carolina blacks faced a society hostile to their civil rights and unyielding in its devotion to white supremacy. Denied the vote and physically separated from whites residentially and in public accommodations, African Americans struggled to earn a living, to educate their children in underfunded and inferior facilities, and to contest the limits placed on their social, economic, and political lives. For blacks the age of segregation appeared on the surface to be one of repression and powerlessness. But beneath an apparent resignation to such conditions black anger seethed.

Ironically, during the half century after disfranchisement North Carolina enjoyed a reputation for having harmonious race relations. Compared to many other southern states, North Carolina did appear moderate. But white leaders—and occasionally some black spokesmen—exaggerated the state's self-styled progressivism. John Larkins, the state's black consultant for social services, asserted during the Second World War that white North Carolinians had demonstrated "confidence, understanding, fair treatment, and liberalness" toward blacks. Yet he went on to catalog a series of "aggravated social problems"—including "delinquency, crime, low standards of living, ill health and undernourishment"—that he attributed to a failure "to employ Negroes according to their abilities." Whites mistook blacks' cautious, carefully calculated statements for acquiescence and complacency. In fact, African Americans never gave up the struggle for equality.

The era before the Second World War was one of important demographic changes for blacks. The number of black farmers in the South peaked in 1920 at 915,595. Of those, 701,471 were tenants. North Carolina reflected such trends. In 1910 there were 64,456 black farmers in North Carolina, fully two-thirds of them (67.2 percent) tenants. The number of black farm operators in North Carolina decreased from 74,849 in 1920 to

74,636 in 1930 to 57,428 in 1940. The total amount of farmland blacks cultivated dropped from 3.3 million acres in 1920 to 2.7 million in 1940. In the latter year three-fourths of North Carolina's black farmers remained tenants. In 1930, 56.8 percent of the state's black males were employed in agriculture; ten years later the percentage had shrunk to 41.2.

In 1910 there were 64,456 black farmers in North Carolina, two-thirds of whom were tenants. The total number of black farmers in the state peaked in 1920 and declined slowly thereafter, mirroring a general trend away from agriculture and ruralism. These black laborers are shown on the Wayne County strawberry farm of Calvin Brock, a black farmer, about 1907. From Clarence Hamilton Poe, "The Rebound of the Upland South," *World's Work*, XIV (May 1907), 8971.

The black population was changing in other important respects as well. During the antebellum period blacks constituted about one-third of North Carolina's population. After 1880, however, that percentage steadily eroded. By 1940 only 27.5 percent of the state's population was black. Whereas eighteen North Carolina counties had black majorities in 1900, only nine did in 1940.

The reasons for the changes included movements from farm to city and from South to North. In 1920, 80 percent of North Carolina blacks lived in rural areas; two decades later that figure had declined to 70 percent. Of those blacks not working on farms, nearly one-fourth were employed in personal and domestic services in 1940. One in seven black workers found work in manufacturing. Only 4.6 percent of black North Carolinians in nonagrarian sectors belonged to professional classes. Indeed, there were only twenty-six black lawyers in the entire state in 1940.

Outside of the farm, blacks found few opportunities for employment except in traditional "Negro jobs." Those included lumbering, naval stores, and railroad construction and maintenance. Jobs in the textile and furniture industries remained unavailable to blacks, but tobacco was an exception. Unionization also hurt black workers. The number of black trainmen in the

Outside of farm work, North Carolina's African Americans found few opportunities for employment except for traditional "Negro jobs" in the early years of the twentieth century. Among the few jobs available to black workers were construction and maintenance of railroads in the state. Shown at top are black construction workers on the Tallulah Falls Railway into Macon County about 1904. At bottom is a black railroad section gang photographed in 1911 while doing repair work, probably in Chatham County. Photo at top from Lucy Morgan Group, North Carolina Photographic Collection; at bottom (by C. Horton Poe, Moncure) from original owned by H. T. Eddins, Durham; both supplied by North Carolina Collection.

South actually declined from 41.3 to 33.1 percent between 1910 and 1930 because of union hostility toward black workers.

Black earnings and property values remained well below those of whites. A study of Chatham County in the 1920s revealed that 102 black tenants averaged only $257 in income; 41 black farm owners averaged $529. Comparable statistics for white farm owners and tenants were $626 and $225 respectively. Throughout the South, landownership was becoming increasingly concentrated in fewer hands. A little more than one-half of all farmers, black and white, were landowners, and they held nine-tenths of the South's real property. But the gap between black and white wealth was profound. The value of real property owned by North Carolina blacks in 1940 averaged $826 per person, compared to $2,071 per person for whites.

Confronted by such disparities and restricted avenues toward economic opportunity, middle-class black leaders counseled patience and accommodation in the years immediately following disfranchisement. When they did lodge mild protests against unfair treatment and discriminatory practices, they nonetheless urged blacks to build their communities through self-help and self-reliance. In 1903 Booker T. Washington addressed the annual fair of the North Carolina Industrial Association. He advised North Carolina blacks to content themselves as an agrarian people, to eschew migration, and to seek the type of education that would promote community building. Seated on the platform with Washington were James H. Young, the leading black Fusionist of the 1890s and a former Wake County legislator, and black educators Simon G. Atkins, James B. Dudley, and James E. Shepard. Their presence implicitly endorsed Washington's advice.

After 1900, as historian John H. Haley has commented in his astute study of the era's racial politics, both whites and blacks remarked on the decline in harmonious race relations. At Emancipation Day ceremonies in Durham in 1907 blacks criticized Jim Crow railroad cars, mob violence, and election frauds. But they also looked to white friends for assistance and sympathy. The answer they received was not always reassuring. In 1912 Clarence H. Poe, editor of the *Progressive Farmer* (Raleigh), noted: "There has been . . . a tie of affection between the negroes and the families of their former owners that made strongly for peace between the races—a tie now rapidly weakening." In 1913 Poe launched a two-year crusade to establish rural segregation throughout the South. He modeled his plans on the policies then being enacted in South Africa. In 1915 the North Carolina Senate narrowly defeated an amendment to the state constitution that would have ordained separate agricultural districts for blacks and whites.

Educators, clergymen, and businessmen were the principal spokesmen for the black community. They preached a middle-class morality that cultivated cooperation with whites and emphasized character building. Black leaders encouraged African Americans to abjure immorality and crime. James E. Shepard, founder of the National Religious Training School in Durham (forerunner of North Carolina College for Negroes), decried the effects of "moving picture shows, ignorance, superstition, and the use of cocaine or dope by youth." In a 1912 Emancipation Day speech, Charles N. Hunter, a Raleigh educator, urged blacks to remain in the South. Clearly aiming his remarks at whites as well as blacks, Hunter declared: "There are no negro anarchists, nihilists, or socialists, there are no dynamiters with their bombs. . . . [The Negro] is not given to strikes and the wide range of destructive lawlessness that prevailed in the North. . . . From such menaces the South is practically free."

Yet by the eve of the First World War, a different tone had entered black discourse, as Haley's study shows. Poe's rural segregation plan awakened blacks to the hazards of not protesting racial injustices. James B. Dudley, president of the Agricultural and Mechanical College for blacks at Greensboro, began speaking out against the consequences of segregation—rural and otherwise—in 1914. He was especially concerned about poor health conditions in black residential areas. The wooden Jim Crow cars on railroads also troubled him. In 1913 a friend of Dudley's had been killed in a train accident. The flimsy wooden cars were sandwiched between modern steel coaches in which whites rode. For his candor, Dudley was accused of advocating social equality.

Blacks also turned a critical eye toward the inadequate schools their children attended. In 1916 Professor Charles H. Moore, a respected educator in Salisbury and Greensboro, became the full-time field organizer for the North Carolina State Teachers Association. The black teachers' association, founded in 1881, instructed Moore to survey the state's black schools. What he saw appalled him. Moore confirmed the findings of Nathan C. Newbold, the white state agent for rural schools, two years earlier. At that time Newbold reported: "the average negro school house is really a disgrace to an independent civilized society." Newbold conceded that the condition of black schools revealed "injustice, inhumanity, and neglect on the part of white people."

Moore also confirmed that blacks did not receive a fair share of the tax moneys for schools. In 1909 Charles L. Coon, superintendent of the

On the eve of World War I, black educators James Benson Dudley (1859–1925; *left*) and Charles Henry Moore (*right*) began to call attention to the economic and social consequences of racial segregation as manifested in poor health conditions and inadequate schools in black residential areas of North Carolina. Photographs from Ethel Stephens Arnett, *Greensboro, North Carolina: The County Seat of Guilford* (Chapel Hill: University of North Carolina Press, 1955), facing 108.

In 1914 Nathan C. Newbold, North Carolina's white state agent for rural schools, sharply criticized the conditions prevalent in the state's schools for blacks. This school for black students, located near Lake Waccamaw in Columbus County, was photographed about 1900. Photograph courtesy North Carolina Collection.

Goldsboro schools, produced statistics to show that black schools were not a burden on white property owners. Coon asserted that money was actually being diverted to whites to hire more teachers, build more schools, and extend school terms. Coon's allegations created a sensation. They were all the more ironic because earlier efforts to divide school moneys on the basis of what each race paid in taxes had been thwarted.

Coming on the heels of those disclosures, D. J. Jordan's tirade against President Woodrow Wilson generated new tensions between the races as America entered the Great War. Jordan, a history professor at Dudley's A&M College in Greensboro, excoriated Wilson's stand on race issues at the same time the president was defending the rights of Europeans and others around the world. In an open letter to the president published in the *Independent* (Raleigh) in 1917, Jordan warned that Americans should not take blacks' loyalty for granted. "Is this the kind of Democracy I am asked to give my fortune and my life to make safe in the world?"

Jordan's bold comparison of Wilson's democratic rhetoric with actual conditions in America stunned white North Carolinians. The *Raleigh Times* editorialized that black educators should promote racial harmony. The newspaper insisted that North Carolina was "exceptionally free from race oppression, enmity, and malice." Gov. Thomas Walter Bickett, whom many thought to be liberal on race issues, was outraged. He considered Jordan's letter treasonous and sent a copy to the United States attorney general. With dispatch, black leaders closed ranks and apologized for Jordan's remarks. They claimed that nine-tenths of the black community disapproved of the college professor's views. Charles N. Hunter assured Raleigh lawyer James H. Pou: "There is not a traitor among us."

In the stormy racial climate that followed the First World War, Haley demonstrates, North Carolina blacks proclaimed their unhappiness with segregation and discrimination. At Emancipation Day ceremonies in Raleigh in 1919, an assembly of 3,000 blacks passed strongly worded resolutions warning whites that blacks would not be content to sacrifice their lives in a war for democracy and return to bigotry at home. The resolutions condemned lynching, demanded the boycott of Jim Crow facilities, and urged parents and teachers to instill race pride in black children.

The *New York Age* applauded the stand made by North Carolina blacks. The newspaper pointed out that the blacks who complained loudest also owned property, educated their children, and supported the war effort. "If these do not constitute the better element, the more sensible and patriotic colored people of North Carolina," the paper asked, "we should like to know who does?" The New York journal said that blacks who continued to advise patience and forbearance were losing the black community's respect. Whites who claimed to understand blacks and denounced the resolutions had little comprehension of the "agony of soul that the race goes through, . . . of its hopes and aspirations."

Such attacks from the northern black press disconcerted southern whites. They considered the National Association for the Advancement of Colored People (NAACP) a radical organization, and they deplored the outspoken W. E. B. Du Bois, editor of the *Crisis*. The *Charlotte Observer* urged black leaders to protect their people from the "contamination" of the NAACP. Labeling the NAACP's doctrine "objectionable," Dr. Frank Trigg, black president of Bennett College, a Methodist school for black women in Greensboro, banned the *Crisis* from campus. Nevertheless, NAACP branches took root in North Carolina. Raleigh, Greensboro, and Durham organized the state's first three branches, chartered in 1917. Three years later more than 1,000 black North Carolinians, in an act requiring moral and physical courage, belonged to ten NAACP branches.

By the 1920s—the decade of the so-called "New Negro"—verbal assaults on segregation had intensified. Addressing 2,000 blacks at Emancipation Day observances in 1923, the Reverend D. Ormonde Walker, minister of St. Paul's AME Church in Raleigh, rebuked the Ku Klux Klan, American imperialism in Haiti, and Marcus Garvey's "Back to Africa" movement. He also upbraided the Republican Party for abandoning its founding principles. Walker cautioned whites that they were no longer dealing with former slaves but rather with a new generation of blacks.

Walker's point was well taken. If black leaders tried to minimize the harmful effects of segregation and injustice, they were accused of appealing to the "white gallery of the Old North State." Indeed, younger blacks began to question the continued commemoration of Emancipation Day. It was too much of a reminder of slavery, they feared, which whites used to justify discrimination. Growing disenchantment with the observance culminated in 1928 when Professor William S. Turner of Shaw University delivered a revisionist interpretation of the Emancipation Proclamation. Turner denied Lincoln's humanitarian motives and argued that Lincoln issued the proclamation to further the war effort and infuse the Union cause with idealism. Turner even questioned the proclamation's constitutionality.

Turner's historical revisionism notwithstanding, whites and blacks perceived the Civil War in strikingly different ways. In 1929 Durham's black newspaper, the *Carolina Times*, edited by Louis E. Austin, continued to agitate for the freedoms that emancipation and Reconstruction had supposedly given blacks. Austin denied that northern and southern blacks had disparate objectives. African Americans in both regions sought equal justice, opportunity, and political rights. In the South, however, such views had to be disguised, Austin explained. The blunt-speaking editor said whites were fooled if they believed blacks were happy and content. Behind the "hypo-critical smile" and "feigned goodwill" was a "hatred hidden by fawning." In response the *Raleigh Times* ridiculed such talk and those blacks who believed the Civil War "amendments may yet be put into effect" when the South had "made their nullification a religion."

It was no coincidence that such unblinking candor and unsentimental analysis, evident in the crusading *Carolina Times*, emanated from the black community in Durham. Durham occupied a special place in the lives of all black southerners. It was there that the self-assertive, successful, proud, and impatient "New Negro" flourished. A raw new town without an antebellum aristocracy, Durham accorded self-made black businessmen and professionals high status. As early as 1903 Booker T. Washington praised Durham as "The City of Negro Enterprises." By the mid-1920s the black press dubbed it the "Capital of the Black Middle Class" and the "Black Wall Street of America."

Durham epitomized the New South ethos. Its cult was progress. The first black newspaper in Durham announced in 1906: "Everything here is push, everything is on the move, every citizen is looking out for everything that will make Durham great. The Negro in the midst of such life has caught the disease and . . . has awakened to action." When W. E. B. Du Bois visited Durham in 1912 he found a thriving black middle class. Writing in the *World's Work*, he reported 15 grocery stores, 8 barbershops, 7 meat and fish dealers, 2 drugstores, a shoe store, a haberdashery, and an undertaker.

Anchoring the black middle class in Durham was the North Carolina Mutual Life Insurance Company. Established in 1898, the company began doing business in 1899 with three employees: John Merrick, Dr. Aaron McDuffie Moore, and Charles Clinton Spaulding. Within a half century it grew to be the largest black-owned business in the United States. Merrick, who owned five barbershops, started the company because of his experience with fraternal orders that provided health and life insurance. Blacks had difficulty obtaining insurance or else paid exorbitant rates. As treasurer of the Royal Knights of King David, a benevolent society,

Merrick recognized the comprehensive insurance needs of the black community.

The success of North Carolina Mutual led to the growth of other middle-class enterprises. In 1908 Richard Burton Fitzgerald and William Gaston Pearson established Mechanics and Farmers Bank. James E. Shepard's religious training school, begun in 1910, eventually widened to include agriculture, horticulture, and domestic science. The school struggled until the 1920s, when the state took over and made it a liberal arts college. Renamed the "North Carolina College for Negroes" in 1925, it consisted of sixteen faculty members and encompassed thirty-three acres. During the 1920s C. C. Spaulding was secretary-treasurer of the "National Negro Business League," one of Booker T. Washington's initiatives. By 1925 Durham boasted the largest chapter, and it was regarded as a model for other cities.

After the turn of the twentieth century the Piedmont North Carolina city of Durham achieved a special status as a black middle-class business, commercial, and professional center. Booker T. Washington recognized the city's unique qualities as early as 1903. This view of one of the town's principal black business streets was made about 1910. From Booker T. Washington, "Durham, North Carolina, a City of Negro Enterprises," *Independent*, LXX (March 30, 1911), 643; photo reproduced courtesy North Carolina Collection.

Durham became the home of a vibrant black culture. "Christian music" and blues originated in the tobacco factories. To ease their toils, black laborers often sang while at work. The steamy workrooms in Durham's factories swayed with the rhythm of gospel music that soon developed into public performances. The parents of nationally renowned gospel singer Shirley Caesar went to work for the Liggett and Myers Company in 1926. Her father formed a quartet called "Just Come Four." Most gospel groups sang a cappella, but guitar music accompanied a few. White Rock Baptist Church and St. Joseph's AME Church attracted black celebrities and businessmen and nurtured black religious music.

Between 1900 and 1940 Durham hosted a remarkable group of blues musicians. Unlike Christian music, the blues had a low-down, slightly disreputable air. Middle-class blacks thought the blues sinful. Most blues musicians worked at unskilled jobs during the day and played music at night. A few were disabled and depended on music for their livelihoods. The masters of the Durham blues included Blind Gary Davis, Blind Sonny Terry (Saunders Terrill), Bull City Red (George Washington), and Blind Boy Fuller (Fulton Allen). Whereas gospel inspired and uplifted, blues growled with life's hardships and disappointments. Aimed at working-class people, the blues reflected the loves, fears, hopes, and frustrations of the laboring black masses. Fuller recorded 135 songs between 1935 and 1941. In his hit song "Big House Bound," he sang:

> Lord, I never will forget the day,
> they transferred me to the county jail.
> I had shot the woman I love,
> and ain't got no one to come go my bail.

The blues singers captured the gritty reality of life in urban ghettos. A survey conducted by the Durham Business League in the 1920s revealed that 80 percent of the city's black residents lived in rented housing. The housing was substandard, cheaply constructed, and overcrowded. Surface privies symbolized the unsanitary conditions, poor health, and malnutrition blacks endured. An exposé of the Queen City's slums by the *Charlotte News* in 1937 told much the same story. Two or three families were crammed into a single shotgun house. Many suffered from diseases, and murder stalked the community. Whites tended to ignore the problem because the victims were black. In 1940, after the city housing authority received

Durham's North Carolina Mutual Life Insurance Company, founded in 1898 by John Merrick, Dr. Aaron McDuffie Moore, and C. C. Spaulding, became the largest black-owned business in the nation. This photograph of clerical workers in the company's "Industrial Department" was made about 1920. Photo from Durham Historic Photographic Archives, Durham County Library.

federal funding, more than 5,000 dwellings still lacked proper toilets, and more than 10,000 lacked bathtubs.

In 1940 black birth and death rates exceeded those of whites, while black deaths from tuberculosis, syphilis, and malaria were one-and-one-half times as great as whites' deaths from the same diseases. There was one white physician for every 1,127 white persons, but only one black physician for every 6,499 black persons. Deaths from homicides were twice as high among blacks as among whites.

Durham's proud black middle class and vibrant institutions could not conceal the brutal existence endured by the vast majority of black North Carolinians. A report on black urban housing in North Carolina in 1939–1940 showed that 80 percent of black families lived in substandard housing, and two-thirds of black households earned less than $800 per year. Such statistics help to explain why, when an opportunity to move north beckoned during the First World War, many Tar Heel blacks seized the chance.

The "Great Migration" that began during World War I and continued into the 1960s represented both a "northern pull" and a "southern push." An estimated one million blacks moved north between 1916 and 1925. The migration from North Carolina in the World War I era, while substantial, actually continued a pattern dating back to the 1880s. More blacks left North Carolina between 1880 and 1900 than between 1900 and 1920. Indeed, outmigration from other states during the First World War, especially Mississippi, Georgia, and South Carolina, was much greater than that from North Carolina. An estimated 57,000 black North Carolinians left between 1910 and 1930, but an even greater number (222,000) migrated between 1930 and 1950. In terms of percentages, North Carolina lost 5 percent of its black population during the decade of the First World War, 7.6 percent during the Great Depression, and a whopping 14.8 percent during the 1940s.

Migrants moved in stages. They went first to southern cities and then proceeded to northern urban areas. By 1940, 58 percent of all urban blacks had migrated from other urban areas, including cities in the South. North Carolina blacks tended to concentrate in the Northeast, especially New York, New Jersey, and Pennsylvania, but some went to Virginia and West Virginia as well.

The reasons for the massive movement of people were not difficult to surmise. Low wages, poor housing, poor schools, unfair treatment of tenants by landowners, and legal discrimination in courts and daily life pushed people out of the South. Floods, the boll weevil, and increasing mechanization also destroyed agricultural jobs for blacks. The war, of course, created a great demand for labor that pulled blacks toward better-paying jobs in the North. With the outbreak of war, foreign immigration to the United States dwindled from 1,218,000 in 1914 to only 110,618 in 1918, creating a severe labor shortage. Wages in northern industries were appreciably higher. The average daily wage for a black farm laborer in the South was $1.00. Wages in the North averaged $2.00 to $4.00 per day. In New Bern, for example, a black laborer in a sawmill or cotton oil mill earned between $1.50 and $1.90 per day. In contrast, a black North Carolinian employed in a Pennsylvania steel plant received 30 cents per hour and could work 12 hours a day, 7 days a week. His income over a two-week period totaled $48.00 to $54.00.

Railroads and the United States mails became conduits for the movement and communication of blacks on either side of the Mason-Dixon line. Every black man who succeeded in the North wrote friends and family and sent money for wives and children to come north. News spread by word of mouth, and other groups joined the burgeoning exodus. Because of the dramatic increase in passenger traffic, railroads had to add extra cars to northbound trains. A 1919 report by the United States Department of Labor noted: "The Negroes just quietly move away without taking their recognized leaders into their confidence any more than they do the white people about them."

The *Chicago Defender*, published and edited by Robert Abbott, played an important role in the migration. Abbott urged southern blacks to move north to find better jobs and better living conditions. Between 1916 and 1918 the circulation of his newspaper jumped from 10,000 to 93,000. He depended on black railroad men and black entertainers to distribute the paper in the South. Emmett J. Scott, special assistant to the United States secretary of war, collected letters from the hopeful migrants to document the reasons for the massive shift in population. From Hamlet, North Carolina (a railroad town), a forty-two-year-old teacher and printer by trade expressed a strong interest in moving his wife and four children. He said he was "very desirous of changing [his] location. . . . Will accept any kind of work with living wages, on tobacco farm or factory." He described himself as a "sober, steady worker."

Ultimately, the treatment of blacks was the primary reason for the migration. As the Department of Labor reported in 1919: "The average white man...seems to have little knowledge or appreciation of this feeling among Negroes." One African American who relocated in Iowa offered the following explanation for blacks' migration: "The first reason they give for coming North is to educate their children; the second is to get better wages and shorter hours; and the third is to have the privilege of voting."

Southern whites recognized the calamitous effect on labor the migration would have. The Southern University Commission on Race Relations, an expression of the region's nascent interracial movement, listed a number of remedies to stanch the exodus: "Fair treatment, opportunity to labor and enjoy the legitimate fruits of labor, assurance of even-handed justice in the courts, good educational facilities, sanitary living conditions, tolerance, and sympathy." The Southern Sociological Congress in 1917 recommended the same solutions and suggested higher wages and fairer dealings with black tenants. The *Charlotte Observer* argued: "The Negroes must be given better homes and better surroundings. Fifty years after the Civil War they should not be expected to be content with the same conditions which existed at the close of the war." In contrast, the *News and Observer* of Raleigh advised blacks that the "best friend of the North Carolina Negro is the North Carolina white and the best job for the North Carolina Negro is on North Carolina farms and in North Carolina industry."

The scarcity of black farm labor proved especially acute. In 1916 eighty-seven of the state's one hundred counties reported labor shortages. Cotton-producing counties were particularly hard hit. In Mecklenburg County farmers had to sow grass and raise livestock because there were not enough black workers to chop and harvest cotton. In other counties land remained untilled. A North Carolina editor complained about "outrageous wages" of $1.25 per day that farmers were forced to pay if they could find any laborers. Even white women in towns and cities discovered they could no longer depend on loyal domestics who had departed for the North.

Once North Carolina blacks arrived in the North, their welcome was not always cordial. In Philadelphia, for example, a labor agent recruited a group of blacks to work as strikebreakers at an oil refining company. They were known as the "North Carolina gang." The company, at its own expense, fed and housed the black workers in "an old building until the trouble was past." By breaking the strike, the blacks became one-fourth of the company's labor force. They had displaced foreign laborers.

Unfortunately, justice for blacks was not a high priority for northern industries. If employers sometimes hired blacks to smash strikes, many unions constitutionally or through discriminatory practices simply barred blacks from membership. Caught in the middle, blacks often found themselves suddenly thrust into fierce labor disputes about which they had no previous knowledge. In the North blacks faced a new set of challenges and tensions, but still they boarded the Jim Crow cars heading north.

Southern whites' reaction to the Great Migration combined a mixture of paternalism and solicitude for blacks' welfare with veiled warnings about blacks' absorbing northern values. In a 1920 message to the General Assembly, Governor Bickett declared: "In North Carolina we have definitely decided that the happiness of both races requires that white government shall be supreme and unchallenged in our borders. . . . [W]hen we deny to the negro any participation in the making of laws, we saddle upon ourselves a peculiar obligation to protect the negro in his life and property. . . ." He chided blacks who received a northern education and then returned to teach high school. Bickett said that "the ideals of the North" made such teachers "unfit . . . to be useful citizens in the South."

When race riots erupted in Chicago in the summer of 1919, Bickett, ignoring recent racial disturbances in Winston-Salem and Fayetteville, reiterated the belief that "the South is the best place in the world for a decent negro to make a decent living." He said North Carolina would welcome back 25,000 blacks who had migrated to the North. "But if, during their residence in Chicago, any of these negroes have become tainted or intoxicated with dreams of social equality or of political dominion, it would be well for them to remain where they are, for in the South such things are forever impossible."

In 1921 Bickett addressed the black students at Hampton Normal and Agricultural Institute in Virginia. He condemned "negroes with brilliant minds who are using their talents in sowing seeds of hate between blacks and the whites." The former governor said blacks were "entitled to equal and exact justice before the law" but admitted that whites did not "always deal justly by the negro." Bickett counseled blacks "to rest your case on the white man's sense of justice, and to keep it there." Any other course would lead to race war, a revival of the Ku Klux Klan, and mounted Red Shirts once again.

Bickett's successors in the governorship delivered much the same message. At the "Negro State Fair" in Raleigh in 1925, Gov. Angus W. McLean insisted: "There is no longer a real race problem in the South. It exists only in the minds of those, white and colored, who are seeking selfish advancement; who are trying to intimidate others, and have no better weapon than the cowardly appeal to racial prejudice and racial antipathy." McLean characterized the African American as "a most valuable element in our population because he controls our labor supply, in the agricultural districts especially." But he told blacks that in education they should emphasize vocational training, chiefly in agriculture. In the governor's opinion, blacks received too much instruction "along academic and theoretical lines." Four years earlier, Gov. Cameron Morrison, a leader in the white supremacy campaigns of 1898 and 1900, informed black schoolteachers that their people were receiving "as much education as you are ready for. You cannot use the highly organized system that is provided for whites."

Such attitudes perpetuated a system of institutional racism through North Carolina's segregated schools. When the Department of Public Instruction organized a "Division of Negro Education" and named Nathan C. Newbold its director, he inaugurated a series of interracial conferences on black education during the 1920s. Newbold liked to call that decade the "Golden Age of Negro Education." He worked hard to equalize the curricula in urban and rural as well as black and white schools. Nevertheless, differences and inequities were apparent.

In 1931 Newbold delivered a speech at the George Peabody College for Teachers in Nashville, Tennessee. In it he compared two Winston-Salem schools: Reynolds High School (white) and Atkins High School (black). College preparatory courses were the same, according to Newbold. Vocational training for young black and white women likewise was similar. Young women received training that emphasized domestic skills, though blacks also received instruction in "maid service." Vocational training for the young men, however, indicated wide disparities in expectations, as shown in the following comparison.

Whites	Blacks
Mechanical drawing	Auto mechanics
Sheet metal	Barbering
Cotton mill math	Bricklaying
Tobacco manufacturing	Carpentry
Electricity	Chauffering
Furniture manufacturing	Janitorial services

Newbold concluded that such distinctions grew "out of actual working situations. It is an effort to fit pupils of both races for the work they hope to do in mature life, and does not attempt to say that members of either race must do certain things because they may be white or black." Nonetheless, he conceded that more blacks would likely enter "industrial work." Segregation and subordination extended to the workplace in North Carolina society.

The Great Depression had a devastating impact on black education when it already lagged far behind what was available for white children. In a report to the State School Commission in 1933, Newbold termed conditions "pathetic." Some black classrooms had 60, 70, 80, or even 100 students. Only 7 percent of black students—compared to a meager 17 percent of white students—attended high school. Newbold characterized the problems with black schools as follows: "short, inadequate non-standard school terms for slightly more than half the children; no high schools within reasonable distance of many hundreds of children who are ready for high school; nearly a thousand teachers now in the service who have not had even a good high school education; and many classrooms crowded and congested beyond all hope of serving the children with any degree of satisfaction."

As late as 1938 a wage differential of 25 to 30 percent existed between black and white teachers. On the eve of the Second World War, Newbold, a longtime advocate of better schools for blacks, admitted "that it is natural and logical for intelligent Negroes to exhibit a feeling of unrest, whether wisely or unwisely, over conditions which to them seem to mean there is no hope for equality of educational opportunity for them in a great State like North Carolina."

In areas other than education, rudimentary social services for blacks got under way in 1925 with the creation of the "Bureau of Work among Negroes" under the State Board of Charities and Public Welfare. It was the first program of its kind in the nation and became a model for other states in the South and Midwest. Although the agency and board underwent name changes during the next two decades, three black men supervised the bureau's work: Lieutenant Lawrence A. Oxley, who left in 1934 to begin a distinguished career with the United States Department of Labor; the Reverend William Randolph Johnson; and John R. Larkins, who joined the agency in 1942. Larkins held a bachelor's degree from Shaw University and a master's degree in social work from Atlanta University.

A $60,000 grant from the Laura Spelman-Rockefeller Memorial Fund made possible the establishment of the bureau. The grant allowed the state to set up pilot programs for social services in four selected counties. To organize social work in each county, Oxley turned to the black community for assistance and leadership. In Alamance County, for example, the "Negro Advisory Committee" to the County Board of Public Welfare consisted of three clergymen and a woman. In 1926 the committee adopted

Nathan Carter Newbold (1871–1957), a native of Pasquotank County and a graduate of Trinity College, began his career as an educator. He became North Carolina's first state agent for negro schools in 1913 and continued to serve in that capacity until he retired in 1950 at the age of seventy-nine. Newbold is generally credited with effectively managing the daunting task of expanding educational opportunities for North Carolina's black citizens at a time when such opportunities were virtually nonexistent. Photograph from the files of the Office of Archives and History.

John Rodman Larkins (1913–1980), a native of Wilmington, joined the North Carolina Department of Public Welfare (successor agency to the State Board of Charities and Public Welfare) in 1942 as a consultant for social work among blacks. During the ensuing twenty years he carried on the work pioneered by Lieutenant Lawrence A. Oxley in 1925. After 1962 he remained active in a number of state government positions and as a member of numerous boards and commissions. Photograph from Hugh Victor Brown, *A History of the Education of Negroes in North Carolina* (Raleigh: Irving Swain Press, 1961), 137.

a budget of $1,000 and then had to go out and raise the money. A typical quota was $25.00 from each black urban church and $15.00 from each black rural church. The committee also solicited pledges from fraternal orders such as the Masons, Odd Fellows, and Knights of Pythias. Black schoolteachers contributed $1.00 each and black schoolchildren 5 cents each. Individuals pledged an average of $10.00 apiece.

By 1928 Oxley had raised more than $120,000 statewide "for Negro welfare projects." Roughly one-third had come from public funding, one-third from private sources, and one-third from blacks themselves. The bureau's areas of concern included industrial workers, broken homes, hospital services, recreation facilities, truants, and delinquent children. By the time Oxley left, welfare services for blacks had been organized in at least thirty-five counties.

In 1926 there were only thirteen black social workers in the entire state. They encountered attitudes that were not always receptive to services for blacks. In Greensboro, Oxley found that the black social worker, a native of Ohio, had "difficulty adjusting herself to conditions as she finds them. . . . She is very much dissatisfied, and . . . intends to resign unless certain changes are made." Oxley said that "personal likes and dislikes are small factors in a program of service, and . . . there are many matters it is wiser not to discuss. . . ."

Oxley's conservative, circumspect method of dealing with white officials proved politic. He had not misread the depths of white prejudice that black social workers and the larger black community faced. In 1929 the Rosenwald Fund provided money for Oxley's agency, in association with the Institute for Research in Social Science and the School of Public Welfare at the University of North Carolina, to study child welfare among blacks. As part of the study, four social workers, including Oxley and one other black, conducted a survey of leading local officials across the state. At least thirty-eight of the one hundred counties were surveyed. Most of them lay in rural areas of the east and west, though a number of Piedmont counties participated in the survey. Various officials were interviewed, including the clerk of court, the superintendent of education, the superintendent of welfare, the farm demonstration agent, the home demonstration agent, and the county doctor. Interviewers asked four basic questions: What was the general attitude toward blacks in each respective county? How much and what kind of education were appropriate for them? Should blacks own land? Should blacks be allowed to vote?

The results were sobering. What began as a study of child welfare among blacks became inadvertently a penetrating look at white racial attitudes three decades after disfranchisement. When the final published report appeared in 1933, the director of the study, Professor Wiley Britton Sanders of the School of Public Welfare, omitted the survey's results. He feared they "would serve no useful purpose . . . and might lead to misunderstanding and criticism."

Public officials reflected stubborn prejudices that relegated blacks to a sharply defined laboring class. Few acknowledged blacks' aspirations to receive a high school education, to vote, or to be anything but farmers and laborers. The prejudice ran as deep, perhaps more so, in Mountain counties as in counties along the Coastal Plain. Most officials couched their responses in the language of white superiority, and a number cited biblical authority for their views.

Several respondents thought blacks needed to be taught more respect and deference for whites. The superintendent of welfare in Beaufort County, for instance, criticized the Catholic school in Washington, North Carolina, because the nuns treated blacks as equals. "This is causing the negroes to be more uppity," he concluded. The clerk of court in Camden County opposed any education for blacks. "It makes them too biggety," he said, "and they forget their places." He also opposed black landownership:

"It makes them too independent. They should always be made to feel that they are under the white man."

The public officials' attitudes toward black education confirmed the opinions Governors Morrison and McLean had expressed. The clerk of court in Burke County argued that blacks should not be educated beyond what their tax moneys could provide. In his view, "The white people should not be taxed in order to put money into something that is of no value. 'Educate a negro and you ruin a good servant.'" The superintendent of schools in Burke agreed. Educating blacks beyond the seventh grade was "a waste of time and money." College-educated blacks, he commented, were "more immoral" and had a "bad influence on the other negroes in the community." The county doctor in mountainous Mitchell County stated that blacks were fit only for picking cotton, and they did not need an education for that. Blacks, he asserted, "were much better off a[s] slaves." The home demonstration agent in Richmond County called high school education for blacks "useless." She contended that blacks "should be taught to be better cooks, farmers and laborers."

A few respondents grudgingly agreed that blacks should receive a "good" education so long as it did not lead to social equality. The superintendent of welfare in Jackson County observed: "The attitude of the south has always been to keep [blacks] as servants. This is wrong." The superintendent of schools in Richmond County admitted that black children attended school "better than the white children in the mill villages." The Jackson County superintendent of schools noted the same pattern. Blacks attended for all six months without prompting. Many black students stayed out during cotton picking but returned as soon as possible. If educators pressed blacks to attend more often, he warned, white land-owners would get "down on negro education." The "colored supervisor" of schools in Wayne County, one of the few blacks surveyed, maintained that blacks attended school as often as possible. Attendance suffered from "a bad crop year" and shorter school term.

On the question of black landownership, opinion was more divided. In general the public officials recognized the stability of property-owning blacks. The Jackson County clerk of court stated: "The landowners give little trouble. They are steady, good citizens." But he believed blacks should own land "in segregated sections." The county doctor in Mitchell County also favored land segregation. The Burke County clerk of court declared: "Many good towns are ruined by negroes owning property within town limits." Admitting that he did not do as much work among black farmers as among white, the farm demonstration agent in Richmond County noted that the "landowning negro follows directions . . . pretty well. The tenant is harder to reach." The Wayne County superintendent of welfare said succinctly: "Wherever you find landowning negroes you find a good set."

Attitudes toward black suffrage had not changed in thirty years, however. Most respondents opposed blacks' voting except in certain circumstances. Several would have extended suffrage restrictions to the "low type of white person," for "half of the white voters do not understand what they are doing." The Jackson County clerk of court thought black landowners who were educated and met "other requirements of the law should be allowed to vote." But, he cautioned, "Promiscuous voting among the negroes should not be allowed. It would bring about race riots." One mountain official, revealing the limits of white liberalism, asserted that blacks should have the right to vote except in areas where they constituted a majority.

The survey revealed that few blacks were receiving any social services and those services that were made available occurred in a haphazard manner. The county doctor in Lee County, for example, confessed that the county was "doing little" for blacks. When the doctor promoted vaccination and inoculation among blacks, "they have come out." Few blacks, interestingly, sought aid for dependent children, ostensibly one of the survey's principal purposes. "They take care of these children among themselves," said the McDowell County superintendent of welfare. Regular health care and training for blacks extended only as far as licensing midwives. Other clinics were limited or unavailable to blacks. Dental checkups were for whites only.

The Rosenwald survey hinted at class and color distinctions among blacks. The superintendent of schools in Scotland County said that he favored as a teacher a "black negro that has only finished the 10th or 11th grade. Some of the mulatto teachers are keen and have splendid teaching technique but they look down on the other negroes in the community." Similarly, the Wayne County superintendent of schools asserted: "It is hard to get good negro teachers to go into the rural sections on account of the homes that they have to live in." Even the "Colored Home Demonstration Agent" in Wayne County insisted blacks could take better advantage of education. "The college woman or man is the one that gets along these days," she said. Unfortunately, only 4 percent of the black students in rural parts of Wayne County attended high school. Like other social services, education was still a dream for the majority of blacks.

The onset of the Great Depression and the sunny promises of the New Deal gave North Carolina blacks fresh hope that the federal government would address their urgent needs. But the New Deal left, at best, a mixed legacy. While it raised blacks' expectations and provided some material benefits, it also hurt the state's black workers, reinforced blacks' low status, and in agriculture accelerated the unrelenting departure of black sharecroppers from the farm.

The National Recovery Administration (NRA) largely ignored the state's black workers, who made up 17 percent of all laborers. The NRA's codes did not cover "Negro jobs" on farms and in domestic service. In cases where it did oversee certain jobs, the agency's codes stipulated higher wages than those paid in many southern industries, such as tobacco. Thus, industry leaders sought and received a wage differential in order to maintain a cheap supply of black labor. Lawrence Oxley vigorously opposed the lower NRA wage for blacks, but to no avail. Moreover, Oxley reported that many blacks lost traditional "Negro jobs" to unemployed whites. A black cashier at a Durham bank observed: "The Depression and now the New Deal, with its higher wages, is just forcing us Negroes out of our jobs." By 1940 the percentage of black laborers in the tobacco industry had declined to 54.9, whereas ten years earlier it had stood at 76.1. Aptly, black leaders called the NRA the "Negro Removal Act."

The Agricultural Adjustment Administration (AAA) perhaps had an even more ruinous impact on black sharecroppers and tenants. The AAA displaced thousands of propertyless farmers in eastern North Carolina. Its policies of acreage control and limited production forced sharecroppers off the land. In 1934 Lorena Hickok, a New Deal official from Washington, estimated that there were 10,000 displaced tenants in eastern North Carolina, 60 percent of whom were black.

Mandatory crop controls aided large commercial farmers but not small family farmers and tenants. Landlords refused to share benefit checks from the AAA with tenants and sold tenants' crops so as to collect all the proceeds. The number of black farm owners and tenants consequently dwindled, while the number of black farm laborers increased.

Relief programs told a similarly grim story of discrimination and neglect. The Federal Emergency Relief Administration (FERA) paid white families $12.65 per month but black families only $8.31. Although the FERA ostensibly paid a minimum wage of 30 cents per hour for relief work, administrator Harry Hopkins relented to southern pressure and agreed to pay the "prevailing wage." When cotton and tobacco farmers complained that they could not compete with FERA wages for black laborers, Annie Land O'Berry, director of the North Carolina Emergency Relief Administration, suspended work relief in areas of the state where it might interfere with the labor demands of agriculture.

Despite such shortcomings, the New Deal proved popular among blacks, who overwhelmingly supported Franklin D. Roosevelt. Black disenchantment with the Republican Party had been growing since disfranchisement. The state GOP had adopted a "lily-white" policy as early as 1902, and during the 1920s the national Republican Party under Herbert Hoover had pursued the same strategy.

The estrangement between blacks and the GOP became an open rift during congressional hearings affecting the appointment of two North Carolina Republicans to important federal posts. In 1921 black North

During the 1930s the tobacco industry successfully lobbied the National Recovery Administration (NRA) to exempt it from codes specifying the higher wages for workers whose jobs the agency oversaw. As a consequence, the number of blacks employed in the tobacco industry declined dramatically during the decade. These workers are transferring tobacco from a trailer to baskets at a tobacco warehouse in Durham in 1939. Photograph from [Howard W.] Odum Subregional Photo Study, Southern Historical Collection.

Carolinians—led by David C. Suggs, president of Livingstone College, and Charles N. Hunter of Raleigh—bitterly contested the nomination of Frank A. Linney as United States attorney for the Western District of North Carolina. Linney, as the Republican candidate for governor in 1916, had supported Clarence Poe's scheme to segregate the races in rural districts. In 1920, as chairman of the state GOP, Linney sent a letter to white women voters in which he endorsed disfranchisement and pledged the total removal of blacks from politics. During his confirmation hearings, Linney was forced to disavow his lily-white pronouncements and promise to enforce the law impartially, even if that meant prosecuting a white registrar who refused to register qualified black voters.

Linney was confirmed, but John J. Parker did not fare as well. In 1930 President Hoover nominated Parker to a seat on the United States Supreme Court. During his 1920 gubernatorial campaign in North Carolina, Parker, like Linney, had endorsed disfranchisement. His lily-white comments ruined his chances for confirmation. The NAACP, hailing Parker's rejection as African Americans' finest political moment since the Civil War, led the fight that prevented Parker's elevation to the bench. But it was a black North Carolinian—Dr. A. M. Rivera of North Carolina Mutual— who quietly provided the damning evidence.

In short, blacks were edging toward the Democratic Party before the New Deal. Roosevelt's programs did not exclude blacks, and that in itself was a sign of progress. Additionally, FDR denounced lynching and appointed blacks to more important posts than they had ever held. In the end, tangible economic benefits in the form of relief, highly visible black New Dealers, and the genuine sensitivies of Eleanor Roosevelt took precedence over the fight for racial equality.

In June 1940, a meeting of 700 African Americans calling themselves the "United Negro Democrats of North Carolina" unanimously endorsed FDR. That year three-fourths of an estimated 40,000 black voters in North Carolina supported the president. The black middle class in Charlotte, Durham, Greensboro, Raleigh, and Winston-Salem, which had become increasingly active politically during the 1930s, comprised most of the black voters in the state. C. C. Spaulding of North Carolina Mutual continued to espouse the bootstrap philosophy of Booker T. Washington, but he also became the state's most ardent black New Dealer.

Even more than the New Deal, the Second World War was a great divide for southerners. During the war 3.2 million people left the rural South to seek new jobs and opportunities. Between 1940 and 1960 the

Rural blacks received little benefit from New Deal agricultural legislation. Shown at top are black tenant farmers of Iredell County aboard a hay wagon, about 1935; at bottom is the wife of a sharecropper on the front porch of her house in Person County in 1939. Photo at top from North Carolina Emergency Relief Administration Papers, State Archives; at bottom from Odum Subregional Photo Study.

TOP: A black sharecropper pauses for a photograph with his wife outside their tin-roofed log cabin in Person County, 1939. BOTTOM: Black women workers cut fish in a factory in coastal North Carolina, possibly Colerain, in the late 1930s. Photograph at top from Odum Subregional Photo Study; at bottom from Charles A. Farrell Photograph Collection, State Archives.

Despite shortcomings in New Deal programs, particularly those affecting rural blacks, President Franklin D. Roosevelt and his legislative initiatives remained popular among North Carolina's African Americans. New Deal agencies such as the Works Progress Administration provided funds to underwrite public-sector jobs for the unemployed of both races. In this photograph, black WPA workers are installing a sewer pipe in Ahoskie in November 1936. Photo from a print in the Lee A. Wallace Photograph Album, North Carolina Collection.

number of southerners remaining on the land declined by more than 50 percent, from 14.6 million to 7 million. Economic, demographic, and social trends affecting blacks and dating back as far as the First World War quickened during the Second World War. Blacks continued to leave farms for southern as well as northern cities. During the 1940s more than two million blacks migrated to northern and western industrial centers. Within the South another one million moved from farms to cities. Sharecropping gave way to seasonal wage labor and hand labor to mechanization.

In North Carolina patterns of black employment persisted in the traditional areas of common labor, personal service, domestic service, and farming. Black women in particular faced acute child-care needs. More than one-half of African American women over age fourteen worked full or part time, whereas only 20 to 30 percent of white women did. The ongoing migration of blacks from the farm to the city also aggravated a seasonal labor shortage in agriculture. At one point during the war John R. Larkins, the state's black consultant for social services, advised Gov. J. Melville Broughton to parole blacks from the state prison and to conscript the high number of black "rejectees" from the Selective Service for work on farms.

The Second World War also increased racial tensions. Whites expected the war to preserve the status quo, whereas blacks were not eager to join the war effort unless their participation led to equal rights. Nationwide at least 6 civilian riots, 20 military riots and mutinies, and 40 to 75 lynchings occurred. Rumors of black disloyalty and fifth columns abounded.

In 1942 rumors about so-called "Eleanor Clubs" swept the South. Blacks, according to gossipmongers, were organizing the clubs, named in honor of Eleanor Roosevelt, to promote "social equality." Louis E. Austin, the feisty editor of the *Carolina Times*, denounced the stories. In a full-page, signed editorial he offered a $100 reward to anyone who could provide conclusive proof that such a club existed anywhere in the South. "Social equality," Austin averred, "is the age-old scarecrow that is always brought out of the attic and dusted off to frighten the weak minded whenever Negroes ask for better jobs, better wages, better schools and other improvements that will tend to raise their economic standard. . . ." Austin noted that despite laws and other barriers "our streets are crowded with Negroes, the color of whose skin bears testimony to the fact that there are individuals in both races who have been engaging in the highest point of social equality." Austin called on both blacks and whites "to scotch these rumors" during the national crisis. He defended blacks as loyal and true to the American cause. African Americans, Austin declared, sought the same rights as everyone else.

In pursuing those rights, however, blacks unsettled North Carolina's vaunted harmonious race relations. Blacks clung to a vision of equality. Whites were convinced that blacks voluntarily agreed with policies of segregation. Those clashing perceptions left the two races fundamentally at odds.

At a meeting of the North Carolina Conference for Social Service in 1939, Nathan C. Newbold presented a report titled, "Race Relations in North Carolina: What Nine Prominent North Carolina Negroes Think." During the war he presented the same report to seminars on race relations. Newbold's survey disclosed that black leaders appreciated efforts to increase black teachers' salaries and black representation on some planning boards. The race leaders also applauded the absence of lynching in North Carolina. But they pointed to many problems. "Officers of [the] law are sometimes too quick on the trigger, and sometimes tend to assume that an arrested Negro is guilty," commented one respondent. Another stated: "There is a tendency in many rural sections to deny well-qualified Negroes the right to vote." Others mentioned the abominable conditions under which tenants

This proprietor of a barbershop in Oxford in 1939 is representative of the increasingly visible—and politically active—black middle class that emerged during the 1930s. Photograph from Odum Subregional Photo Study.

and sharecroppers labored and the "tendency to shut the door of employment in the face of Negroes . . . even in occupations in which Negroes have traditionally engaged." The race leaders also said that blacks resented wage disparities in cases where blacks and whites performed the same work.

Newbold's report reflected a growing consensus among black leaders and people that would take concrete form during the war. In the *Carolina Times*, Louis Austin published weekly a platform demanding equal pay for teachers; "Negro policemen where Negroes are involved"; equal educational opportunities; black jurymen; higher wages for domestics; full participation of blacks in all branches of the armed services; abolishment of the "double-standard wage scale in industry"; greater black participation in politics; black representation in city, county, state, and national governments; and better housing.

Austin did not stop there. In 1942 he called on President Roosevelt to issue "an edict declaring a new birth of freedom for the thirteen million

During World War II, a time of increasing racial tension, Louis Ernest Austin, combative editor of the *Carolina Times*, a Durham newspaper aimed at the black community, countered rumors of the existence of clubs to promote "social equality" for black Americans by offering a generous cash award to anyone who could prove that such a club existed anywhere in the South. Photograph (ca. 1950s) from Durham Historic Photographic Archives.

Negroes in the United States." Blacks, he argued, were being asked to fight "for a democracy that is infested with deception, hypocrisy, deceit, unfairness and subversive measures toward one-tenth of the nation's citizenship."

A few black leaders, including James E. Shepard, cautioned against using the war as an occasion to wring concessions from white Americans. Others viewed the national emergency as an opportunity to demand equal rights. The war offered an opening for economic and racial justice inconceivable only a few short years earlier. Working-class blacks, impatient with the pace of reform, seized the initiative.

In 1943 black tobacco workers in Winston-Salem led a strike against the R. J. Reynolds Tobacco Company. The black strikers sought union recognition, the right to collective bargaining, higher wages, and better working conditions. Black middle-class spokesmen urged the strikers to resist the appeals of union organizers and to preserve "friendly" relations with white industrialists.

Black laborers remained unimpressed. One woman declared: "Our [black] leaders always look clean and refreshed at the end of the hottest day, because they work in very pleasant environments. . . . All I ask our leaders is that they obtain a job in one of the factories as a laborer and work two weeks. Then write what they think." Another asserted that the city's black middle class professionals "have always told us what the white people want, but somehow or other are particularly silent on what we want." With the help of the National Labor Relations Board, the Reynolds workers, represented by the Congress of Industrial Organizations (CIO), secured a contract in 1944.

That union victory was only an opening wedge. Local NAACP membership soared. By 1946 Winston-Salem boasted the largest NAACP branch (1,991 members) in North Carolina. The CIO also conducted a voter registration drive that increased the number of black voters tenfold. In 1947 Kenneth Williams, a minister, won a seat on the Board of Aldermen. In so doing, he became the first black city official in the twentieth-century South to defeat a white opponent.

The black middle class, which traditionally brokered small concessions from the white elite, could not remain reticent in the face of such working-class ferment and the rapidly changing conditions brought on by the war. In October 1942, the Southern Conference on Race Relations met at James E. Shepard's institution, North Carolina College for Negroes in Durham. Fifty-nine African American representatives from ten southern states gathered to draft a "new charter for race relations in the South." Prominent educators such as Charles S. Johnson, Benjamin Mays, and Gordon B. Hancock joined Plummer B. Young, editor of the *Norfolk Journal and Guide* and a native North Carolinian, and other luminaries in religion, business, and social welfare to attend the conference.

Two months later a committee headed by Charles S. Johnson of Fisk University issued a document that became known as the "Durham manifesto." The document candidly acknowledged that the war had generated "increased racial tensions, fears and aggressions, and an opening up of the basic questions of racial segregation and discrimination, Negro minority rights and democratic freedom." Calling for a wartime victory in both "arms and ideals," the statement demanded complete voting rights for blacks and an end to white primaries, evasions of the law, and intimidation. It urged the equalization of teachers' salaries and school facilities for both races. Finally, it insisted on equal access to all jobs, denounced unions that barred blacks, and encouraged service workers to organize into unions.

The Durham manifesto represented a brave departure for many of its sponsors. When the Southern Conference on Race Relations convened in Durham, Louis Austin dismissed it as too conservative. To have any credibility, he contended, the conference must include Walter White of the NAACP or A. Philip Randolph, head of the Brotherhood of Sleeping Car Porters. The *Carolina Times* editorialized: the "Negro masses . . . are suspicious of all Negro leaders who are so smart they never ruffle the feathers of the oppressors."

After Johnson's committee issued its December document, however, Austin conceded that the declaration did not have the "'Uncle Tom' flavor" of the Durham meeting. "Frankly we do not think that the statement as released will do any harm," Austin predicted, "nor do we think it will do any good. About the only purpose it can serve is to give Negro intellectuals in the South an opportunity to show off by appearing profound. . . ." His fury building, Austin thundered: "Most of the white people who howl about Negroes not being loyal are those who have had a part in promoting the nefarious system against the Negro and they cannot understand how in the hell the Negro can remain loyal when he knows he

By winning a seat on the Winston-Salem Board of Aldermen in 1947, Kenneth R. Williams, a minister, became the first black candidate in the twentieth-century South to outpoll a white opponent in a municipal election. Williams (*second from right*) posed with his newly elected fellow aldermen at a swearing-in ceremony in Winston-Salem on May 12, 1947. Photograph by Frank Jones; reproduced courtesy Frank Jones Photography Collection, Forsyth County Public Library, Winston-Salem.

has and is getting for the most part a raw deal in employment and in the armed services of the country."

In this case Austin misjudged the Durham manifesto's impact. The conference that enunciated those principles became the impetus for the establishment of the Southern Regional Council in 1944. An interracial organization with headquarters in Atlanta, the Southern Regional Council became a staunch proponent of racial, industrial, economic, and social progress throughout the South.

One reason for Austin's lukewarm response to the Durham manifesto could be attributed to his efforts, as president of the Durham NAACP, to bring together into a single organization the state's twenty-two branches of the NAACP. Ella Baker, a native North Carolinian and director of branches for the NAACP, had proposed the idea to Austin, Kelly Alexander of Charlotte, T. V. Mangum of Statesville, and others. At a meeting in Charlotte in 1943, influential branch presidents inaugurated the North Carolina State Conference of NAACP Branches. The state conference signaled a growing maturity in the methods used to fight racial oppression. It created a network to concentrate protests against Jim Crowism and to set a unified agenda for reform. As already seen in Winston-Salem, NAACP membership mushroomed in the mid-1940s. During the Second World War the number of NAACP branches in North Carolina more than doubled, and total membership approached ten thousand.

Whatever differences Austin had with the framers of the Durham manifesto, he had not misjudged the chasm between white and black perceptions of the racial situation in the South. Gov. J. Melville Broughton articulated the prevailing view among whites. Ironically, his comments came in response to a survey on race relations being conducted by Charles S. Johnson, one of the authors of the Durham manifesto.

In October 1943, Governor Broughton offered six reasons for his belief that "[r]ace relations in North Carolina have been exceptionally good for many years." The governor asserted: "North Carolina is traditionally a conservative state and her people have not been inclined to listen to demagogues who would use race prejudice as a means of obtaining political power or preferment." He credited "strong Negro leadership" that he characterized as "conservative and reasonable." Cooperation, Broughton observed, accomplished more than "agitation." The governor continued: "The principle of segregation of races as to housing, schools, churches, and similar public activities is on the whole accepted by both races as being sound and sensible." Broughton said the state's policy was to give blacks equal public services in health, education, and agriculture, though he admitted that that goal had not yet been attained. As evidence of whites' good faith, he cited a recently enacted $1 million supplement to black teachers' salaries to equalize them with those of white teachers. (Broughton neglected to mention the role of NAACP lawsuits in forcing southern states to equalize black teachers' salaries.) Finally, the governor commended the state's public and private institutions of higher education for blacks. In his estimation, all of them rendered "fine service."

Broughton acknowledged the need for better housing, recreation facilities, and health care for blacks. He also defended constitutional prohibitions on interracial marriages and encouraged both races to pursue a policy of "purity and high standards." Progress would continue, the governor declared, if North Carolina were "spared outside interference and the agitation . . . stimulated by a radical Negro press. . . ."

When juxtaposed, the Durham manifesto and Broughton's optimistic appraisal of race relations disclosed just how far apart white rhetoric and black aspirations remained. The so-called "conservative" leaders acclaimed by Broughton had helped draw up the Durham manifesto. No matter how cordial personal relations between the races appeared, enormous anger and frustration boiled just beneath the surface. Working-class blacks, such as the tobacco workers in Winston-Salem, challenged the black middle class's leadership and pushed insistently for change. Not "outside agitators," as Governor Broughton remarked, but black laborers and respectable middle-class blacks schooled in the ways of racial etiquette were creating a climate for protest and upheaval. On the eve of the great civil rights struggles of the 1950s and 1960s, few whites seemed to sense that a half century of segregation—customs, laws, and traditions their politicians promised would never end—teetered on the brink of destruction.

VIII

With All Deliberate Speed

Public and Private Education, Including Colleges, 1865–1900

Before the state of North Carolina made education in its public schools available to blacks, various private organizations sponsored schools for the former slaves. Prior to 1865, members of the religious Society of Friends (Quakers) taught black children in their interdenominational schools. Immediately after the Civil War, black adults and children began receiving the rudiments of education under the auspices of the Freedmen's Bureau. During Reconstruction, church and missionary societies operated schools for blacks in North Carolina. The American Missionary Association of New York was the first and largest benevolent society to establish formal educational institutions for blacks in the South.

Roman Catholics, Presbyterians, Baptists, Episcopalians, and Methodists likewise established black schools in North Carolina and the South. North Carolina's private black colleges began under the auspices of religious denominations as normal or collegiate institutes and subsequently developed into four-year institutions. The American Baptist Home Mission, for example, established Shaw University in 1865 as Raleigh Institute; the facility later became the South's first institution of higher learning for blacks. Other denominational schools followed: Biddle Memorial Institute (Presbyterian) at Charlotte in 1867; Saint Augustine's Normal School and Collegiate Institute (Episcopalian) at Raleigh in 1867; Scotia Seminary (Presbyterian) at Concord in 1867; Bennett Seminary (Methodist) at Greensboro in 1873; and Zion Wesley Institute (AME Zion) at Salisbury in 1879.

The emphasis in black education in North Carolina from 1876 to 1900 was on normal schools and teachers' institutes. Most of the schools began with one or two buildings. Additional facilities were added as financing was secured. Benefactors of the schools generally were white northern philanthropists, but black self-help groups and white southern support from denominations such as the Methodist Episcopal Church, South also provided a foundation for the education of blacks.

Public Education, 1868–1929

North Carolina's state constitution of 1868 required the General Assembly to "provide for a general and uniform system" of free public schools for all children between the ages of six and twenty-one. The document did not make separation of the races in the public schools compulsory, but an amendment adopted in 1875 ordained separate but equal educational facilities for white children and black children. Thus began in North Carolina the racially segregated system of public education that remained in place for more than eighty years. Indeed, North Carolina administered a triracial system of education for whites, blacks, and Indians.

Because funding came from counties or local communities, black schools were substandard. When Charles W. Chesnutt, the black novelist, arrived in Mecklenburg County in 1874 to teach summer school, he learned that local officials had expended all available school funds to erect a schoolhouse for blacks and had no money left to pay a teacher. Chesnutt found another black school located in a church, which "was a very dilapidated log structure, without a window." In 1880 North Carolina reported an enrollment of 161,262 white and 95,160 black pupils. School terms rarely exceeded four months. Among white and black students ages ten to fourteen, rates of illiteracy were 45 and 76 percent respectively. Poverty and the grossly unequal distribution of school funds meant that black students had fewer teachers, shorter terms, and inferior facilities and supplies.

It was not until 1897 that money from the state treasury was made available to help finance operation of the public school system. School districts that approved local school taxes could receive additional support from a $50,000 fund established by the General Assembly. The General Assembly appropriated funds to support a statewide system of public education in 1907. With such funding available, the State Department of Public Instruction began to build schools. In 1907 the state authorized the establishment of secondary schools for whites in rural areas. A total of 156 high schools were constructed in eighty-one counties during the first year. By 1911 some two hundred rural schools had been established in ninety-three of the state's one hundred counties.

By 1910 public elementary schools for blacks began receiving state funds. Three years later the state established the office of supervisor of rural elementary schools to promote the education of blacks, and Nathan C. Newbold became the first state agent for Negro schools. He subsequently became the first director of the Division of Negro Education when that agency was created in 1921. Out-of-state philanthropic agencies such as the Peabody, Rosenwald, Jeanes, and Slater funds, along with the General Education Board, supported Newbold's work. Moneys from the Jeanes Fund made possible the hiring of supervisors for rural schools, and the Rosenwald Fund financed the construction of schools. A number of county training schools built in rural districts with the aid of those philanthropies developed into public high schools. Aside from high-school work conducted in private academies, institutes, and some larger city schools, the only secondary school courses available to black students were in the preparatory departments of black colleges.

Berry O'Kelly School opened in the Method community of Wake County in 1910 as a private vocational training school for blacks. In 1917 a Baltimore newspaper acclaimed it as the "finest and most practical rural training school in the entire South." Like many of its counterparts, Berry O'Kelly subsequently developed into a public high school for blacks and was one of the first four such institutions to be accredited. Shown here is vocational teacher Charles Davis conducting a class at the school about 1915. Photograph from the files of the Office of Archives and History.

For many years a high-school education was virtually prohibited for blacks enrolled in public schools, and the first public secondary school for blacks was not established until 1918. Most such facilities offered fewer than four years of work, and almost half of them were limited to only one or two years. Between 1923 and 1929, public secondary schools for blacks were concentrated in the more progressive counties of the state, including Durham, Forsyth, Guilford, Mecklenburg, and Wake.

Annie Wealthy Holland played a major role in the realm of education for rural blacks, as well as in the North Carolina Congress of Colored Parents and Teachers, the first Negro parent-teachers association in the state, which she founded in 1928. She traveled extensively, promoting education in black elementary schools, holding meetings, organizing fund drives, and teaching demonstration classes.

Annie Wealthy Holland (1871–1934) of Gates County worked for the Division of Negro Education for a number of years. She subsequently founded the North Carolina Congress of Colored Parents and Teachers, the first such organization for blacks in the state. Photograph from Brown, *A History of the Education of Negroes in North Carolina*, 140.

The North Carolina General Assembly gave the task of supervising the state's public schools for blacks to the Division of Negro Education, created in 1921 as part of the State Department of Public Instruction. North Carolina continued to maintain its totally segregated educational system until the 1950s, when the separate-but-equal doctrine in education and public accommodations was overturned in the federal courts.

Public and Private High Schools, 1930–1967

By the 1930s many North Carolina counties had established public secondary schools for blacks. The majority of those facilities housed elementary and secondary grades in the same building. Schools were located on small lots in cities or towns, on the perimeter of cities and towns, and in some instances in open country. Public secondary schools for blacks were made available only in areas of North Carolina in which there resided sufficient numbers of black students to justify the expense of building and maintaining such facilities. In counties in which public secondary schools were not available, black parents were obliged either to send their children to a private institute—if one existed—or simply to forgo additional education for their children.

One elementary school for blacks that later became a high school and college was located in the community of Bricks in Edgecombe County. The school, which dated back to 1895, began as the Joseph Keasley Brick Agricultural, Industrial and Normal School and then became a junior college. The institution focused on reading and writing, as well as on trades, blacksmithing, carpentry, and other skills that blacks needed to provide for their families. Most schools followed the Booker T. Washington doctrine of industrial education, while others prepared black men and women to become teachers. A large percentage of African American men entered the teaching profession because few other occupations were open to black male college graduates.

The Freedmen's Board of the United Presbyterian Church established Henderson Normal Institute in Vance County in 1887, and in 1925 the state of North Carolina assumed responsibility for operating the facility's eighth grade and high school. Edgecombe County became the owner of the school in 1951 when it purchased from the Presbyterian church the property on which the school stood. The facility became known as the Vance County High School for Negroes and later part of Eaton-Johnson Junior High School. Thus, Henderson Institute began as a private school operated by a religious denomination and became a black public high school.

Black families also sent their children to private schools that developed from the work and dedication of the schools' founders, particularly those black visionaries who saw the pressing need to establish educational institutions for blacks in rural North Carolina. Palmer Memorial Institute, located in Sedalia, Guilford County, was such an institution. Nineteen-year-old Charlotte Hawkins Brown opened the school in 1902 and named it for her friend and benefactor, Alice Freeman Palmer, the first female president of Wellesley College in Massachusetts. As was then customary, Palmer Memorial began with both elementary and high-school instruction offered. By the mid-1920s the institution also included an accredited junior-college program. Brown worked tirelessly to see the school grow

Charlotte Hawkins Brown (1883–1961), the granddaughter of former slaves and a native of Henderson, established Palmer Memorial Institute in eastern Guilford County in 1902. She served as president of the institution for more than fifty years, during which time more than one thousand students graduated from it. This photograph of Dr. Brown was made about 1907. Photograph from the files of the Office of Archives and History.

from an institution that emphasized agricultural methods and industrial pursuits into one of the better-known black preparatory schools in the nation. Following Brown's death in 1961 financial problems beset the school. In 1971 fire destroyed the school's administration and classroom building, forcing the institution's trustees to close the school. The state of North Carolina reopened the facility in 1987 as the Charlotte Hawkins Brown Memorial State Historic Site, a reminder of the contributions of blacks to education in North Carolina and a center for the study of black history.

The only independent black-owned high school still in existence is Laurinburg Institute. Emmanuel McDuffie and his wife, Tinny Etheridge McDuffie, opened the school in 1904 in the Scotland County town of Laurinburg. The McDuffies went to Laurinburg at the suggestion of their former professor, Booker T. Washington, from the Snow Hill School, an Alabama branch of Washington's Tuskegee Institute. For many years Laurinburg Institute was the only school for blacks in Scotland County. Laurinburg Normal and Industrial Institute served as the county's lone high school for blacks until the early 1950s. Emmanuel McDuffie, like Charlotte Hawkins Brown, served as principal of his school until his death in 1953.

Northern philanthropists contributed generously to Laurinburg Institute, and Scotland County also lent financial support. In the 1950s the facility endured hard times when Scotland County established three public high schools for blacks. Once the county had done this, it withdrew its financial support for the institute. Moreover, the new county facilities eroded the enrollment at the institute, as did the subsequent implementation of racially integrated public schools.

Without federal grants or state funds, Laurinburg Institute passed into the third generation of McDuffies to operate the school. Its survival can be attributed to a new mission: educating children from Third World nations instead of those from Scotland County. Although Brick Agricultural, Industrial and Normal School; Henderson Institute; and Palmer Memorial Institute are defunct, those private institutions and others throughout North Carolina educated black Carolinians after emancipation, before and after public elementary and high schools for blacks were built, and before the advent of racially integrated public schools.

The Gaines *Decision and Its Impact on Graduate Education in North Carolina*

The NAACP first attempted to overturn racial segregation in state-supported higher education in the case of *Hocutt v. Wilson* (1933). In 1933 Thomas Raymond Hocutt, a black 1927 graduate of Durham's Hillside High School, applied for admission to the School of Pharmacy at the University of North Carolina in Chapel Hill (UNC). He was accompanied by Louis E. Austin, black editor and publisher of the *Carolina Times* (Durham), who supported Hocutt's efforts to break the barriers of racial segregation at the university. Hocutt's application was rejected, and he was advised to pursue college studies at one of the five state-supported institutions for the exclusive use of blacks. After being rejected by UNC, at which the state's only pharmacy school was located, Hocutt brought suit against the university. Dr. James E. Shepard, president of the all-black North Carolina College for Negroes, refused to recommend Hocutt or to supply UNC with a copy of Hocutt's undergraduate transcript.

Shepard believed that African Americans could do their best work only in their own schools. He desired to have a graduate school for blacks established in Durham. Increased opportunities for competent black students and faculty would result, in Shepard's view, from the expansion of existing facilities at his institution. Among his contemporary African Americans, Shepard was the only public figure to urge the establishment of separate graduate schools.

The judge in the *Hocutt* case ruled that UNC had the discretion to determine who might be admitted to its student body, that the university had considered Hocutt's application in good faith, and that Hocutt had neither supplied the necessary evidence of qualification for admission nor

Dr. James Edward Shepard (1875–1947), founder and longtime president of Durham's North Carolina College for Negroes (now North Carolina Central University), believed that black students could do their best work only in their own institutions of higher learning. He opposed the efforts of his contemporaries to overturn racial segregation in North Carolina's graduate schools and instead sought legislative approval to establish such a facility at his all-black institution. Photograph from Brown, *A History of the Education of Negroes in North Carolina*, 98.

established his clear legal right to be admitted. On the other hand, the court noted that the ruling had no bearing on the question of whether the university had a duty to admit blacks to its professional schools in instances in which the state failed to provide "equal opportunity for training in . . . its state supported negro schools. . . ."

By 1939 growing black activism in the realm of voting rights; opposition to lynching; the formation of additional NAACP chapters; and *Missouri ex rel. Gaines v. Canada*, a key decision by the Supreme Court of the United States, combined to bring new pressures on higher education in North Carolina. In 1936 Lloyd Gaines, a twenty-five-year-old Missourian, applied to the all-white University of Missouri law school. Gaines was a graduate of Lincoln University in Jefferson City, Missouri. Lincoln, a facility exclusively for blacks, did not have a law school. When Gaines was denied admission to the University of Missouri, he brought suit. In December 1938, the Supreme Court ruled that the state of Missouri had to provide Gaines with facilities for a legal education equal to that which the state afforded persons of the white race or else admit Gaines to the law school at the University of Missouri.

The *Gaines* decision forced states with separate systems of education for whites and blacks to provide opportunities for graduate and professional training at facilities already in operation. On the other hand, *Gaines* provided North Carolina and other southern states a legal and convenient method of preventing blacks from attending all-white state-supported schools by requiring only that those states make available to blacks educational opportunities deemed "equal" to those accessible to whites.

In an address to the North Carolina General Assembly in January 1939, Gov. Clyde R. Hoey responded to the new conditions imposed by the *Gaines* decision by recommending that professional courses in law, pharmacy, and medicine be made available at North Carolina College for Negroes in Durham and, if necessary, that additional graduate courses in agriculture or technology be offered by the State Agricultural and Technical College for Negroes in Greensboro. Hoey made a point of remarking, however, that "North Carolina does not believe in social equality between the races." Photograph from the *News and Observer* Negative Collection.

In January 1939, North Carolina governor Clyde R. Hoey responded to the new conditions imposed by the *Gaines* ruling. In an address to the General Assembly, Hoey, following the recommendations of a specially appointed "Commission on Higher Education for Negroes," proposed that professional courses in law, pharmacy, and medicine "as deemed necessary and essential" be made available at the North Carolina College for Negroes in Durham and that if "added courses are required in agriculture or technology they should be provided at the Agricultural and Technical College in Greensboro." At that time, those schools were the two largest state-supported institutions of higher learning for blacks in the state. Three others, located at Elizabeth City, Fayetteville, and Winston-Salem, specialized in the training of black educators. Hoey told legislators that his recommendations could be implemented without requiring the state to expend large sums of money if black colleges did not duplicate courses. "North Carolina does not believe in social equality between the races," Hoey declared, "but we do believe in equality of opportunity in their respective fields of service. . . ."

Before North Carolina established professional schools for blacks, its African American citizens had extremely limited resources available to them within the state. In the late nineteenth and early twentieth centuries, Shaw University in Raleigh, a private institution of higher learning for blacks, had supported both a law department and Leonard Medical School. By 1918, however, both programs had been terminated. North Carolina blacks who attempted to prepare themselves for nonteaching professions or to enter graduate schools were obliged to attend colleges and universities in other states, and many southern states offered to pay tuition fees for black students who agreed to attend out-of-state institutions.

In November 1938, two months prior to Hoey's address to the General Assembly, Pauli Murray, a young black woman of Durham, had unsuccessfully applied for admission to graduate school at the University of North Carolina in Chapel Hill. Murray was born in Baltimore, Maryland, in 1910 but was reared in Durham by her maternal grandparents and three aunts. After graduating from Durham's Hillside High School, she moved away in 1928. The University of North Carolina rejected Murray's application with the explanation from the dean of the graduate school that "members of your race are not admitted to the University." The university also informed Murray that the governor would be making an official statement on the *Gaines* decision when the legislature convened. Not only did Governor Hoey clarify his position on the subject of higher education for blacks, but his response to the *Gaines* decision also gave legitimacy to the university's denial of Pauli Murray's request to study at the institution. Murray returned to North Carolina in 1977 as an ordained Episcopal priest to administer the Holy Eucharist at the Chapel of the Cross, an Episcopal house of worship in Chapel Hill in which her slave grandmother, Cornelia, had been baptized in 1854.

By the late 1940s many blacks throughout the South were seeking entrance to professional schools of southern universities. North Carolina and other southern states were confronted with the problem of how to educate blacks who sought to attend state-supported graduate and professional schools. Finally, in April 1951, the University of North Carolina School of Medicine accepted the application of Edward O. Diggs. In the summer of that year four black men—including Floyd B. McKissick—began studies at the university's law school.

Parochial Schools and Desegregation, 1953

Despite North Carolina's small Roman Catholic population, Catholic schools were viable institutions in educating whites, blacks, and Indians. Schools provided elementary and high-school education for the state's Catholics as well as some Protestants. White nuns were in charge of most of those schools, but there were communities served exclusively by black nuns within the Catholic Church. In North Carolina two groups of black nuns operated schools: the Oblate Sisters of Providence at Saint Alphonsus School in Wilson and at Our Lady of Consolation School in Charlotte, and the Franciscan Handmaids at Christ the King School in High Point and at Saint Thomas School in Wilmington.

Roman Catholic schools were open to black and Indian children, but the majority of black children who attended such schools lived in black parishes. In Raleigh, black children attended Saint Monica, a black elementary school, and Cathedral Elementary School also enrolled Indians and a few blacks. When Sampson County closed the Eastern Carolina Indian Training School in 1966, some of the children went to live with families in Raleigh so that they might attend Cathedral Elementary. Saint Monica and Cathedral Elementary merged in 1967. Saint Monica was closed, and black students were transferred to Cathedral Elementary when the Catholic high school moved to a new location in Raleigh. In some instances white children went to black schools. Catholic High School in Washington, North Carolina, the only such institution in the town, furnished an example of that practice.

The Catholic Church in North Carolina began to end segregated practices in its parishes before other institutions in the state did likewise. Bishop Vincent S. Waters began the process of desegregating the Catholic schools in North Carolina. The bishop's 1953 pastoral letter to all parishes in the Raleigh Diocese (which then encompassed all of North Carolina) called for an end to racial segregation. Beginning in 1953, segregated Catholic churches and schools were merged on orders from the bishop, whose directives specified when, where, and how desegregation would occur. African American parishes in eastern North Carolina that were in Bishop Waters's Raleigh Diocese are listed in Table 1 below.

Table 1
African American Parishes in Eastern North Carolina
Included in the Raleigh Diocese under Bishop Vincent S. Waters

City	Parish	School
Durham	Holy Cross	
Elizabeth City	Saint Elizabeth	X
Fayetteville	Saint Anne	X
Goldsboro	Saint Mary	X
Greenville	Saint Gabriel	X
Kinston	Our Lady of the Atonement	X
Lumberton	Saint Madelyn Sophie Barrett[1]	X
New Bern	Saint Paul	X
Newton Grove	Saint Benedict[2]	X
Raleigh	Saint Monica[3]	X
Rocky Mount	Immaculate Conception	
Southern Pines	Saint Anthony of Padua	X
Washington	Mother of Mercy	X[4]
Wilmington	Saint Thomas	X[5]
Wilson	Saint Alphonsus	X

[1] Now known as Saint Francis de Sales
[2] Now known as Our Lady of Guadalupe
[3] Now known as Saint Joseph
[4] Elementary and high school
[5] Early childhood and elementary school

Reaction to the Brown *Decision: Initial Delays in Desegregation*

The legal assault on school segregation began with careful planning by the NAACP and Thurgood Marshall, attorney for the plaintiffs in *Brown v. Board of Education of Topeka* (1954). The NAACP-sponsored case challenged the doctrine of separate but equal with evidence that racial segregation made equal educational opportunity impossible. Chief Justice Earl Warren, writing for a unanimous court, stated: "in the field of public education the doctrine of 'separate but equal' has no place. Separate educational facilities are inherently unequal." One year later the Supreme Court ordered the states to proceed "with all deliberate speed" to integrate their schools.

Did the North Carolina public school system move to integrate its classrooms as the Supreme Court had ordered? Was the process of desegregation too protracted? Could it have been accomplished in less time? Some historians argue that North Carolina proceeded in direct opposition to the Supreme Court mandate in the desegregation of its public school system. Others believe that the state did indeed follow the high Court's decree to proceed with all deliberate speed. De facto and de jure segregation were firmly entrenched in the South through social pressures, laws, and judicial decisions. North Carolina was unwilling to accept immediate change in the status quo. As a result, it took more than three decades of court-ordered desegregation to deinstitutionalize the racial policies that had been in effect in the state since before the *Brown* decision of 1954.

Prior to 1951 the courts were unanimous in declaring that no constitutional guarantees against racial discrimination had been abridged in the distribution and use of public school funds. Nevertheless, in the case of *Blue v. Durham Board of Education* (1951), a North Carolina court found that in the matter of unequal public school facilities, black children had been discriminated against on the basis of their race. As a result of that finding, school officials conceded the existence of disparities between facilities available to white children and those available to black children. Unequal physical facilities clearly existed within the North Carolina public school system. White schools had more abundant space, while black schools tended to be crowded. White schoolchildren enjoyed such advantages as better supervision, greater opportunities for extracurricular activities, better laboratory equipment, better recreational facilities, better buildings, and lighter teaching loads.

The separate-but-equal doctrine in regard to North Carolina's public schools had been firmly ensconced long before 1940. But in the years after 1940 the per capita expenditure for educating black children had increased. Even so, in no way did it approximate the per capita expenditure for white children. The number of one-teacher elementary schools for blacks decreased from 777 in 1939–1940 to 100 by 1952. The number of one-teacher elementary schools for whites dropped from 274 to 34 during the same period. By the 1952–1953 school year, the number of black high schools with six or more teachers had increased from 73 to 153; for white high schools, the numbers were 371 and 521 respectively. Comparisons of numbers of elementary and high schools; enrollment; numbers of teachers, principals, and supervisors; and numbers of high-school graduates in the two-year period immediately prior to the *Brown* decision of May, 1954, are shown in Table 2 below.

The ruling by a North Carolina court in the case of *Blue v. Durham Board of Education* (1951) prompted school officials to concede the existence of disparities between facilities available exclusively to white children and those available to black children. That such disparities had long existed is suggested by this view of a black schoolroom made about 1950. From a pictorial series titled "Negro Life" derived from a movie titled *The Tar Heel Family*, produced in 1951 by the Department of Public Instruction, North Carolina Resource-Use Education Commission.

Table 2
The North Carolina Public School System, 1952–1954
A Brief Statistical Summary

1952–1953

	Whites	Blacks
Number of Elementary Schools	1,378	926
Number of High Schools	694	236
Number of Students Enrolled in Elementary and High Schools	652,622	276,401
Number of Teachers Employed in Elementary and High Schools	21,800	8,300
Number of Principals and Supervisors Employed in Elementary and High Schools	1,352	468

1953–1954

	Whites	Blacks
Number of Students Enrolled in Elementary and High Schools	683,284	284,782
Number of Teachers Employed in Elementary and High Schools	22,596	8,460
Number of Principals and Supervisors Employed in Elementary and High Schools	1,367	483
Number of High School Graduates	27,133	8,353

SOURCE: *Biennial Report of the Superintendent of Public Instruction of North Carolina for 1952–1953 and 1953–1954.*

Brown v. Board of Education held that segregation of children in public schools solely on the basis of race was unconstitutional. The decision set aside the separate-but-equal doctrine established by the Supreme Court in 1896 in *Plessy v. Ferguson. Brown* was one of five cases brought before the Supreme Court by the NAACP in attacking legally sanctioned public school segregation in seventeen states and the District of Columbia, as well as in four states in which racial segregation of public schools existed not in state law but as a local option.

Ironically, officials at Fort Bragg, the federal military installation located outside Fayetteville, had quietly desegregated their elementary school in 1951 with little excitement. Nevertheless, the majority of North Carolina's political leaders was shocked and disturbed by the *Brown* decision, and efforts to desegregate the state's public schools were delayed for several years. William B. Umstead, who had become governor on January 8, 1953, was "terribly disappointed" by the court's ruling. Former governor W. Kerr Scott had "always been opposed to Negro and white children going to school together," while Charles Carroll, superintendent of public instruction, believed that change, if it were to endure, would require the consent of a firm majority of the people who were obliged to live with it.

In August 1954, Governor Umstead created a "Governor's Special Advisory Committee on Education" to examine the potential problems that might result in North Carolina as a consequence of the *Brown* decision and to make recommendations for consideration by the 1955 General Assembly. Umstead named as chairman of the committee Thomas J. Pearsall, a prominent farmer and businessman of Rocky Mount and formerly Speaker of the North Carolina House of Representatives. Umstead also appointed as members of the committee three blacks: Dr. Ferdinand Douglas Bluford, president of A&T College; Dr. J. W. Seabrook, president of Fayetteville State Teachers College; and Mrs. Hazel Parker of Tarboro, home agent for blacks in Edgecombe County. In its final report, delivered December 30, 1954, the committee declared that "The mixing of the races forthwith in the public schools throughout the state cannot be accomplished and should not be attempted" and recommended "that North Carolina try to find means of meeting the requirements of the Supreme Court's decision within our present school system before consideration is given to abandoning or materially altering it." To this end the report called for legislation to give local school boards control of enrollment and assignment of children in the state's public schools and aboard its school buses.

In May 1955, at the urging of Gov. Luther H. Hodges, who had become North Carolina's chief executive on the untimely death of William B. Umstead, the General Assembly enacted legislation that removed references to race from the state's school laws and granted to the respective county and city boards of education responsibility for school administration, pupil assignment, enrollment, and transportation. Consequently, the State Department of Public Instruction was no longer responsible for statewide administration of North Carolina's public school system, and the problems inherent in implementing desegregation were to be handled on the local level. This delaying tactic meant that legal challenges would have to be filed with individual counties instead of with a centralized statewide authority.

In August 1954, Gov. William B. Umstead created a "Governor's Special Advisory Committee on Education" to examine the potential problems that might result in North Carolina as a consequence of the *Brown* decision and to make recommendations for consideration by the General Assembly of 1955. Members of the committee are pictured here. Standing in the foreground, third from left, are *(left to right)* Dr. Ferdinand D. Bluford, president of A&T College; Mrs. Hazel Parker, home agent for blacks in Edgecombe County; and Thomas J. Pearsall of Rocky Mount, chairman of the committee. Governor Umstead is seated at his desk. Photograph from the *News and Observer* Negative Collection.

From the outset, the black community recognized the dilatory strategy that North Carolina's white state officials were pursuing. When the General Assembly's Joint Committee on Education held a hearing in February 1955, a delegation of prominent blacks appeared before it. Serving as spokesman, John H. Wheeler, a black banker and lawyer of Durham, declared: "We wish to point out that in our opinion, the proposed legislation affecting the public schools seeks by various means to avoid the execution of the Supreme Court's decision and to slow down or retard the process of integration." Blacks sought to centralize authority in the State Department of Public Instruction so as to "enable it to implement integration, according to the mandate of the Court, firmly and impersonally."

In May 1955, the Supreme Court issued an order requiring the imple-mentation of desegregation "with all deliberate speed" in compliance with the *Brown* decision. Implementation and enforcement of the decision were to be carried out by school authorities; federal district courts would decide if such activities were being conducted in good faith. Even with the 1954 *Brown* decision and the court's 1955 compliance order, North Carolina's public schools did not initiate integration in the 1955–1956 school year. In response to the 1955 order, Governor Hodges, while publicly disagreeing with the action of the high Court, on August 8, 1955, recommended a plan of voluntary school desegregation in North Carolina on the part of both races. The governor, desiring to secure acceptance of his proposal from the state's black leadership, appealed to the North Carolina State Teachers Association, a professional organization composed entirely of black schoolteachers, to adopt a policy of "voluntary segregation." The Teachers Association rejected the governor's request, and local chapters of the NAACP were critical of his proposal. Hodges's plan encountered similar opposition among the state's black college students; booing students repeatedly interrupted the governor during a speech at A&T College in Greensboro on November 4, 1955.

Meanwhile, the General Assembly in April 1955, created a seven-member "North Carolina Advisory Committee on Education" as a successor to the "Governor's Special Advisory Committee on Education" established in August 1954, by the late governor Umstead. In June Governor Hodges appointed the members of the new committee and named as its chairman Thomas J. Pearsall, who had served as chairman of the Umstead committee. The 1955 committee became popularly known as the Pearsall Committee. It held a series of meetings, conferences, and hearings and subsequently recommended adoption of an amendment to the state constitution that would empower the General Assembly to enact legislation to appropriate funds to pay for the private schooling of any child assigned against the wishes of his or her parent or guardian to an integrated school; to permit local communities to suspend the operation of public schools if forced integration resulted in conditions deemed intolerable; and to amend the state's existing pupil assignment law so as to enable parents or guardians dissatisfied with assignments made by a local board of education to apply for reassignment of their children to a different public school.

In essence the so-called "Pearsall plan" stipulated that parents who did not wish to send their children to a school with children of another race did not have to do so. Parents could withdraw their children from the public

In April 1955, the General Assembly created a seven-member "North Carolina Advisory Committee on Education" as a successor to the committee established by the late governor Umstead. In June 1955, Luther H. Hodges, who had become governor on the death of Umstead in November 1954, appointed the members of the new committee and named Thomas J. Pearsall as its chairman. The 1955 body became popularly known as the Pearsall Committee. Seated, left to right, are North Carolina Attorney General Harry McMullan, Governor Hodges, Pearsall, William T. Joyner of Raleigh, and Robert O. Huffman of Morganton; standing, left to right, are state Representative Edward F. Yarborough of Louisburg, state Senator W. Lunsford Crew of Roanoke Rapids, state Senator William Medford of Waynesville, and state Representative H. Cloyd Philpott of Lexington. In July 1956, Governor Hodges in a special address televised statewide described the so-called "Pearsall plan" recommended by the committee and announced that the plan would be submitted to the people in a referendum in September 1956. Photographs from the *News and Observer* Negative Collection.

schools and enroll them in private institutions with the aid of state grants to pay tuitions. The Pearsall plan thus conferred upon parents the legal authority to ignore the mandate of the Supreme Court. After an extra session of the General Assembly officially adopted the Pearsall plan in July 1956, residents of the state signified their overwhelming approval of the scheme by voting in a public referendum (September 8, 1956) to adopt an amendment that made the Pearsall plan part of the state constitution. Thus, in 1956 North Carolinians voted by a margin of five to one to maintain racial segregation in the state's public schools. It was not until 1969, in the case of *Godwin v. Johnston County Board of Education*, that a federal court ruled the Pearsall plan unconstitutional.

In Greensboro, however, officials responded promptly to the *Brown* decision and began studying ways of desegregating the city's schools.

The Greensboro School Board demonstrated leadership in responding to the *Brown* decision by swiftly passing a resolution to abide by the decision and instructing Ben L. Smith, the city's superintendent of schools, to prepare a report on how such compliance might be implemented. Smith is pictured here. Photograph from Ethel Stephens Arnett, *For Whom Our Public Schools Were Named* (Greensboro: Piedmont Press, 1973), 378; photo reproduced courtesy Greensboro Historical Museum.

On May 18, 1954, by a vote of six to one, the Greensboro School Board passed a resolution to abide by the decision and directed Ben L. Smith, the city's school superintendent, to compile a report on how such compliance might be effected. David D. Jones, the only African American member of the Greensboro School Board, expressed the opinion that by initiating the first steps, Greensboro could set an example for the community, the state, and the South.

In 1957 school boards in Greensboro, Charlotte, and Winston-Salem admitted a total of twelve black students to previously all-white schools. Craven and Wayne counties followed in 1959, and Chapel Hill, Durham, and other cities began the process of integrating their schools in 1960. Most of the state's school districts were integrated by the end of 1965.

Nevertheless, desegregation of public schools in North Carolina was often accomplished in an atmosphere of defiance rather than compliance, and the process was frequently hindered by tactics employed for that purpose. As previously noted, North Carolina's pupil assignment law had prolonged segregation by enabling parents to dictate where their children were to be educated. Under the freedom-of-choice plan, enacted in 1965, school boards opened the doors of previously all-white schools to black children and black schools to white children. The plan permitted a parent or guardian to choose the specific school his or her child would attend. If reassignment to another school was preferred, the school board would either grant or refuse each request on a case-by-case basis.

With freedom of choice the burden of implementing desegregation fell to blacks. Students who requested reassignment, as well as their families, faced intimidation. During the three years in which the freedom-of-choice plan was operative, 85 percent of the state's black schoolchildren continued to attend all-black schools, and not a single white child elected to attend such a facility. In short, freedom of choice proved entirely ineffective as a means of integrating North Carolina's public schools. In 1968 a federal court ruled in the case of *Boomer v. Beaufort County Board of Education* that freedom of choice for pupils was unconstitutional and an impermissible means of desegregating county public schools. The judge in the *Boomer* case directed Beaufort County's board of education to implement a plan of active desegregation consistent with the decision of the Supreme Court. African American parents, in many cases with the assistance of the NAACP Legal Defense Fund or the NAACP Education Fund, filed suits against North Carolina school boards.

With the push for desegregation of the state's public school system came a corresponding increase in the number of private schools for whites. Public school officials expressed concern over the accelerating withdrawal of white students from the public schools.

Complete desegregation of North Carolina's public schools did not occur until the 1970s. Segregated buses carried black students to black schools and white students to white schools in county systems. The cases of *Teel v. Pitt County Board of Education* (1967) and *Boomer v. Beaufort County Board of Education* addressed certain issues raised by this system of bus transportation. In *Teel* the United States District Court for the Eastern District of North Carolina declared invalid Pitt County's previously accepted freedom-of-choice plan. In the *Boomer* decision the same court held that buses used to transport pupils to county schools had to accommodate *all* students on each bus route, without regard to the race or color of those students. In some areas of North Carolina, elementary schools were integrated before high schools were. School boards and human relations councils held meetings to discuss how faculty and extracurricular activities would be merged. Methods that had worked successfully in the state's county-school system could not be applied to city systems.

Dramatic shifts in housing patterns during the 1960s presented additional obstacles to desegregation of the state's public schools. In North Carolina and other southern states, white families moved in large numbers from cities and towns into newly developed suburban and rural areas where there were relatively few blacks. This pattern tended to leave fewer and fewer white children available to attend what previously had been urban all-black schools.

In 1970 a federal district court ordered the Charlotte-Mecklenburg County Board of Education to inaugurate a program of cross-town busing of students as one means of effecting racial balance in that system's schools.

LEFT TO RIGHT: John L. Brandon, Ralph Frazier, and Ralph's brother Leroy Frazier, three graduates of Durham's Hillside High School, applied for admission to the University of North Carolina in 1955 and were denied admission. The three youths were enrolled after the NAACP sought relief in federal court, resulting in a ruling by a special three-judge panel that the university must process the applications without regard to the applicants' race or color. Photographs from the *News and Observer* Negative Collection.

The court, in *Swann v. Charlotte-Mecklenburg Board of Education*, also ordered the creation of "attendance zones" and the "pairing" of schools. The *Swann* case tested the constitutionality of pairing predominantly black schools in the city of Charlotte with predominantly white schools in Mecklenburg County and the cross-busing of children to and from the paired schools in order to achieve desegregation. *Swann* involved appeals by Julius LeVonne Chambers, a black Charlotte attorney, and the NAACP Legal Defense and Education funds. The decision of the court in the *Swann* case was upheld by the Supreme Court of the United States in 1971 as being necessary to break the pattern of segregated schools. From that beginning, the busing of schoolchildren to achieve racial integration in the public schools spread throughout the South in 1971 and 1972 and subsequently to other parts of the nation.

The path to desegregating institutions of higher learning in North Carolina also proved bumpy. In the spring of 1955 three black graduates of Durham's Hillside High School applied for admission to the freshman class at the University of North Carolina in Chapel Hill. They were denied admission, and in response the NAACP threatened to take the matter to federal court. Leroy Frazier, seventeen years of age, and his brother Ralph, along with John L. Brandon, both age eighteen, were enrolled after a three-judge federal panel ruled that the university must process their applications without regard to their race or color. The three students were admitted in September 1955, under a federal court order, thus becoming the first black undergraduates to attend the university.

With that court order the University of North Carolina also became the first state institution of higher education in the South to admit blacks into its undergraduate classes. The Supreme Court outlawed segregation in tax-supported colleges and universities on March 5, 1956. Gradually other colleges and universities in North Carolina began to accept blacks. In 1961 Davidson College and Duke University, both private institutions, admitted African Americans into their undergraduate programs.

Efforts to desegregate North Carolina's state-supported white colleges and universities moved slowly, however. The Civil Rights Act of 1964 outlawed racial discrimination in hotels, theaters, restaurants, buses, and all public accommodations and provided for the termination of funding to federal projects in which racial discrimination was practiced. The act also created the Equal Employment Opportunity Commission and authorized the attorney general of the United States to initiate lawsuits on behalf of private individuals in cases involving desegregation or discrimination. Civil rights organizations utilized Title VI of the Civil Rights Act of 1964 to challenge racial segregation in institutions of higher learning. Title VI provides that no person in the United States shall, on the basis of race, color, or national origin, be excluded from participation in, be denied the benefit of, or be subjected to discrimination under any program or activity receiving federal financial assistance. By 1969 the Office of Civil Rights (OCR) of the United States Department of Health, Education, and Welfare (HEW), responding to such legal challenges, required several states to develop and implement desegregation plans for their institutions of higher learning or risk the loss of federal funding.

North Carolina was one of ten states that OCR charged with violating Title VI. Five of the states proposed plans that the OCR did not accept, while others did not respond. Because of the inability of the OCR to carry out its responsibilities, the NAACP Legal Defense Fund, in the case of *Kenneth Adams v. Elliott Richardson* (1972), sued HEW for defaulting in administering Title VI. North Carolina, one of the so-called "Adams states," subsequently reached an agreement with HEW.

On July 13, 1981, officials of the University of North Carolina system signed and submitted to the United States Department of Education (a successor agency of HEW) a consent decree. In the document, which essentially settled an eleven-year dispute between the university and HEW, UNC pledged to eliminate all vestiges of separate-but-equal higher education for blacks and to establish an integrated system of higher education in North Carolina. Provisions in the decree called for establishment of a five-year plan to increase the average percentage of white students at traditionally black campuses to 15 percent by 1986 and to ensure that students were informed as to the state's policy of nondiscrimination. Also included was a proposal for new programs and additional appropriations for the five traditionally black universities. UNC was released from the provisions of the consent decree at the expiration of the five-year plan in 1986.

With the efforts to desegregate public institutions of higher learning in North Carolina also came the rallying cry to "save black schools." On October 25, 1971, approximately 3,000 students marched on behalf of the state's five predominantly black universities—Elizabeth City State, Fayetteville State, North Carolina A&T, North Carolina Central, and Winston-Salem State.

Under the administration of Gov. Robert W. Scott (1969–1973), a restructuring of institutions of higher learning took place. To prevent duplication of programs and to reduce inefficiency between the UNC system and the smaller institutions, a study committee appointed by Governor Scott recommended that all sixteen of North Carolina's state-supported institutions be consolidated under one governing board. A thirty-two-member board of governors to be appointed by the General Assembly and the governor would have the authority to regulate the growth of curricula on all sixteen campuses and decide which degrees each institution could grant. Black students protested against the reorganization scheme. Prior to the plan for restructuring, the board of trustees of each institution governed that institution. Under the restructuring plan, local boards of trustees would retain some authority over faculty and student affairs on the respective campuses, but major policy decisions would be the exclusive domain of the board of governors.

The black students' outcry against adoption of the reorganization plan was aimed at preserving the existence and autonomy of their institutions. The students proposed that the local board of trustees at each of the five predominantly black institutions continue to have full governing authority and financial power. They also called for 80 percent black representation on the local board of trustees and a 30 percent representation on the board of governors. Howard N. Lee, the black mayor of Chapel Hill and spokesman for the student protesters, called the proposed reorganization plan the end of the state's predominantly black universities. At the same time, leaders of the state NAACP were calling for the total desegregation of higher education. In spite of the student protests, the state's five historically black universities joined their eleven white counterparts in a reorganized University of North Carolina system effective July 1, 1972.

Through a long and at times seemingly unbending process, desegregation of North Carolina's public school system came closer to reality. Formal desegregation occurred through voluntary, court-ordered, or negotiated compliance and as a result of class-action lawsuits. County school boards throughout the state drafted plans to integrate their facilities in voluntary compliance with the *Brown* decision. When private suits were successfully entered, courts ordered school boards to comply. The Office of Civil Rights intervened against those school districts that received federal funding and discriminated on the basis of race. Class-action suits permitted one judicial ruling to apply to school districts in a multitude of jurisdictions. In the end, such landmark decisions as *Brown* and *Swann* made the desegregation of North Carolina's public schools possible.

IX

The Civil Rights Movement of the 1960s

The fundamental impetus for the civil rights movement of the 1960s extended from the institutionalization of slavery during antebellum days to the disfranchisement of blacks that characterized the post-Reconstruction period to the "color line" of the Jim Crow era. In the days of slavery the lives of black North Carolinians were restricted by various laws that held blacks in perpetual bondage and treated them as property. The struggle to maintain freedom continued even after passage of the Thirteenth, Fourteenth, and Fifteenth amendments to the United States Constitution. Blacks were apprehensive about reenslavement as sharecropping, tenant farming, and the convict lease system became established in the southern economy. The quest for full equality occurred as disfranchisement and racial segregation pushed blacks into second-class citizenship during the Jim Crow era. Segregation had attempted to define the actual physical place of blacks in southern society, as well as their place in a caste system.

As early as the 1930s southern blacks, increasingly restive under such discriminatory conditions, began organizing against institutional segregation. Within three decades they carried their protest to the courts and adopted nonviolent tactics, including sit-ins, boycotts, demonstrations, freedom rides, and marches throughout the South. The struggle on behalf of blacks—with the aid of some sympathetic whites—was for equality in America.

Organized opposition to segregation took several forms in North Carolina. In 1932 black ministers in Raleigh refused to take part in a ceremony to dedicate the new War Memorial Auditorium. Blacks boycotted the ceremony because they were confined to a small section of the balcony of the new structure. They sought a fairer allocation of separate facilities rather than outright desegregation of the facility. In 1938 students

In this early civil rights demonstration (1949) by North Carolina African Americans, placard-carrying students from the North Carolina College for Negroes march in front of the North Carolina State Capitol in Raleigh to demand better law-school facilities at the Durham institution. Photograph from Capus M. Waynick, John C. Brooks, and Elsie W. Pitts (eds.), *North Carolina and the Negro* (Raleigh: North Carolina Mayor's Cooperating Committee, 1964), 240.

in Greensboro initiated a theater boycott that spread to other cities. The students objected to a statement by the North Carolina theater owners' convention that censured "the appearance of colored people in scenes with whites on an equal basis." In the 1940s the NAACP helped organize school boycotts against inferior segregated education. In Lumberton hundreds of students marched downtown in 1946 to protest inadequate educational opportunities. Students from Durham's North Carolina College for Negroes picketed the State Capitol in 1949 to demand improvements at that institution's law school. And in Durham in 1957, a group of seven black activists led by the Reverend Douglas E. Moore, a Methodist minister, sought service in the white section of a local ice cream parlor. They were arrested and convicted of trespassing, but their sit-in presaged a decade of conflict and social revolution.

Black life in the 1950s remained circumscribed by the laws of North Carolina and by city ordinances enacted after 1898. Those laws mandated the segregation of citizens by race or color in the realms of amusements, recreation, prisons, training schools, employment, restaurants, the National Guard, tax records, police, libraries, hospitals, travel, and housing. Although some of those laws and regulations had been repealed by the 1950s, blacks still were forced to adhere to rigid practices that ensured de facto racial segregation. Segregation manifested itself in the signs first seen during the Jim Crow era—signs that read COLORED and WHITE. In 1947 Hubert A. Eaton Sr., a black physician practicing in Wilmington, was shocked to find Bibles so labeled when he was sworn in to give testimony in court. Although labels were not always visible, segregation was a way of life for blacks in the South.

Burial of the dead, too, was governed by segregation ordinances. Municipal cemeteries were designated for blacks or whites. Some black sections could be found in white cemeteries. It was unlawful for a white person to purchase a burial plot set aside for blacks in a municipal cemetery or for a black person to purchase a plot in a section reserved for whites. In order to ensure that one of its municipal cemeteries was totally segregated, the Greensboro City Council was empowered to authorize the removal of dead bodies from one cemetery to another. A June 1947 ordinance in the Charlotte city code specified that city property on North Summit Avenue known as North Pinewood Cemetery be used for the burial of blacks. During the previous year, land along Albemarle Road known as Elmwood Cemetery was designated for the burial of whites. As late as 1969 a wire fence separated the two city-owned cemeteries. Through the efforts of black civil rights advocates Kelly Alexander Sr., and his brother, Fred Alexander, a member of the Charlotte City Council in 1969, the council voted to remove the fence, then the city's last visible sign of segregation. The fence had stood as a symbol that people of different races could not associate, alive or dead.

Some North Carolina cities maintained separate recreational facilities. Public swimming pools were either segregated or all-white, or there were no pools at all. City ordinances generally stipulated whether pools were for the exclusive use of whites or blacks. In 1959 the city of Greensboro sold its two municipal pools to settle a dispute over integration. The following year Charlotte desegregated its public swimming pools, and Winston-Salem desegregated its municipally owned Reynolds Park pool in 1962. The Raleigh City Council closed the all-white Pullen Park pool and the all-black Chavis Park pool in 1962. The closings resulted when four black youths went swimming in the Pullen Park facility.

Signs first seen during the Jim Crow era institutionalized racial segregation until the 1960s and circumscribed everyday life for most African Americans. Separate "Colored" and "White" drinking fountains such as these examples from a tobacco warehouse in Lumberton abounded. Photograph (probably August 1945) from Standard Oil (New Jersey) Collection, Photographic Archives, University of Louisville; reproduced by permission.

TOP: In the spring of 1956, in response to a court ruling, Duke Power Company, which then operated municipal bus lines in various North Carolina municipalities, ordered Jim Crow signs removed from its fleet of buses. The signs had been an accepted fixture aboard North Carolina's buses since the 1930s. Greensboro *News & Record* photograph by Jack Moebes; reproduced by permission. BOTTOM: Signs directed patrons of an Edenton launderette to separate restroom facilities as late as February 1965, the date this photograph was made. Photograph from the *News and Observer* Negative Collection.

On many occasions when blacks attempted to use recreational facilities, they were arrested and charged with trespassing. Such was the case with a municipal golf course in Greensboro. Blacks seeking permission to play at the course were arrested. In December 1956, the Guilford County Superior Court found them guilty of trespassing and sentenced them to thirty days in jail. The defendants appealed the decision, and the North Carolina Supreme Court reversed it on a technicality. The defendants were tried and convicted again in February 1958. This time they were sentenced to fifteen days in jail, and again they appealed the decision. The state supreme court found no error, and the Supreme Court of the United States refused to review the case. On November 11, 1960, Gov. Luther Hodges commuted all of the jail penalties upon the payment of $7,000 in court costs.

These men, arrested and charged with trespassing for attempting to play golf at Greensboro's Gillespie Park municipal course in December 1956, were fined and sentenced to thirty days in jail. They were released on bail without being jailed, but a protracted appeals process through several courts failed to produce a reversal of their original convictions. Gov. Luther H. Hodges subsequently commuted the sentences. Greensboro *News & Record* photograph by Jack Moebes; reproduced by permission.

Several of North Carolina's larger cities—Greensboro, Winston-Salem, and Asheville—adopted ordinances that established separate residential areas for black and white citizens. For many years ownership of substantial amounts of residential property was restricted to whites. Developers of residential subdivisions imposed deed restrictions that forbade the sale or occupancy of dwellings by blacks. Some deed restrictions excluded Jews, Roman Catholics, and Orientals as well. In 1948 the Supreme Court of the United States, in *Shelley v. Kraemer*, ruled that restrictive covenants in real-estate transactions could not be enforced. Nonetheless, de facto, if not purely legal, segregation continued to be practiced in the realm of housing.

Many social problems faced North Carolina and America at mid-century. Perhaps the three most compelling ones were civil rights, poverty, and economic inequality. Even allowing for the monumental *Brown* decision in 1954, the Montgomery bus boycott of 1955, and the forced integration of Central High School in Little Rock, Arkansas, in 1957, the decade of the 1950s was a relatively placid period. But as the 1960s approached, the issues of civil rights, poverty, and urban decay swept across

During his early years as minister and civil rights advocate, the Reverend Martin Luther King Jr. occasionally journeyed to North Carolina to deliver a sermon or speech. Here Dr. King is speaking to an integrated audience in the auditorium at Raleigh's Needham B. Broughton High School on February 10, 1958. Photograph by Archie Henderson Jr.; from the files of the Office of Archives and History.

the South and the nation. Blacks were becoming tired of continued discrimination and impatient with the slowness of change. The successful boycott of the Montgomery bus system had placed Martin Luther King Jr. in the national spotlight and identified him with the nascent civil rights movement. Within a year King had perfected his strategy of civil disobedience through peaceful resistance. The emergence of a trained professional class of black lawyers and the important role of black churches and voluntary institutions created a base from which to attack Jim Crow laws and institutionalized inequality in America.

In 1960 students began adopting civil disobedience as a means of challenging segregation in restaurants and other public facilities. On February 1, 1960, four students at North Carolina A&T College in Greensboro sat down at a lunch counter in the F. W. Woolworth five-and-dime store in downtown Greensboro, a facility at which service was available only to whites. The students protested against being allowed to shop in the store but not being permitted to eat at the store's lunch counter. The sit-in was peaceful. The four students—Joseph McNeil, Franklin McCain, David Richmond, and Ezell Blair Jr.—were not served, but they remained at the lunch counter until the store closed. This action by the four Greensboro students is generally credited with being the opening salvo of the sit-in movement of the early 1960s—notwithstanding the lesser-known act of principle engaged in by the group of activists at a Durham ice cream parlor in 1957.

Additional black students at A&T College joined in the demonstrations, and soon white female students from Greensboro College and Guilford College, as well as black female students from Greensboro's Bennett College, began to participate in the protest—not only at Woolworth's but also at S. H. Kress, another five-and-ten-cent store in downtown Greensboro. In response to the demonstrations, members of the Ku Klux Klan and local white teenagers vied with the black students and their supporters for seats at the Woolworth lunch counter. A telephoned threat that a bomb had been placed in the store's basement forced the store to close on Saturday, February 6; the Kress store closed also. The "sit-ins," as they came to be called, subsequently spread to Charlotte, Durham, Elizabeth City, Fayetteville, High Point, Raleigh, and Winston-Salem.

A lunch counter sit-in protest began in Raleigh on February 10. Some 150 students took part in demonstrations against stores with white-only lunch counters. Students from Shaw University and Saint Augustine's College took seats at the lunch counters at Woolworth's, S. H. Kress,

McClellan's, Walgreen's, Eckerd Drugs, and Hudson Belk, a department store. When black students sat down at the lunch counters, white patrons immediately vacated them. The management of McClellan's and Hudson Belk closed their lunch counters. McClellan's posted a sign that read: "Restaurant Temporarily Closed." In McClellan's lunch counter the lights were turned off, but the students continued to sit. At other times when black students entered the stores, the lunch counters closed immediately. Signs that read "Closed in the Interest of Public Safety," "Luncheonette Temporarily Closed," and "We Reserve the Right to Serve the Public as We See Fit" were made in advance and quickly put on display when black students entered the establishments. Students from Shaw and Saint Augustine's continued their vigil in shifts. Sometimes bystanders threw eggs at the students. Store managers frequently stopped news photographers from taking pictures or blocked their view to prevent the store from receiving adverse publicity in newspapers.

Black college students also carried picket signs as they marched in protest in front of stores. Forty-one students were arrested at privately owned Cameron Village, a Raleigh shopping center. The Raleigh arrests were the first to be made in the widespread protest demonstration by black students in North Carolina. Each student was booked and fingerprinted at the Wake County jail and released under $50.00 bond. George Green, a black attorney in Raleigh who represented a number of the students, declared that the Raleigh arrests were "shameful and a violation of the students' constitutional rights." The students were charged with trespassing as they stood on privately owned shopping-center sidewalks in front of the F. W. Woolworth store in Cameron Village.

Students who picketed in protest at Raleigh's privately owned Cameron Village shopping center were the first demonstrators in North Carolina to be arrested for trespassing during the sit-in era of the early 1960s. Each student was booked and fingerprinted at the Wake County jail and released under bond. Photograph from the *News and Observer* Negative Collection.

The management of Raleigh's Woolworth's store responded to the threat of sit-in demonstrations in typical fashion—it closed its lunch counters to the public. The sign at left is typical of those posted at lunch counters in many North Carolina locations. Photographs from the *News and Observer* Negative Collection.

In the now-famous photograph at top, the four original sit-in demonstrators—David Richmond, Franklin McCain, Ezell Blair Jr., and Joseph McNeil—at the Woolworth's lunch counter in Greensboro on February 1, 1960, are leaving the store by a side exit on the afternoon of the initial demonstration. The February 1 sit-in quickly spawned protest marches on the outside of the Greensboro store and subsequently in other major cities throughout North Carolina. Greensboro *News & Record* photographs by Jack Moebes; reproduced by permission.

Sit-ins and protest marches in various North Carolina cities during the winter of 1960 closely followed the pattern established in Greensboro on Feburary 1. These photographs, made February 16, 1960, on Fayetteville Street in Raleigh, show black protest marchers demonstrating in front of Woolworth's and McClellan's, two dime stores that offered dining services at lunch counters. Photographs from the *News and Observer* Negative Collection.

The first arrest of whites during the demonstration in Raleigh came on February 18. Two white men were arrested after a scuffle with black youths who were picketing on a sidewalk in downtown Raleigh. One of the men received a sixty-day road sentence for slapping a picketer across the wrist with a dog chain.

As the movement against the Woolworth chain of stores spread throughout the South and to stores in the North, the Greensboro store eventually was forced to make concessions. By the end of February, black picketers had left the Kress store in downtown Raleigh. The store's strategy had been to open the main-floor lunch counter and offer stand-up service to both races. Stools had been removed from the counter area, and black students and white customers drank coffee and ate sandwiches while standing. Students from Shaw and Saint Augustine's continued to picket those downtown Raleigh stores that closed their lunchroom facilities rather than make them accessible to black people.

J. Melville Broughton Jr., an attorney for the North Carolina Association of Quality Restaurants, a lobbying organization, advised member restaurants that it was their right to refuse to serve anyone in their private places of business and to press trespass charges if persons refused to leave after being denied service. With respect to the sit-in demonstrators, Raleigh mayor W. G. Enloe thought it "regrettable that young blacks would risk endangering race relations in the city by trying to change a long-standing custom in a manner that is all but destined to fail."

The desegregation of restaurants and public accommodations met the same resistance that the desegregation of the public school system had encountered. Demonstrations and legal pressure brought some relief, but the bastions of segregation were slow to fall. The Ku Klux Klan, White Citizens' councils, and segregationists in general were influential in determining the status of race relations in the state and throughout the South.

The civil rights movement gained momentum as students, assisted by various organizations, developed new forms of protest to take advantage of mass participation at the grass-roots level. These novel forms of protest were frequently devised in response to particular situations. From the initial sit-ins at all-white lunch counters the protests evolved to picket lines in which demonstrators carrying signs marched in front of restaurants, theaters, stores, hotels, and other public facilities. Then came wade-ins (at public swimming pools), read-ins (at public libraries), and kneel-ins and pray-ins, during which students kneeled and recited the Lord's Prayer as a

Efforts by North Carolina's African American citizens to effect the desegregation of public facilities in the 1950s and 1960s met with open resistance from segregationists, members of White Citizen's councils, and the Ku Klux Klan. This billboard, probably located in Harnett County, openly invited the public to "Join and Support the United Klans of America." Photograph (May 1967) from the *News and Observer* Negative Collection.

form of protest. Individuals and black organizations offered their services to help train demonstrators in the techniques of nonviolent protest. Those techniques taught protesters how to avoid certain actions and thus prevent law enforcement officers from arresting them either for assault or merely for

Beginning as sit-ins at lunch counters, the civil rights movement branched into other types of marches and demonstrations aimed at calling attention in a nonviolent manner to racial inequities. These marchers picketed a Greensboro movie theater with separate facilities for white and black patrons. Greensboro *News & Record* photograph by Jack Moebes; reproduced by permission.

College students, not limited by the threat of dismissal of jobs, spearheaded the civil rights demonstration of the 1960s in North Carolina and throughout the nation. These students at the University of North Carolina at Chapel Hill resorted to peaceful civil disobedience to protest Chapel Hill's "Candy-Coated Racism." Photograph (January 31, 1964) from the *News and Observer* Negative Collection.

being a public nuisance. Those who instructed demonstrators on their behavior emphasized love and nonviolence in order to bring about strictly peaceful protests.

On February 16, 1960, Martin Luther King Jr. spoke to approximately 1,200 persons—an estimated fifty of whom were white—at a civil rights rally at White Rock Baptist Church in Durham. The evening rally packed the church to capacity, and the crowd overflowed onto the church grounds. Earlier that same day King had addressed a group of 100 black student leaders in Durham. The students met to ask questions and to learn how to practice the techniques of nonviolence at sit-in demonstrations. Students and the masses kindled the fire of the civil rights movement of the 1960s. Students on college campuses could protest without the threat of losing jobs. Once the struggle became a movement of the masses, it was impossible to keep aggressive blacks in line by threatening dismissal from jobs, denial of loans, or foreclosures of mortgages.

Black organizations such as the NAACP, the Congress of Racial Equality (CORE), the Southern Christian Leadership Conference (SCLC), and the Student Nonviolent Coordinating Committee (SNCC) spear-headed the sit-ins, picket lines, freedom rides, and economic boycotts. CORE, SCLC, and SNCC organized workshops on tactics of passive resistance. (In addition, CORE protested the use of trespass ordinances as a means of stopping sit-ins in the South.) The organizations staged mock confrontations between police and demonstrators in an attempt to teach protesters how to react in adverse situations. Support also came from the United Presbyterian Church, the largest Presbyterian body in the nation. The protest movement, along with the court system, hammered away at racial injustice in America. Nevertheless, the role of indigenous community groups, civic leagues, and private institutions was indispensable to the success of the civil rights movement.

CORE

The Congress of Racial Equality (CORE), an interracial action group founded in 1942, pioneered the sit-in demonstrations. When the sit-ins began to spread throughout the South, the organization dispatched "field secretaries" to bail students out of jails, share their experiences with demonstrators, and help organize protests. In organizing the sit-in protesters, the field secretaries instructed the students to be courteous, friendly, and not to strike back or curse if abused. The students were counseled not to block entrances to the target stores or shopping aisles within those stores. They were cautioned against engaging in conversation with employees of the stores in which they conducted demonstrations. They were told to sit straight and to face the counter at all times. The field secretaries emphasized personal restraint in the face of harassment and the importance of being nonviolent at all times during the demonstrations. The students adopted as their protest anthem "We Shall Overcome," an old gospel song that subsequently came to be the freedom refrain of the larger civil rights movement.

CORE's first foray into North Carolina occurred in 1947. The "Journey of Reconciliation" was a two-week interracial trip designed to test compliance with *Morgan v. Virginia* (1946), the Supreme Court decision against segregation in interstate bus travel. Eight black and eight white men left Washington, D.C., in April 1947, to desegregate both Greyhound and Trailways buses. Organizers of the trip obtained assistance along the way from local blacks, who fed and housed the travelers. The organizers arranged thirty speaking engagements, mostly at black churches, colleges, and NAACP chapters.

The riders, some of whom were pacifists, adopted a strategy of nonviolence. Eugene Stanley, former treasurer of CORE, then a teacher at North Carolina A&T College, joined the riders at Durham and Chapel Hill and lost his job as a result. Riders were arrested in Durham, Asheville, and Chapel Hill. Only in Chapel Hill did violence threaten. The "Journey of Reconciliation" became the model for the "Freedom Ride" of 1961.

The mastermind of the freedom rides was James Farmer, a longtime civil rights activist who resigned as program director of the NAACP to become national director of CORE. Farmer had been involved in civil rights issues before Martin Luther King Jr. and nonviolent protest became a visible movement. Under Farmer's leadership CORE initiated the freedom rides. One year after the first sit-ins in Greensboro, freedom riders traveled by bus through Virginia, North Carolina, South Carolina, Georgia, and Alabama to challenge segregation in interstate bus terminals. The freedom riders began their trip south in May 1961. There were no reported incidents when the bus carrying the freedom riders stopped at the Raleigh terminal. The riders met resistance on May 14 in Anniston, Alabama, where they were attacked by angry segregationists. "Jail—no bail" was implemented as a CORE tactic when the freedom riders were arrested for attempting to ride the buses, refusing to move to the rear of the vehicles, and for attempting to use white-only rest rooms on their trip through the South. The freedom riders—black and white—who were arrested were found guilty of trespass and fined $200 each. They elected to be taken to jail rather than pay the fines.

Farmer, along with about 300 other freedom riders, was arrested in the summer of 1961 and held until August of that year. Although the riders faced reprisals, they were successful in desegregating southern bus terminals. On September 22, 1961, the Interstate Commerce Commission (ICC) ruled that passengers on buses and trains operating on interstate routes would be seated without regard to race and that separate terminals for blacks could not be used. Commercial airlines had never been segregated, and those blacks who traveled by air avoided the discriminatory practices of the bus lines and railroad companies. The Greyhound and Trailways bus terminal on Morgan Street in Raleigh, with its separate waiting rooms for whites and blacks, eventually merged the two facilities. The ICC ruling in 1961 removed for blacks the humiliating experience of having to move from seats in the front of buses to those in back once a bus reached the Mason–Dixon line.

The Greyhound and Trailways bus terminal in downtown Raleigh had long featured separate waiting rooms for "White" and "Colored" travelers. These photographs were made in January 1956. From the *News and Observer* Negative Collection.

Following the freedom rides, CORE shifted its attention to the desegregation of public accommodations. "Freedom Highways" focused on the Howard Johnson's chain of restaurants. CORE organized and staged protests in Raleigh, Durham, Greensboro, Burlington, Graham, and Statesville. The demonstrations helped thrust into national prominence Durham attorney Floyd B. McKissick. By August 1962, half of the Howard Johnson's restaurants in North Carolina had been desegregated. White resistance had diminished, and some white customers of the Howard Johnson's restaurant in Durham even told the manager that they supported the demonstrators.

CORE's largest, most disruptive demonstrations in North Carolina occurred in the spring of 1963 when civil rights demonstrators targeted various cities in the Piedmont for a variety of protests designed to bring about desegregation of public accommodations. Hundreds of arrests resulted. These students at Raleigh's Shaw University are being fingerprinted at police headquarters in downtown Raleigh after being arrested for participating in such a demonstration. From the *News and Observer* Negative Collection.

CORE's largest, most disruptive demonstrations came in the spring of 1963. In order to desegregate hotels, restaurants, and public accommodations, demonstrators employed such tactics as sit-ins, picketing, and daily marches. In particular CORE targeted major cities in the Piedmont— Greensboro, High Point, Durham, and Chapel Hill. Hundreds of arrests followed. Indeed, one of CORE's tactics was to fill a jurisdiction's jails to beyond capacity. Jesse Jackson, then president of the student body at North Carolina A&T College, led marches and sit-downs in Greensboro. Although largely unsuccessful in achieving its overall goals, CORE realized many of its major objectives with the enactment of the Civil Rights Act of 1964.

Floyd McKissick succeeded James Farmer as national director of CORE in 1966. McKissick was chief administrator of the organization for two years, during which time he launched a major fund-raising campaign. At its 1966 convention, held in Durham, CORE officially changed its direction. Instead of emphasizing nonviolent direct-action demonstrations, CORE turned to organizing black communities to obtain economic and political power. In addition to his responsibilities for overseeing the activities of CORE, Floyd McKissick served as North Carolina state youth director of the NAACP Young Commandos, the militant branch of the organization. Moreover, as a lawyer, McKissick defended demonstrators who had been arrested for various civil rights activities. In 1968 he resigned as director of CORE, which chose for its new director Roy Innis. Along with SNCC, CORE began emphasizing a more militant philosophy that emphasized black nationalism. CORE's philosophy tended to become more radical with the approach of the 1970s.

SCLC

Sixty black leaders, mostly ministers from ten southern states, founded the Southern Christian Leadership Conference (SCLC) in January 1957. The Atlanta-based civil rights organization elected Martin Luther King Jr. as its first president. King, whose home had been bombed in January 1956, became known for his advocacy of Mohandas K. Ghandi's theories on passive resistance. Blacks were angry about the bombing, and King made an appeal for nonviolence that the newspapers carried. Thereafter, the media characterized King as an advocate of nonviolent protest. King had successfully demonstrated nonviolent methods during the Montgomery bus boycott, which lasted for more than a year.

In 1962 Dr. King asked Golden A. Frinks of Edenton, whom he had met in 1957, to serve as North Carolina field secretary for the SCLC. Frinks was active in civil rights demonstrations in North Carolina and other southern states.

Golden Asro Frinks of Edenton served as North Carolina field secretary for the Southern Christian Leadership Conference and was tireless in his leadership of protests for a variety of causes in several North Carolina cities and towns in the 1960s and 1970s. Photograph from Waynick, Brooks, and Pitts, *North Carolina and the Negro*, 167.

In North Carolina, he organized protests for employment opportunities for blacks in the town of Hertford and assisted the blacks of Williamston in their attempts to have trash collected in their community. Indeed, he went to jail in Williamston for six months in 1963–1964. Frinks, also an activist for school desegregation, housing, and voting rights, led five marches in Raleigh between 1963 and 1974.

SNCC

The Student Nonviolent Coordinating Committee (SNCC) was a student organization founded in April 1960, on the campus of Shaw University in Raleigh by Ella J. Baker. Baker was a Shaw graduate who was then serving as executive director of the Southern Christian Leadership Conference. The visionary Baker, realizing that the students involved in the civil rights movement needed an organization of their own, persuaded the SCLC to finance a conference of student demonstrators for the purpose of keeping the spirit of the movement alive by ensuring that the energies of students did not dwindle. The result was an organization that the students could use to maintain their interest and help them coordinate their efforts in the civil rights struggle.

More than two hundred delegates attended the organizational meeting of SNCC at Shaw University. The nascent organization continued to work with the SCLC, CORE, and the NAACP. SNCC, like other civil rights organizations, devised a protest strategy. One of SNCC's techniques was the task force. Student task forces were assigned to live with blacks in the rural South, to teach them, and to build their self-esteem. Members of SNCC endured insults and risked their lives in order to register blacks to vote in the Deep South.

Eventually, Ella Baker's fear of student apathy toward the movement was realized. By the mid-1960s members of SNCC had become disillusioned. Students feared that black leaders were settling for less than full equality. When Stokely Carmichael became chairman of SNCC in 1966, members were expressing reservations about working along traditional lines to achieve equality. Carmichael was a strong advocate of "black power" and black nationalism. Although little has been written on Ella Baker's role in the civil rights movement, she nurtured the "children" of the movement, the student activists of the 1960s.

One of North Carolina's civil rights pioneers was Kelly Miller Alexander Sr. (1915–1985), who reorganized the dormant Charlotte chapter of the NAACP in 1940 and embarked on a forty-five-year career as an activist. This early view of Alexander shows him delivering an address in North Wilkesboro in 1949. Photograph from Kelly M. Alexander Sr. Papers, J. Murrey Atkins Library, University of North Carolina at Charlotte.

NAACP

The National Association for the Advancement of Colored People (NAACP) was founded in 1909 and formally organized in May 1910. From its inception the organization pledged to work for the abolition of all forced segregation, equal education for black and white children, the complete enfranchisement of blacks, and the enforcement of the Fourteenth and Fifteenth amendments to the United States Constitution. In its first year of operation the NAACP campaigned for more police protection for blacks and a crusade against the lynching of blacks in the South, and it chartered branches in various states to carry out the work of the parent organization on the local level.

In North Carolina, Kelly Alexander Sr. reorganized the dormant Charlotte chapter of the NAACP in 1940 and thus embarked on a forty-five-year career as a civil rights activist. Alexander chose to work for civil rights through the NAACP because it was a legal, nonviolent, and Christian organization. After serving as president of the Charlotte chapter, Alexander became president of the North Carolina State Conference of NAACP Branches in 1948, a position he held until 1984. Alexander worked unceasingly to build the state organization through memberships and annual fund drives. In 1950 he was elected to serve the organization at the national level as a member of the board of directors. By 1955 the NAACP in North Carolina boasted 83 chapters or affiliates and more than 10,000 members. Alexander remained active in the national organization of the NAACP until his death in April 1985.

One of the advantages Kelly Alexander had in building the NAACP in North Carolina was that he and his brother, Frederick Douglas Alexander, did not work for white people. As owners of a funeral home founded by their father, the two brothers could agitate and speak out for black rights without fear of economic reprisals from segregationists.

The NAACP Legal Defense Fund (LDF) represented numerous black plaintiffs in desegregation suits in North Carolina. Families that allowed the LDF to represent them in test cases frequently shared certain similarities with the Alexanders of Charlotte. Like the Alexanders, they risked reprisals by attempting to dismantle the entrenched system of racial segregation. Though insulated from the loss of their jobs, civil rights activists such as the Alexanders often received visits from the Ku Klux Klan or had their homes bombed. On November 22, 1965, the homes of Charlotte civil rights activists Kelly Alexander, Fred Alexander, Julius Chambers, and Reginald A. Hawkins were bombed. The party or parties responsible for the bombings were never arrested, even though the bombings made national headlines.

The outlook of the black community in North Carolina underwent a gradual change in the late 1960s. This period gave birth to a more radical

By the 1960s Kelly Alexander (*left*) was a recognized leader in the field of civil rights, particularly for his leadership of the NAACP at the national level. In 1962 he attended a conference of community leaders on equal employment opportunity in Washington, D.C., hosted by then Vice-President Lyndon B. Johnson. Photograph from Kelly M. Alexander Sr. Papers, J. Murrey Atkins Library, University of North Carolina at Charlotte.

philosophy and the Black Revolution movement. Some blacks who emerged as the spokesmen of various organizations advocated immediate changes in the system. These militant activists expressed dissatisfaction with the manner in which Kelly Alexander ran the NAACP. In 1969 Golden Frinks, field secretary for the Southern Christian Leadership Conference, labeled Alexander an "Uncle Tom." Frinks complained that Alexander was the biggest obstacle to desegregation in the state and that the Charlottean was resistant to the ideas of the young.

The March on Washington

In 1963 the struggle for jobs, social justice, and equality moved to the nation's capital. Twenty-two years earlier A. Philip Randolph, founder and longtime president of the Brotherhood of Sleeping Car Porters, threatened President Franklin D. Roosevelt with a march on Washington by 50,000 black people to protest job discrimination. Although the march never materialized, it did help to bring about creation of the Fair Employment Practices Commission during World War II. A. Philip Randolph; Roy Wilkins, then executive secretary of the NAACP; and Martin Luther King Jr. organized the Washington Prayer Pilgrimage, which took place on May 17, 1957. The demonstration to protest discrimination and the slow pace of desegregation drew some 35,000 participants. The August 28, 1963, March on Washington for Jobs and Freedom was the largest public demonstration in the nation's history. As North Carolina field secretary for the Southern Christian Leadership Conference, Golden Frinks assisted in planning the march. Cars and bus caravans from throughout the nation converged on Washington, D.C., where an estimated 200,000 people marched and heard speeches in front of the Lincoln Memorial from leaders in the civil rights movement. One year after the march, Congress passed the Civil Rights Act of 1964, and President Lyndon B. Johnson enthusiastically signed the measure. The landmark legislation ended discrimination in public accommodations.

More sweeping legislation was needed if blacks were to achieve true equality in America. Throughout the South, blacks had been systematically disfranchised; they now looked to Congress to abolish that practice.

The Voting Rights Act

President Dwight D. Eisenhower submitted a civil rights bill to Congress in 1957. The resulting act authorized the federal government to bring civil

Enactment by Congress of the Voting Rights Act of 1965 opened doors long closed to North Carolina's black citizens. The focus of some demonstrations turned to encouraging eligible voters to exercise their newly won franchise by registering and voting. Photograph (March 1966) from the *News and Observer* Negative Collection.

suits in cases in which people were denied the right to vote or were threatened with reprisals if they exercised that right. The law also created a Civil Rights Division in the United States Department of Justice, as well as a United States Commission on Civil Rights. It authorized the commission to investigate denials of the right to vote. The civil rights commission held hearings on black voting in several cities. It found and reported that certain white southern registrars were denying blacks the right to vote. In 1960 Congress enacted another civil rights bill, which strengthened the federal government's enforcement of voting rights. The Civil Rights acts of 1957,

1960, and 1964 did not eliminate voter discrimination, but with enactment of the Voting Rights Act of 1965 the protections offered by the Fourteenth and Fifteenth amendments were made real to a number of black people who had been systematically prohibited from exercising their franchise.

The act made illegal all qualifying tests, such as those based on literacy, previously used to bar blacks from registering to vote. It authorized the attorney general of the United States to take legal action against local boards of election, and it stipulated that federal examiners could be sent to a jurisdiction to register black voters who had been turned away by officials of that jurisdiction.

The Voting Rights Act of 1965 opened the door of political power to all black citizens. It enabled thousands of blacks who previously had been disfranchised to participate in the election process. Instead of protesting to achieve gains, blacks could focus their attention on political participation by helping to elect officials who would work for their entire constituency. As registered voters, blacks could participate in the question of whether southern congressmen who did not vote for significant civil rights legislation should return to Washington.

Additional legislation in 1965, 1968, and 1970 in the area of voting rights lowered other barriers to black voting in North Carolina. The "grandfather clause," the poll tax, and the literacy test had been used to prevent blacks from voting in the Tar Heel State. The Supreme Court of the United States declared the grandfather clause unconstitutional and overturned the poll tax. The Voting Rights Act ended the literacy test as a requisite for blacks to have the franchise.

In many southern states black men and women were elected to political office as a result of the increase in the number of black registrants. Statistics compiled by the North Carolina State Board of Elections in 1965 showed black voter registration at 244,684; for 1966 the figure was 281,134. An apparent increase in the number of black voters in the state contributed to the election of blacks as city councilmen or councilwomen, mayors, county commissioners, judges, state legislators, and members of school boards. Beginning with the elections of 1968, a black returned to the North Carolina General Assembly after an absence of seven decades. Henry E. Frye, a Democrat of Guilford County, was elected to the state House of Representatives. In 1974 the voters of Mecklenburg County elected Frederick Douglas Alexander of Charlotte to the state senate, and voters in Wake County chose John W. Winters of Raleigh to represent them in that body.

The Voter Education Project

Under the administration of President John F. Kennedy and with his support, CORE, SNCC, SCLC, the NAACP, and the Urban League embarked on a Voter Education Project (VEP) in April 1962. The North Carolina VEP, founded in 1967, was based in Durham. The VEP, a two-and-one-half-year project, encouraged voter registration but failed to provide for the protection of civil-rights activists and blacks who attempted to register to vote. The organization was hampered in its efforts to register voters because it tried to appease whites at the same time it was attempting to register blacks. Golden Frinks directed the SCLC voter-registration campaigns in North Carolina. A 1964 voter-registration drive in Mecklenburg County under the direction of Reginald Hawkins added 15,000 new voters to the rolls. In that instance, Hawkins and Fred Alexander dealt directly with VEP headquarters in Atlanta.

In some cases black tenant farmers who attempted to register to vote were evicted by white landlords. There were incidences of wholesalers' refusing to deliver food and supplies to the black owners of stores. Murders of black and white civil rights workers were reported in some areas of the South. White hostility to government-sponsored efforts to enforce civil rights legislation continued, as did marches and violence. The 1965 Selma-to-Montgomery march was a five-day, fifty-mile trek to protest discrimination against blacks in voter registration and to push for additional voting-rights legislation. President Lyndon B. Johnson federalized the Alabama National Guard to protect the demonstrators on the road from Selma to Montgomery. The march led to the passage of the Voting Rights Act of 1965.

The Poor People's March

Before Martin Luther King was assassinated on April 4, 1968, he was organizing his Poor People's March on Washington. After he was assassinated, some black people became disillusioned with the philosophy of peaceful protest. Riots broke out in many of the cities in the North and South, and mayors were forced to implement curfews and impose certain other emergency measures. Dan K. Moore, governor of North Carolina, appealed to citizens of the state to remain calm and to refrain from violence. The governor dispatched National Guard troops to Raleigh, Greensboro, Goldsboro, Wilmington, Wilson, and Durham. The following day he expressed condolences to the King family and issued a statement that declared: "for violence to surround the death of Dr. King is a denial of his life's work. Those who honor his memory and mourn his passing should pay their tribute by keeping the peace."

After King's death, the Reverend Ralph David Abernathy and other leaders of the Southern Christian Leadership Conference continued to plan and organize the Poor People's March, which Dr. King had envisioned as a means of dramatizing the plight of the nation's poor. Blacks from throughout the United States set up makeshift housing, tents, and shanties in Washington, D.C. King's widow, Coretta Scott King, and Roy Wilkins, executive director of the NAACP, were among the speakers who addressed the encampment of poor people in the nation's capital on May 20, 1968.

Good Neighbor Councils

The demonstrations that began in Greensboro in 1960 had in no way diminished by the summer of 1963. As a method of improving race relations in North Carolina, Governor Terry Sanford established the twenty-four-member biracial North Carolina Good Neighbor Council on January 18, 1963. Among the black citizens who served on that body were Dr. Reginald A. Hawkins, Dr. John R. Larkins, John S. Stewart, John H. Wheeler, John W. Winters, and Robert J. Brown.

As its mission the Good Neighbor Council was charged with encouraging employment of qualified people in the state without regard to race and urging the state's youth to become better trained and qualified for employment. Governor Sanford believed that a cooperative effort would be necessary to carry out those objectives. He asked mayors and county commissioners to establish Good Neighbor councils at the local level. He appealed to state government, private business, industry, church leaders, pastors, and civic organizations to support the objectives of the Good Neighbor councils. At a meeting at the State Capitol in June 1963, the governor called on black leaders to seek means other than mass demonstrations to address the plight of blacks. He told the black leaders that mass demonstrations had been effective in calling attention to the situation in the beginning but that the effectiveness of such demonstrations had diminished over time. It was his opinion that mass demonstrations had destroyed goodwill between the races, created resentments, alienated friends, and ceased to produce the results earlier demonstrations had engendered.

The Good Neighbor Council and the Mayors' Cooperating Committee that Governor Sanford proposed on July 5, 1963, were designed to seek ways in which greater economic opportunities could be extended to blacks. The governor believed that through good faith, goodwill, and a determination on the part of North Carolinians, the citizens of the state would work to ensure that all people, regardless of race or color, might have the chance to achieve a rewarding life. His was an appeal to the consciences of Carolinians to do the right thing. He went on to reiterate that programs were in place to train minorities in the skills they needed to acquire better jobs.

Sanford helped produce a positive atmosphere in the realm of race relations by recognizing the legitimacy of black aspirations for freedom and equality. His policies, however, had little substantive effect. Hiring practices in state government did not change. The North Carolina Good Neighbor Council lacked administrative muscle to secure equal employment opportunities. In the end, improvement in race relations depended upon local leaders, who might or might not move voluntarily toward Sanford's vision of racial justice.

Racial Unrest: The New Militancy

North Carolina blacks were making progress, but the problem continued to be the pace of change. With discrimination still rampant, militancy increasingly took hold in the late 1960s and 1970s. Baptist, Methodist, and other denominational churches were the meeting places at which plans to end discrimination and desegregate the state's public school system were discussed.

Gregory Congregational United Church of Christ in Wilmington was the scene of a 1971 meeting of one hundred students to plan a school boycott to protest the closing of the previously all-black Williston High School. Before the boycott and other disturbances were over, Gregory Congregational had attained notoriety. Two weeks prior to the meeting at Gregory Congregational, students had been suspended for attempting a sit-in to protest the refusal of school officials to permit a program to be held in commemoration of the birthday of Martin Luther King Jr. Fights between white and black students occurred, and police were assigned to active duty at three of Wilmington's high schools. Tensions ran high, and the police were accused of harassing black students. The Reverend Leon White of the

North Carolina-Virginia Commission for Racial Justice, an agency of the United Church of Christ, attended the students' second meeting at Gregory Congregational. The students had requested White's presence at the meeting to help them organize the boycott. The following week Ben Chavis, a twenty-four-year-old minister, arrived in Wilmington on orders from the Commission for Racial Justice. Chavis was asked to help organize the protest and plan strategy.

The students' demands included a request for Williston High School to be reopened as a black high school, Martin Luther King Jr.'s birthday to be observed as a school holiday, and a course on black history to be offered in the Wilmington schools. Racial strife spread from the schools and besieged the community as shooting, rock throwing, and bombing occurred. Wilmington police and the National Guard seized Gregory Congregational Church. As the violence continued, the mayor imposed a curfew on Wilmington. Eventually the schools were closed.

On March 18, 1971, Golden Frinks of the Southern Christian Leadership Conference set up headquarters in Wilmington. At a mass meeting he had called, Frinks stated that student leaders and concerned citizens had invited the SCLC to Wilmington. Frinks told the group that there would be a protest march to Raleigh. The marches, boycotts, destruction of property, and violence ended after the Wilmington Board of Education went to United States district court on March 22, 1971. The board asked Judge Algernon Butler for a restraining order to prevent Ben Chavis, the Reverend Leon White, the Reverend Eugene Templeton, the white pastor of Gregory Congregational, Golden Frinks, the North Carolina-Virginia Commission for Racial Justice, the Southern Christian Leadership Conference, and others from interfering in the operation of the New Hanover County school system. The battle over desegregation of the New Hanover County public schools continued in the courts after the violence and demonstrations ended.

On March 16, 1972, the Reverend Ben Chavis was arrested and charged with fire bombing Mike's Grocery Store, a white-owned establishment that stood opposite Gregory Congregational Church, and for conspiring to assault firemen and policemen with firearms. Eight other black men—Joe Wright, Jerry Jacobs, James McKoy, Reginald Epps, Willie Earl Vereen, Wayne Moore, Marvin Patrick, Connie Tindall—and one white woman— Ann Shepard Turner—were arrested and likewise charged. All ten were convicted and were given prison sentences ranging from twenty-three to thirty-four years for the nine men and seven to ten years for the white woman. The North Carolina Court of Appeals upheld the conviction in 1974, and the Supreme Court of the United States declined to review the case in 1976. The one aspect of the case that was not subject to review in the appellate courts was the length of the sentences. North Carolina law permitted the review of the appropriateness of the sentences by the governor and not an appellate court.

On January 23, 1978, Gov. James B. Hunt Jr., appeared on television with an official statement on the "Wilmington 10," as the defendants in the case had been dubbed. Governor Hunt remarked that the trial had been fair, that the jury had made the right decision, and that the appellate courts had reviewed the case and ruled properly. "I cannot and I will not pardon these defendants," the governor declared. He concluded that the sentences imposed on the nine black men for fire bombing an unoccupied building were too long and reduced them; but he did not reduce the sentences imposed for conspiring to shoot at firemen and policemen. Governor Hunt let stand the sentence imposed on Ann Shepard Turner, deeming it appropriate for her participation in encouraging the other defendants to fire bomb the grocery. In 1980 a federal court of appeals overturned on technical grounds the conviction of the Wilimington 10.

In 1973, in an episode reminiscent of the 1898 Wilmington race riot, a black newspaper in Wilmington was attacked. This time the *Wilmington Journal*, founded in 1901, was bombed. The editor and publisher, Thomas C. Jervay, had written and published editorials condemning the oppression of minorities. The building was not completely destroyed, and Jervay was able to continue publishing the weekly newspaper.

The struggle for equality and social justice was waged through the court system and through nonviolent protest. This combination was integral to abolishing racial segregation in America. The civil rights movement included not only the outspoken but also those who worked quietly and methodically through the judicial system to bring an end to discrimination. Participants in the movement saw the injustices in American society and tried to right them. People such as Frederick Douglas Alexander, Kelly Alexander Sr., Louis Ernest Austin, Ella J. Baker, Julius L. Chambers, Hubert A. Eaton, Golden Frinks, Reginald A. Hawkins, Jesse Jackson, Thomas Jervay, and Floyd B. McKissick, as well as many others, believed that southern blacks had been denied equal political rights, adequate education, social equality, and economic opportunity for too long.

Many Americans believed that with the passage of the Civil Rights Act of 1964, most of the work in the realm of racial equality had been done. But large-scale protest movements continued long after this legislation had been enacted. Racial segregation was firmly rooted in American society, and no single piece of legislation could undo overnight what had been in place continuously for more than ninety years. Woolworth's lunch counter and other public accommodations had been desegregated, but the lives of most black people remained virtually unaltered. Most blacks still faced humiliation, and the majority of black children still attended segregated schools. What had to be realized was that if America were to be a great society, a just society, certain attitudes and prejudices would have to be eradicated in the minds of the people. There was only so much that the legal system could do. Laws could be passed to end de jure segregation, but an end to de facto segregation in the way a society and its people—all nationalities and ethnic groups—interrelated was required. In short, the persistent racism inherent in American society was a moral and not simply a legal problem capable of being redressed by the enactment of legislation.

The Black Power movement of the late 1960s and 1970s, as Floyd McKissick characterized it, was a response to the "dashed hopes and mangled dreams of a people and a result of the ineffectiveness of the nonviolent movement." Those who study American history will continue to write about and analyze the most pervasive social and political movement of the twentieth century. But the struggle for civil rights did not begin in the 1960s. Rather, it began when slaves resisted their masters' demands, when freedmen gathered in Raleigh in 1865 to demand equality, and when courageous black educators, businessmen, and ministers protested Jim Crowism and disfranchisement in the wake of the Wilmington race riot. Those civil rights activists who followed carried on a proud and brave tradition.

X

The Rise of African American Political Power

Progress and New Dilemmas

In the decades following the civil rights struggles of the 1950s and 1960s, African American political power surged. Whereas a handful of African American legislators began appearing in the North Carolina General Assembly in the late 1960s and 1970s, by the 1990s African Americans had assumed positions of considerable power and influence in both state and local government (see Appendix 2). Between 1970 and 1997 a total of 506 African Americans won elective office in North Carolina. That figure included two representatives to Congress—Eva Clayton in the First District and Mel Watt in the Twelfth District—and more than sixty legislators. At the city and county levels of government, 354 African Americans were elected to office. An additional twenty-nine African Americans in law enforcement and ninety-six in education likewise won election at the county and local level.

Henry E. Frye of Guilford County, the first African American elected to the General Assembly in the twentieth century, in 1968, received appointment from Gov. James B. Hunt Jr. to the North Carolina Supreme Court in 1983. In 1984 and 1992 Frye won statewide elections as associate justice. In 1999 Hunt appointed him chief justice. A year later, however, Frye lost his bid to be elected chief justice. Meanwhile, Ralph Campbell Jr. won elections as state auditor in 1992, 1996, and 2000. In the General Assembly, Dan Blue of Wake County served as Speaker of the House of Representatives from 1991 to 1994. African Americans also received appointments to cabinet positions under both Republican and Democratic administrations in the 1980s and 1990s.

Perhaps most conspicuously in 1990 and again in 1996, Harvey Gantt, former mayor of Charlotte, mounted strong challenges to the reelection of

Republican Jesse Helms, the incumbent U.S. senator first elected in 1972. Gantt lost both elections by nearly identical margins of 53 percent to 47 percent. But the 1990 election in particular turned on a controversial television advertisement by the Helms campaign. It showed a pair of white hands crumpling a job rejection notice. The advertisement tied Gantt to affirmative action and equal employment opportunity policies that many white North Carolinians resented.

Between 1990 and 2000 the African American population grew from 1.461 million to 1.723 million. For the first time, the U.S. Census allowed citizens to identify themselves as "multiracial." A total of 79,965 North Carolinians listed themselves as multiracial, and of that number 33,630 noted black ancestry. The African American population of North Carolina declined slightly—from 22 percent of the total population in 1990 to 21 percent in 2000.

As black political influence broadened, blacks' participation in elections lagged behind that of whites. In 1998, among African Americans of voting age, 65.5 percent registered to vote but only 48.7 percent cast ballots. Comparable figures for whites were 70.4 percent and 56.4 percent respectively. In 1992, 50.3 percent of blacks voted in the presidential election, but only 45 percent participated in 1996. Despite the election of Eva Clayton and Mel Watt to the U.S. Congress in 1992, 1994, 1996, 1998, and 2000, black voter participation in congressional elections was low. In 1992, 40.9 percent of African Americans voted in congressional races. That percentage dropped to 29.3 percent in 1994 and improved only slightly to 36.9 percent in 1996.

African American economic well-being continued to lag as well. Economic disparities remained wide. Black per capita income in 1990 ($7,926) was only 55 percent of white per capita income ($14,450). That same year the poverty rate was 7.1 percent among white males and 10.1 percent among white females. The comparable figures among black North Carolinians were 23.4 percent (male) and 30.2 percent (female).

Regardless of economic indicia, African Americans exercised the greatest political power that they had ever known. At the same time, however, minority voting rights came under attack in the courts. Indeed, North Carolina became a bellwether for minority voting rights throughout the nation as a series of legal cases, beginning with *Shaw v. Reno* (1993), made their way to the Supreme Court of the United States.

TOP: Among a host of African Americans elected or appointed to public office in North Carolina in the years following the civil rights struggles of the 1950s and 1960s were Henry E. Frye , flanked by his wife and a well-wisher, at the time of his appointment as a justice of the North Carolina Supreme Court in 1983 (Frye is also the first African American to have been elected to the General Assembly in the twentieth century); BOTTOM: Ralph Campbell Jr., first elected state auditor in 1992 and here shown at a 1995 press conference; Top photo from *News and Observer* Publishing Company/ Office of Archives and History; bottom photo courtesy of *News and Observer* Publishing Company, Raleigh.

TOP: Dan Blue, speaker of the state House of Representatives from 1991 to 1994 and here shown announcing his candidacy for the U.S. Senate in October 2001. BOTTOM: Harvey Gantt, a former mayor of Charlotte, ran unsuccessfully for the United States Senate against Republican Jesse Helms in 1990 and 1996. Here Gantt is shown at a campaign rally at the University of North Carolina at Charlotte in October 1990. Top photograph courtesy *News and Observer* Publishing Company, Raleigh. Bottom photograph courtesy Robinson-Spangler Carolina Room, Public Library of Charlotte and Mecklenburg County; both reproduced by permission.

Two African Americans—Eva Clayton (*left*) in the First District and Mel Watt (*right*) in the Twelfth District—were elected to Congress from North Carolina each election year between 1992 and 2000. Nevertheless, black voter participation in congressional elections remained low throughout the 1990s. Photograph at left courtesy *News and Observer* Publishing Company; photo at right courtesy, *Charlotte Observer*, Charlotte.

Shaw v. Reno *(1993)*

The Voting Rights Act of 1965 (VRA), renewed in 1970, 1975, and 1982, had produced a dramatic impact on black officeholding by 1990. Virginia became the first state in the nation to elect an African American governor. African American mayors ruled six of the nation's ten largest cities. Nationally, 59 percent of blacks and 64 percent of whites were registered to vote. Amendments to the 1982 VRA had declared that minorities should enjoy the same opportunities as whites "to participate [in elections] and to elect candidates of their choice." In 1993 the number of black and Latino elected officials totaled fifty-seven in Congress and 686 in state legislatures.

In particular, section 5 of the 1982 VRA, as interpreted by the Civil Rights Division of the U.S. Department of Justice, brought great pressure to bear on states to maximize the number of voting districts in which minority groups made up a majority of voters. Those districts came to be known as "majority-minority" districts. They were intended to reflect the proportion of minority voters in a state. For example, in 1990 African Americans constituted 22 percent of North Carolina's total population. Accordingly, one-fifth of North Carolina's congressional seats should represent majority-minority districts. Moreover, the question of bloc voting was crucial to VRA cases. To create majority-minority districts, plaintiffs needed to show that a majority of whites always voted against the candidate favored by a majority of blacks.

The Justice Department, under Republican presidents Ronald Reagan and George Bush and later Democratic president Bill Clinton, aggressively enforced section 5. It was not a theoretical exercise in constitutional law. States that once disfranchised African Americans had to obtain "pre-clearance" from the Justice Department before redistricting. The department refused to give preclearance to states that did not maximize the number of majority-minority districts. Hence, in 1990 many states had drawn congressional districts with bizarrely shaped boundaries.

The insistence on majority-minority districts generated fierce debate among historians, constitutional scholars, and informed citizens. Even some observers sympathetic to African American civil rights after centuries of discrimination found the oddly shaped congressional districts offensive. Conservatives and some liberals viewed majority-minority districts as a new form of segregation, dividing races instead of uniting them. One legal scholar compared the congressional districts to "racial homelands" for voting purposes. Some Republican observers, however, noted astutely that majority-minority districts could make the GOP more competitive in districts once dominated by Democrats.

A conservative majority on the U.S. Supreme Court agreed with critics of the majority-minority districts, comparing the districts to "racial gerry-mandering." The origins of *Shaw v. Reno* began in 1991 and 1992 when the North Carolina General Assembly created one, then two, black-majority congressional districts (see Appendix 3). North Carolina had not sent an African American to Congress since George H. White's reelection in 1898.

Under the 1992 plan adopted by the General Assembly, the First District sprawled over eastern North Carolina. It was overwhelmingly rural in character. The Twelfth District, in contrast, was almost exclusively urban. It followed a very narrow corridor for 160 miles along Interstate 85 from Durham to Charlotte. Each district included 57 percent black majorities; 51 to 54 percent of the registered voters were black. In her majority opinion in *Shaw v. Reno*, Justice Sandra Day O'Connor termed the districts a "political apartheid." Historian J. Morgan Kousser has taken an opposing view. In his careful study of minority voting rights in the 1990s, he has argued that the two North Carolina districts were "the least segregated, most nearly racially balanced congressional districts in the state in the twentieth century," providing African Americans with a fair opportunity for equal representation in Congress.

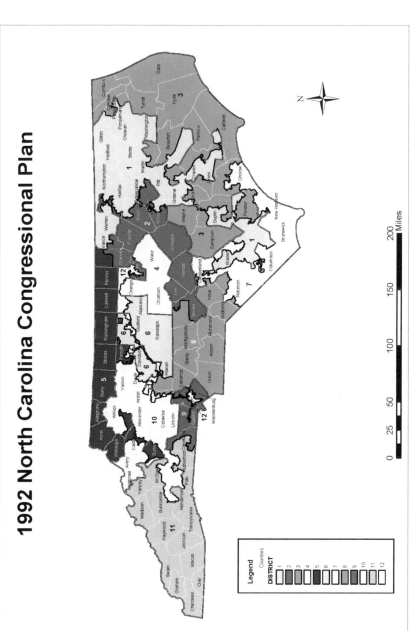

1992 North Carolina Congressional Plan

This map reveals the details of the congressional redistricting plan adopted by the North Carolina General Assembly in 1992. Of particular interest are the First District, in the northeastern portion of the state, and the Twelfth District, which runs in a crescent-shaped swath approximately along Interstate 85 from Durham County southwestward to Mecklenburg County. In the case of *Shaw v. Reno*, the Supreme Court of the United States held that the redistricting plan was unconstitutional as drawn. This map and all subsequent maps are provided by the Information Systems Division. North Carolina General Assembly

Robinson O. Everett, a law professor at Duke University in Durham, initiated the suit that challenged both districts in federal court. Everett served as both a plaintiff and chief attorney. Plaintiffs included four other white residents of Durham. Three of the five lived in neither the First nor Twelfth District, and the two who lived in the Twelfth actually voted for Mel Watt in 1992. The plaintiffs argued that the General Assembly, under pressure from the U.S. Department of Justice, had instituted a "racial gerrymander." In a 1993 brief to the U.S. Supreme Court, Everett asserted: "No court or agency has determined that racial discrimination has ever occurred in the creation of congressional districts in North Carolina. Indeed, it is clear that none has taken place; and so there was no constitutional violation to be remedied by establishing two majority-minority districts."

Robinson O. Everett, a law professor at Duke University in Durham, initiated the lawsuit that challenged the constitutionality of the General Assembly's 1992 congressional redistricting plan, specifically the projected First and Twelfth Districts. Everett characterized the configuration of the two districts as a "racial gerrymander" and alleged that the process infringed the rights of every North Carolinian under the equal protection clause of the U.S. Constitution. Photograph courtesy *News and Observer* Publishing Company.

The facts of North Carolina's political history belied Everett's assertion. During Reconstruction, when Democrats regained control of the General Assembly, they packed African American voters into the Second Congressional District—the so-called "Black Second." Between 1872 and 1900, the Second District elected four black congressmen. The district contained a substantial black majority. According to Kousser's analysis, the total population of the Second District (black and white) was 10 to 18 percent more than the average population of other congressional districts in the state. Moreover, the Second District included almost twice as many blacks as an equal division of the African American population among the other congressional districts would have created. In a state that was approximately one-third black, apportionment confined black political power to one district out of eight or nine, depending on the state's total population in each decade. By packing the Second District, Reconstruction-era Democrats reduced black influence and Republican representation in other congressional districts. Republican governor Tod R. Caldwell described the Second District's shape as "extraordinary, inconvenient and most grotesque." After disfranchisement, with the passage of the 1900 suffrage amendment, Democrats reduced the Second District's size, population, and number of blacks to conform demographically more closely to other congressional districts.

North Carolina's recent political history indicated that racial discrimination remained deeply embedded both in terms of voter registration and the shape and composition of congressional districts. In 1948 only 15 percent of African Americans were registered to vote in North Carolina. As late as 1962 the figure had risen to only 36 percent. Because of the continued use of literacy tests, forty of North Carolina's one hundred counties came under the VRA in 1965. The first time later chief justice Henry Frye attempted to register to vote in 1956, he failed the literacy test because he was unable to name the signers of the Declaration of Independence. Such arbitrary denials soon ended. In 1966 black voter registration cracked the 50 percent mark for the first time since 1900.

The reapportionment of the Second Congressional District by the General Assembly in 1981 showed that black political power was on the ascent. L. H. Fountain, a conservative white Democrat, represented the Second District. In the Democratic primaries of 1968 and 1972, he received unsuccessful challenges respectively from Eva Clayton and Howard Lee, the black mayor of Chapel Hill. In 1981 reapportioning the state's congressional districts took six months. At issue was Durham County, with its long history of black economic and political power. If the General Assembly moved Durham County into Fountain's largely rural Second District, he likely would face a tough Democratic primary opponent. The black political establishment in Durham made it clear that that opponent probably would be black. Conservative white Democratic legislators feared that with a black congressional candidate in the Second District, the Republicans would win the seat. The *Raleigh Times* editorialized bluntly:

"Until now, districting plans' impact on minority political clout and vice versa has been a behind the scenes concern of the powerful people who draft the plans—but rarely an on-the-record one."

The 1981 plan devised by the General Assembly for the Second District resembled a fishhook. It looped around Durham County and ostensibly protected Fountain's reelection chances. But the district looked suspiciously like the original 1812 Massachusetts district of politico Elbridge Gerry, for whom the term *gerrymander* is named. Common Cause, a politically active interest group, reviewed redistricting efforts in thirty-two states and labeled North Carolina's Second District one of two "infamous gerrymanders" of the year.

The NAACP sued the state over the proposed Second District, but the U.S. Department of Justice rejected the district before the courts could rule on the case. The exclusion of Durham County, the federal lawyers maintained, had "the effect of minimizing minority voting strength and was motivated by racial considerations. . . ." The Justice Department noted that the African American population in the Second District had decreased from 43 percent in 1970 to 40.2 percent in the 1971 reapportionment, and to only 36.7 percent in the 1981 plan. The General Assembly drafted a new plan that added Durham County to the Second District and eliminated Alamance and Chatham counties. Thus ended the fishhook.

In 1982 Fountain retired, and Tim Valentine, a Nash County lawyer, won a runoff election with Mickey Michaux, an African American lawyer and former legislator from Durham, in the Democratic primary. The electorate divided deeply along racial lines. Michaux received 91.5 percent of the black vote, and Valentine received 87 percent of the white vote. In the November election Valentine defeated the Republican candidate by a margin of 54 to 46 percent. In the judgment of historian J. Morgan Kousser, by 1984 it was clear that African Americans could not elect a black candidate in a congressional district with a 40 percent black population. African Americans needed a greater population base, perhaps considerably greater.

Before reapportionment could occur in 1991, however, two U.S. Supreme Court decisions further complicated the work of state legislatures in drawing new congressional districts. Reapportionment after each decennial census has always been subject to demographic considerations based on race, partisan maneuvering, and pressures to protect incumbents. In 1983 the Court ruled in *Karcher v. Daggett* that state legislatures must make a "good-faith effort" to create congressional districts with complete population equality insofar as "practicable." As a result, it became more difficult to preserve county, city, and town boundaries. Geographical considerations and local attachments diminished in importance. Henceforth, legislative staffs with robust yet flexible computer programs exercised greater power in devising population balance in each congressional district. Legislators no longer could protect partisan strongholds easily. The decision sharpened partisan politics and empowered social and political groups that transcended traditional local politics and boundaries.

In a second decision—*Thornburg v. Gingles* (1986)—the Supreme Court ruled in effect that whether voting was racially polarized and whether minority candidates usually lost could be criteria to determine violations of the VRA. The case involved North Carolina's legislative districts. The Court scrutinized "at large" or multimember districts wherein minority candidates, even with "racial bloc voting," had difficulty getting elected. The Court found that the "totality of circumstances" could produce "vote dilution." It said that "racially polarized voting; the legacy of official discrimination in voting matters, education, housing, employment, and health services; and the persistence of campaign appeals to racial prejudice acted in concert with the multimember districting scheme to impair the ability of geographically insular and politically cohesive groups of black voters to participate equally in the political process and to elect candidates of their choice." In other words, the VRA applied to any law that had the effect of discrimination on people of color. The decision went far beyond the mere intent to discriminate.

The effect of the *Gingles* decision increased Republican and black representation in the General Assembly as single-member districts replaced at-large systems in several counties. As a result, the number of Republican legislators in the North Carolina General Assembly grew from 20 percent in 1981 to 31 percent in 1991. The rise in African American representation was even more dramatic. Whereas four African Americans served in the General Assembly in 1981, nineteen served a decade later, and Dan Blue was Speaker of the House of Representatives.

The General Assembly of 1991 faced a difficult task in devising new congressional districts. First, the U.S. Department of Justice pressured the state hard to create majority-minority districts. Second, the new plan had to meet the various tests for equality and fairness that the U.S. Supreme Court had determined during the 1980s. Third, partisan considerations were never far from the surface. With the Democrats in the majority in both houses of the General Assembly, Republicans feared that the new apportionment plan could reduce the four seats that they then held in Congress. The first plan drafted by the General Assembly created only one black-majority district out of twelve. The Justice Department rejected it. The second plan, adopted in January 1992, devised a second "urban black district." At the same time, the second plan strengthened incumbents' chances for reelection, both Republican and Democratic.

The stage thus was set for *Shaw v. Reno*. The state acknowledged that it drew the First and Twelfth Districts with race in mind. It was trying to comply with federal court decisions and with the demands of the Justice Department. Robinson Everett argued, however, that such a blatant "racial gerrymander" infringed the rights of every North Carolinian under the equal protection clause of the U.S. Constitution and the Fifteenth Amendment. Everett demanded a "color-blind" process.

In April 1992, by a vote of two to one, the United States District Court for the Eastern District of North Carolina dismissed the claims against both the federal and state defendants. Everett and the plaintiffs, the federal court declared, had failed to prove a discriminatory purpose or discriminatory effects in the reapportionment plan. Even if African Americans won two of the twelve seats, they would not have proportional statewide representation based on their population.

Everett appealed the decision to the U.S. Supreme Court, which handed down its ruling in June 1993. By a vote of five to four, the Court upheld Everett's complaint. Justice O'Connor stated that the two majority-minority districts "rationally cannot be understood as *anything other* than an effort to separate voters into different districts on the basis of race." In her opinion, the state had drawn lines amounting to "racial classification." She denounced the shape of the Twelfth District as "bizarre," "irregular," and "egregious." O'Connor contended that districts should exhibit "compactness, contiguity, and respect for political subdivisions."

Justice Byron White dissented. He denied that a district's shape made any constitutional difference. The justice argued that no injury to whites existed. According to Justice White, the question was not whether voters were classified by race during redistricting; that was a given. "Rather," he asserted, "the issue is whether the classification based on race discriminates against *anyone* by denying equal access to the political process."

Shaw v. Reno shocked advocates of civil rights for African Americans. The decision bewildered specialists in voting rights and many constitutional scholars as well, for it seemed to overturn past precedents. Among the leading critics of the decision was historian J. Morgan Kousser. First, he argued, in the past anyone who challenged a government policy had to prove that that policy had a discriminatory effect and was motivated by a discriminatory purpose. Yet whites in North Carolina and in other *Shaw*-related cases routinely elected equal or higher proportions of members to Congress than their percentage of the population. Second, courts traditionally do not hear cases on abstract questions of public policy. Third, North Carolina was acting at the behest of the Justice Department. If the state were complying with the VRA, why were majority-minority districts now considered unconstitutional? Finally, other states had equally irregular district configurations with white majorities that were deemed constitutional. Clearly, there was an inherent conflict between the VRA and the *Shaw* decision about requiring race-conscious districts.

The *Shaw* decision set in motion a train of complicated and confusing legal maneuvers and decisions that threw North Carolina's electoral process into chaos for the rest of the 1990s. Robinson Everett continued to fight in the courts for the General Assembly to draw what he considered fairer and more constitutionally valid boundaries for congressional districts. The General Assembly struggled to comply with court decisions and demands from the Justice Department while it tried to balance competing partisan interests.

In *Shaw v. Reno* the Supreme Court returned Everett's lawsuit to the U.S. District Court for the Eastern District of North Carolina—the three-judge federal panel that had dismissed it in 1992. In August 1994 that federal court ruled that, although the congressional redistricting plan was based on the racial composition of the population, the General Assembly had carefully drawn the boundaries to meet the needs of the VRA and to remedy decades of discrimination. The federal court stated that the 1994 elections could proceed without redrawing the districts. Political and legal observers expected that decision to be appealed to the Supreme Court once again.

As predicted, in June 1995 the Supreme Court agreed to hear arguments on the Twelfth District. North Carolina attorney general Michael F. Easley urged the Court to offer "guidelines" for all the states that had reapportionment cases pending. "The net effect of these cases," said the attorney general, "is that the court, not the people's elected representatives, ends up drawing congressional districts. This is troublesome. The court's role should be to set guidelines for the states, and it has failed to do so in its three opportunities so far."

Despite the attorney general's pleas, *Shaw v. Hunt* (1996) indicated that the Supreme Court would not accept North Carolina's 1992 reapportionment plan under any circumstances. Chief Justice William Rehnquist, in another five-to-four decision, wrote the majority opinion that declared the plan unconstitutional. As Justice O'Connor before him, Chief Justice Rehnquist criticized the shape of the Twelfth District as too long and narrow. In the view of the majority of the justices, the district was not compact enough. The chief justice chided the state for using race as a "predominant consideration." The state did not deny the criticism. It created two majority-minority districts to comply with the VRA and the demands of the Justice Department. But the chief justice also repudiated the argument that the intent of the districts was to alleviate past oppression. Rehnquist objected to the purported premise of North Carolina's reapportionment plan, namely, that the General Assembly could draw a district anywhere in the state to overcome violations of the VRA. "We find this position singularly unpersuasive," he concluded.

The Supreme Court's decision temporarily placed on hold the 1996 elections in North Carolina. In July the U.S. District Court for the Eastern District of North Carolina ruled by a vote of two to one that the 1996 elections could proceed. However, the federal judges ordered the General Assembly to draw a new congressional map by April 1, 1997. Democratic judges J. Dickson Phillips Jr. and W. Earl Britt prevailed over Republican judge Richard Voorhees in the decision. Many political observers believed that electoral chaos and disorder had been averted for at least another year.

The new redistricting plan that the General Assembly unveiled in the spring of 1997 remained as controversial as the 1992 plan. The number of African Americans in the Twelfth District was reduced from 57 percent to 47 percent. Perhaps more significantly, the 1997 plan reduced the number of African American registered voters from 54 percent to 46 percent. While the district continued to follow a narrow corridor along Interstate 85, it now extended only from Greensboro to Charlotte. The 1997 plan also maintained a partisan balance of six Democrats and six Republicans in Congress. Mickey Michaux, an African American legislator from Durham, was not impressed. "All you have done with the 12th District," he complained, "is knock 60 miles off it." He offered three amendments to increase minority voting strength in the Fifth, Seventh, and Twelfth Districts. All were defeated.

The 1997 plan also reshaped the First District. African Americans now constituted a bare majority (50.2 percent) in the district, but only 45

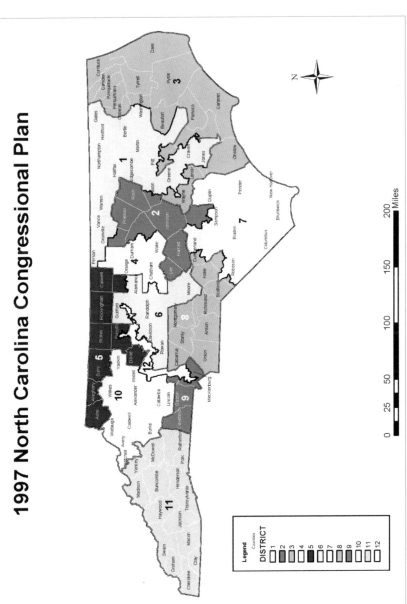

1997 North Carolina Congressional Plan

The 1996 case of *Shaw v. Hunt* indicated that the U.S. Supreme Court would not accept North Carolina's 1992 reapportionment plan under any circumstances and threatened to interrupt the state's 1996 elections. A federal court eventually ruled that the election could proceed but ordered the General Assembly to draw a new congressional map by April 1, 1997. The map shown above reveals the results of the legislature's efforts. Before the proposed plan could be implemented, however, a U.S. district court rejected it and ordered the General Assembly to redraw it. The Supreme Court agreed and upheld the decision.

percent of the registered voters were black. Alma Adams, an African American legislator from Greensboro, declared: "That's a flaw in this [reapportionment]. . . . I don't think it is a good plan for African Americans."

Before the plan could be implemented in the 1998 elections, however, the courts intervened once again. In April 1998 the U.S. District Court for the Eastern District of North Carolina threw out the 1997 plan, ruling that the Twelfth District remained a racial gerrymander. It ordered the General Assembly to redraw the districts again and postponed congressional primaries to September 15. If the legislature failed to devise a new plan, the federal court threatened to draft its own. The Supreme Court agreed and upheld the lower court's decision. Robinson Everett had prevailed for the third time in the Supreme Court.

North Carolina officials scrambled to comply with the court's decision. State senator Roy Cooper of Rocky Mount, chair of the Senate Redistricting Committee, lamented: "The summer just got longer and hotter. I think we are all losers. I can't make a case that this will benefit anybody." Attorney General Easley noted that the federal court had not released an opinion, so the legislators did not know whether to prune the district or start from scratch. "It is difficult to know how long it will take to fix the problem since we have not been told by the court what the problem is," said the attorney general. Everett recommended the appointment of a redistricting commission made up of "a panel of experts with no political interest." When Everett testified before the redistricting committee in May 1998, he declared: "Don't just tweak the 12th District. Don't just tweak the 1st District. Get it right this time." But Mel Watt offered the most stinging rebuke: "I don't think it is fair to the public to allow a court to make that decision. Ultimately, the last chapter has to be written by the voters."

The General Assembly met the federal court's deadline in May. For the second time in two years it approved a plan redrawing districts. Under the 1998 plan the Twelfth District became wider and shorter, running from Winston-Salem to Charlotte. The district now encompassed five instead of six counties and reduced black registered voters still further to 33 percent. Attorney General Easley expressed confidence that the new plan would satisfy the federal court. Everett countered: "We'll be asking the court to reject the plan and draw one of their own."

The 1998 plan deeply divided the black caucus in the General Assembly. Senator Frank Ballance of Warren County supported the plan but without enthusiasm. "The three-judge court gave us an option of presenting the plan or the court would draw a plan," he explained. "With that option, I don't think there was any choice." Senator Bill Martin of Guilford County, from which the 1998 plan eliminated the greatest number of black voters in the Twelfth District, opposed it. "I cannot cast my vote in support," he said, "because I see this plan as further erosion of that which many Americans have fought for and championed since the creation of this nation—particularly Americans . . . who have been disenfranchised, discriminated against, ostracized, ignored, abused and marginalized because of race, nationality or place of origin." Former House speaker Dan Blue likewise opposed the plan. Drawing a historical analogy, Senator Howard Hunter of Northampton County asserted: "I voted against it simply because by voting for it, I send a message to the black community that it's o.k. for African-Americans not to [be] represented at the table. I maintain that we are in our second Reconstruction in this state and gains that African-Americans . . . have made, if they don't open their eyes, will be lost."

In June the U.S. District Court for the Eastern District of North Carolina approved the new districts, opening the way for the September 15 primaries and a general election on November 3. The federal judges warned, however, that their decision affected only the 1998 elections: "the court reserves jurisdiction with regard to the constitutionality of District 1 under this plan and as to District 12 should new evidence emerge." Meanwhile, the state continued to press its appeal of the 1997 plan to the Supreme Court.

In September 1998 the Supreme Court agreed to hear the state's arguments that the 1997 redistricting plan, struck down by the U.S. district court in April, should be considered as a constitutionally acceptable reapportionment. The Court's willingness to hear the state's appeal did not affect the 1998 elections, which proceeded under the 1998 plan. Attorney General Easley observed: "This is an opportunity for the U.S. Supreme Court to get things straightened out once and for all. The justices can finally provide clear guidance to North Carolina and other states as we prepare for another round of redistricting following the 2000 Census." State senator Roy Cooper remarked: "When the General Assembly agreed on the 1997 plan we said it was based on a number of factors, including geography, partisan balance and regional groupings. Race was not the primary factor, and the Supreme Court's decision to hear the case gives weight to our argument."

In May 1999 the Supreme Court determined that the U.S. district court had erred in throwing out the 1997 plan without a trial. It ordered the three-judge panel to conduct a trial. Accordingly, the U.S. District Court for the Eastern District of North Carolina held a trial in Raleigh in November and December 1999 to consider the constitutionality of the First and Twelfth Districts under the 1997 plan. In March 2000, by a vote of two to one, the federal court ruled that the Twelfth District was unconstitutional because race played too large a role in its design. However, the federal court upheld the First District. Though race was a predominant factor in reapportioning the First District, the federal court determined that the boundaries were more narrowly tailored than the Twelfth's to ensure that African Americans achieved equal access to the political process.

The three-judge federal panel now consisted of two Republicans—Richard Voorhees and Terence Boyle—and one Democrat, Lacy Thornburg, who dissented. Judge Boyle stated: "the primary characteristic of the Twelfth District is its 'racial archipelago' stretching, bending and weaving to pick up predominantly African-American regions while avoiding many closer and more obvious regions of high Democratic registration but low African-American population." Judge Thornburg, former attorney general of North Carolina, disagreed. He said that the court was making an "unwarranted intrusion into North Carolina's legislative process." Mike Easley was indignant: "It is frustrating to me as attorney general and as a voter that a three-judge court has again thrown North Carolina's elections process into turmoil." He condemned the court's "inconsistent ruling" for ten years. The state promised to appeal the decision.

In June 2000 the Supreme Court agreed for the fourth time to review the Twelfth District. Attorney General Easley hailed the decision. "This is good news for the voters," he said. He hoped that the Court would provide much-needed guidance for the next legislature as it prepared a new plan for reapportionment. Neil Bradley, associate director of the southern regional office of the American Civil Liberties Union in Atlanta, commented: "There is no need to take a case involving redistricting in the year 2000 unless you are trying to do something you haven't done before." Robinson Everett found the Supreme Court's decision puzzling. "We obviously were disappointed because we didn't think there was any legal issue to hear," he said.

While the case remained on appeal, the Supreme Court's decision had one other ironic effect. When the Supreme Court overturned the lower court's ruling on the 1997 map and ordered a trial, it reinstated the 1997 plan for the 2000 elections. Hence the 2000 elections proceeded under the 1997 plan for the first time.

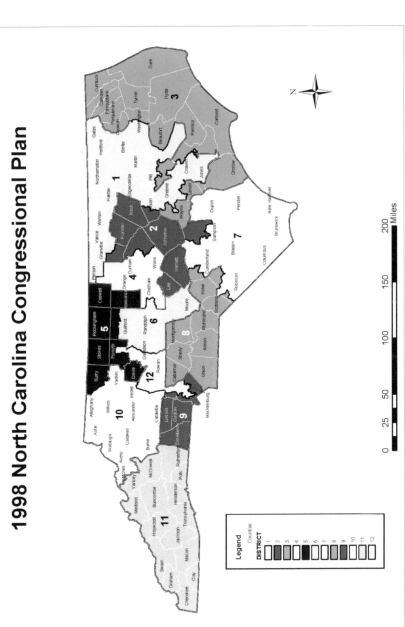

1998 North Carolina Congressional Plan

In May 1998 the General Assembly responded to the district court's rejection of its 1997 redistricting plan by proposing the plan shown above. The district court approved the new plan in order that the 1998 elections could proceed, but in May 1999 the Supreme Court determined that the district court had erred in throwing out the 1997 plan without a trial and ordered a three-judge panel to conduct a trial. The panel subsequently upheld the First District but ruled the Twelfth District unconstitutional because race played too large a role in its design. In June 2000 the Supreme Court agreed for the fourth time to review the Twelfth District, and in April 2001 the Court, by a vote

In November 2000 the Supreme Court heard arguments for the fourth time on North Carolina's congressional districts. Mel Watt, who attended the hearings, commented: "This is not about electing black representatives. It's about minority communities having some opportunity to send representatives of their choice to Washington and have them represent them." Walter Dellinger, a Duke law professor and acting solicitor general for the Clinton administration, argued for the state. He pointed out that the North Carolina General Assembly wanted to maintain a partisan balance of six Democrats and six Republicans in Congress. Under the 1997 plan blacks no longer held a majority in the Twelfth District. Indeed, only 46 percent of the registered voters were black.

The most telling exchange in the hearings occurred between Robinson Everett, attorney for the plaintiffs, and Justice Sandra Day O'Connor. "To say that something is political, or incumbent protection, is very convenient," Everett opined. "It's a nice dodge." Justice O'Connor interjected: "Well, it's not always a dodge." As former majority leader of the Arizona State Senate, O'Connor was the only member of the Court who had firsthand political experience in drawing district lines.

In April 2001, by a vote of five to four, the Supreme Court upheld North Carolina's 1997 redistricting plan. The Court ruled that race was only one factor, not the main factor, in designing the Twelfth District, thereby reversing the lower court ruling. Justice Stephen G. Breyer wrote the majority opinion, and once again Justice O'Connor was the swing vote. Justice Clarence Thomas wrote the dissenting opinion. *Easley v. Cromartie* (2001)—formerly titled *Hunt v. Cromartie*—made little new law, however. Breyer's opinion was based on earlier redistricting cases to attract the support of O'Connor, while Thomas's dissent was mild. Breyer explained his reasoning thusly:

In a case such as this one where majority-minority districts (or the approximate equivalent) are at issue and where racial identification correlates highly with political affiliation, the party attacking the legislatively drawn boundaries must show at the least that the Legislature could have achieved its legitimate political objectives in alternative ways that are comparably consistent with traditional districting principles. That party must also show that those districting alternatives would have brought about significantly greater racial balance.

Roy Cooper, the newly elected state attorney general who had chaired the Senate Redistricting Committee in the General Assembly, praised the decision: "I believe this decision and the plan itself gives the nation a blueprint for how to balance the Voting Rights Act, which requires racial fairness, and the court's directive that race not be the predominant factor in the process."

The decision came just as legislatures throughout the nation began to draft new district boundaries in response to the results of the 2000 census. Ostensibly, both Republicans and Democrats seemed comfortable with the Supreme Court's ruling. Evidently, both parties saw advantages in creating majority-minority districts that helped the Democrats on the one hand and concentrated more whites in Republican districts on the other. As North Carolina's population surpassed eight million in 2000, it picked up a thirteenth congressional district. How would an extra congressional district affect majority-minority districts, and would the new boundaries generate a new round of legal challenges?

At almost the same time that the redistricting cases reached a resolution in the U.S. Supreme Court, a separate lawsuit challenging busing in the federal courts of North Carolina and Virginia portended a coda for the civil rights movement of the 1950s and 1960s.

The Challenge to Busing

In the landmark *Swann v. Charlotte-Mecklenburg Board of Education* (1971), the U.S. Supreme Court ordered mandatory busing to end segregation in the public school system. The Court determined that the city and county were operating two school systems—one for blacks and one for whites. The Court ruled that Charlotte-Mecklenburg must create a single desegregated system and use busing to achieve equality of opportunity in education.

Over the next three decades busing became a significant part of various plans nationwide to assure desegregated schools. In North Carolina both Wake and Mecklenburg counties, among others, established "magnet" schools in downtown areas to draw children from primarily white suburbs. In 1992 Durham became the last predominantly black city school district to merge with the predominantly white county school district. When President Reagan visited Charlotte in the 1980s and made critical remarks about busing, his comments received a chilly response. The Queen City took great pride in the peaceful way that it had accomplished desegregation.

But a backlash among both white and African American parents was not long in coming. In a development known as "white flight," urban whites began moving to the suburbs to escape busing and the integration of schools. Paradoxically, after a promising start, schools became more segregated. Meanwhile, the burden of desegregation fell more heavily on African American families and children. More often it was black children who were bused out of inner cities to suburban schools. The elimination of segregated schools also meant the loss of jobs for African American teachers, principals, and administrators. In Hyde County, North Carolina, in 1968–1969, African American parents and students conducted a yearlong boycott of public schools to protest the closing of two black schools and the integration of black students into a white school. The protest succeeded. A new desegregation plan, approved by the voters of Hyde County in 1969, preserved the two black schools as desegregated elementary schools. The white facility became the county's consolidated high school.

Meanwhile, U.S. Supreme Court decisions began to erode the mandate for busing. In 1991 the Court ruled in *Board of Education of Oklahoma City v. Dowell* that a school district could free itself of court supervision if it could show that it "had complied in good faith with the desegregation decree" and that "the vestiges of past *de jure* segregation had been eliminated to the extent practicable." A year later, in *Freeman v. Pitts* (1992), a case involving the DeKalb County, Georgia, school district, the Court ruled that if schools could demonstrate a "good-faith commitment" to desegregation, they could be released from court orders "before full compliance has been achieved in every area of school operations." The Court determined: "Racial balance is not to be achieved for its own sake, but is to be pursued only when there is a causal link between an imbalance and the constitutional violation. Once racial imbalance traceable to the constitutional violation has been remedied, a school district is under no duty to remedy an imbalance that is caused by demographic factors." Lower courts began to issue rulings that distinguished between segregation caused by government action (illegal) and that caused by circumstances such as housing patterns (legal).

By the late 1990s the legal foundations of and public support for busing came under attack on all fronts. In 1997 the NAACP—faced with white resistance to busing, a conservative judiciary, and criticism inside and outside its ranks—began to rethink its advocacy of integrated public schools. For example, efforts to reduce busing in Guilford County, North Carolina, won black support. The county board of education redrew district lines so as to minimize large-scale busing and preserve neighborhood schools. A group of black ministers known as the Pulpit Forum supported the plan. Amos Quick, a black member of the sixty-member citizens committee that drew the new lines, stated: "Our biggest concern now is whether our schools will be equal. Separate but truly equal would not be so bad."

Julian Bond, a prominent member of the NAACP board, empathized with such frustration over busing but characterized it as "a wrong attitude." In fact, the NAACP board ousted local branch presidents in Bergen County, New Jersey, and Yonkers, New York, for saying that quality schools in black neighborhoods were more important than integrated schools. Just as striking, a 1997 report issued jointly by Harvard and Indiana Universities found that racial segregation in public schools had increased since 1980.

Ironically, the Charlotte-Mecklenburg school district that had initiated busing in 1971 became the test case for the judicial demise of busing. In 1998 a Charlotte parent sued the school district, claiming that his white daughter was denied access to a magnet program because of her race. The case came before the U.S. District Court for the Western District of North Carolina. In September 1999 Judge Robert D. Potter ruled that busing in Charlotte was no longer necessary because all "vestiges of past discrimination" had disappeared. The decision ended almost thirty years of busing. Arthur Griffin, the African American chair of the Charlotte-Mecklenburg Board of Education, greeted the decision with disappointment. He acknowledged, however, that 14 percent of the children in the county now attended private schools and that whites constituted fewer than 50 percent of the pupils. Michael E. Ward, superintendent of public instruction in North Carolina, took a dubious view of the assault on busing. "I am really skeptical of this re-emerging belief that separate can be equal," he declared. "It never has been and I am not convinced it [ever] will be." A half century after the *Brown* decision, the march toward integrated schools that would assure an equal education seemed to be in retreat.

Perhaps the bitterest indictment of busing—its promises and its failures—came from the African American community. The *Carolinian*, an African American newspaper serving Raleigh, expressed little remorse about the decision to end busing. In a caustic editorial, it proclaimed:

An abysmal failure to many years of forced integration [busing] proved to be quite a disappointment for black kids and parents. The schools were integrated by closing black schools and busing the kids to white neighborhoods, sometimes in trips that took up hours each day. They were viewed as outsiders by white kids, and frequently, by white teachers as well. Racial hostility, far from abating, actually seemed to grow. Black kids found themselves resegregated within the schools themselves—"tracked" into programs

In 1998 a Charlotte parent sued the Charlotte-Mecklenburg School District, claiming that his white daughter was denied access to a magnet school because of her race. The case came before the U.S. District Court for the Western District of North Carolina. In September 1999 Judge Robert D. Potter, pictured here, ruled that busing in Charlotte was no longer necessary because all "vestiges of past discrimination" had disappeared. The decision ended nearly thirty years of busing. In November 2000 a three-judge U.S. Circuit Court of Appeals for the Fourth Circuit reversed Judge Potter's decision, but in September 2001, by a vote of seven to four, the full Court of Appeals for the Fourth Circuit overruled the three-judge panel by holding that Charlotte public schools could no longer use race when making student assignments. Photo by Todd Sumlin, *Charlotte Observer*, December 27, 2000.

for "slow learners" that were occupied almost exclusively by other black students. The number of black teachers declined, giving them few role models. All too frequently, white teachers simply didn't know how to relate to or teach black kids, especially black males. They tended to spend a disproportionate amount of time in the principal's office, on suspension or expelled. Black kids began to look at academic excellence as a "white thing." Achievement actually declined. It started as a murmur at first, but before long black parents were saying out loud that integration had been an abysmal failure for black students. That's why the NAACP may have a tough sell, in raising the warning that school integration may soon be gone forever. Many black parents and others in the African-American community are responding, "Good riddance!"

The *Carolinian* no doubt overstated black parents' disillusionment with busing. The great majority did not view the demise of busing as a victory. Rather, the *Carolinian*'s denunciation of busing went to the heart of how complex and disappointing the issue had become. Well-intentioned plans had gone awry with the bad effects decried by the newspaper. Had busing failed society, or had society failed busing?

In the spring of 2000 the Charlotte-Mecklenburg school board appealed Judge Potter's decision to end busing to the U.S. Circuit Court of Appeals for the Fourth Circuit. The U.S. Department of Justice filed a brief that did not take a position but questioned whether the federal district court had assessed fully Charlotte-Mecklenburg's compliance with the Supreme Court's desegregation orders. The Justice Department especially inquired whether the local board of education had placed schools in areas that could "readily serve both races" and whether it provided facilities in mostly black areas equivalent to those provided in white areas.

On November 30, 2000, the U.S. Circuit Court of Appeals for the Fourth Circuit in Richmond, Virginia, voted two to one to reverse the September 1999 ruling by U.S. District Judge Robert Potter in Charlotte. The reversal marked a significant departure from recent federal court rulings involving school integration. The federal appeals court stated: "Today with the Board having had less than 26 years to implement appropriate remedies, we must decide whether the task of desegregating the Charlotte-Mecklenburg schools has reached its end. We hold that it has not."

Judges Diana Motz and Robert King (with William B. Traxler Jr. in dissent) determined that the Charlotte-Mecklenburg schools had not achieved "unitary status." They noted "the return of predominantly one-race schools as a vestige of segregation. . . ." The Charlotte-Mecklenburg schools, they held, had failed to comply with "court orders regarding selection of sites for the construction of new schools. The role of school siting in achieving sustainable desegregation should not be under-estimated." For example, twenty-five of twenty-seven schools built since 1971 had been placed in predominantly white suburbs. The judges continued: "imbalanced-black schools in [Charlotte-Mecklenburg] are in worse shape than those attended by larger proportions of white students. Once we accept that premise, the lone remaining question of any signi-ficance is 'Why?'" The judges acknowledged that Charlotte-Mecklenburg schools had integrated staff and faculty, extracurricular activities, and student discipline practices. However, equity had not been reached in student assignments, transportation, and classroom achievement.

Gloria Browne, attorney for the NAACP Legal Defense and Education funds, praised the decision: "This opinion is great for black children and great for black parents because there are many obstacles for them receiving educational opportunities across the country." Jack Boger, a law professor at the University of North Carolina at Chapel Hill, warned that earlier federal court cases that backed away from using race as a standard for school assignments still could not be ignored. But the opinion on Charlotte-Mecklenburg indicated a different set of criteria. "There have been a number of cases in other circuits that have acted as if the game is over," he commented. "This is a very different signal."

Following Judge Potter's decision in September 1999, the Charlotte-Mecklenburg school board voted narrowly to approve a "race neutral" plan to give parents more choice in selecting a school. The federal appeals court, however, had upheld a "race-conscious lottery" to determine student enrollment in a magnet school program. The day after the federal appeals court's ruling, the Charlotte-Mecklenburg board voted five to four to scrap the parental choice plan. The board reinstated the system for student enrollment based on race. Magnet programs remained at their current schools, and race continued as a factor in lotteries. White parents announced plans to appeal the decision to the U.S. Supreme Court.

Before that appeal could be filed, however, the U.S. Circuit Court of Appeals for the Fourth Circuit announced in January 2001 that the entire court would review the Charlotte-Mecklenburg decision. In September the federal appeals court rendered its decision. By a vote of seven to four, the court ruled that Charlotte public schools could no longer use race when making student assignments. Thirty years of busing came to an end. J. Harvie Wilkinson III, chief judge of the Fourth Circuit, wrote: "If it was important that courts nurture the task of desegregation in its infancy, it is equally essential that a school district one day depart the comforting judicial homestead and strike out on its own." Judge William B. Traxler Jr., who had dissented in the earlier two-to-one decision upholding busing, asserted that "students today are educated in an integrated environment by an integrated faculty. In sum, the 'end purpose' of federal intervention to remedy segregation has been served."

Judges Diana G. Motz and Robert B. King, who constituted the majority in the earlier two-to-one decision, dissented. They argued that the Fourth Circuit had succeeded only "in dashing the hopes of the citizens of Mecklenburg County, particularly those of African-American descent, who have long fought for the fair and equitable implementation of the desegregation plan." The dissenting judges said that the decision failed to recognize the degree to which schools had become resegregated. One-third of the district's 135 schools no longer met the original court standards for an integrated school. Eleven schools were more than 80 percent white, and twenty-seven schools were more than 80 percent minority.

In a unanimous vote, the Charlotte-Mecklenburg school board, which had fought to keep the 1971 busing order in place, announced that it would not appeal the ruling to the Supreme Court. "We want to move to the next stage," Arthur Griffin, chairman of the board, stated.

The Fourth Circuit also ordered Charlotte-Mecklenburg schools to implement a race-neutral student assignment plan by the 2002–2003 school year. The plan adopted after Judge Potter's decision in 1999 cut the district into separate zones and allowed parents to choose any school within the area in which they lived. Superintendent Eric Smith said repeatedly that the new plan would increase segregation among the district's 105,000 students. The emphasis now, he pledged, would turn toward providing the best possible education for all children regardless of where they attended school. Board members pointed to a $275.5 million bond approval in 2000 to repair several older center-city schools as evidence that the community was committed to equality. After thirty years of busing, perhaps Judge Traxler had the final word on the issue of desegregation: "we are confident that de jure segregation is history."

Eventually, Wake County's busing plan came under pressure to return to "neighborhood schools." The school system was the largest in the state. In the 1990s the Wake County school board had abolished race as a criterion for busing and instead had adopted an economic measure to balance the student population at each school. With only a few exceptions, students who qualified for free or low-cost lunches were not to exceed 40 percent of a school's population. Because race and income remained closely related, some parents in more affluent neighborhoods resented having their children bused to schools farther away. Low-income students, on the other hand, were bused to affluent neighborhoods to provide economic and racial balance. In practice few students from affluent areas were bused for diversity. In fact, only 1–2 percent of students (about 2,000) overall were bused to improve socio-economic diversity. Rather, students either attended magnet schools by choice or could not attend the closest school because of overcrowding or a different calendar. Even so, 86 percent of Wake County students attended schools within five miles of their home. In October 2009 forces opposed to busing captured a 5-to-4 majority on the

Wake County school board. The new majority immediately promised to reduce busing, to end mandatory year-round schools, and to assign students to schools closer to home.

Despite the election results there was surprising opposition to the end of Wake County's busing plan from white as well as black parents. Wake's school system had received national attention for making busing work with a system of magnet schools, enrichment programs, and year-round schools. Between 1997 and 2007 the percentage of black students' performing at or above grade level doubled from 40 percent to 82.5 percent. With moral fervor, proponents of the busing plan resisted a return to what they deemed the Jim Crow policies of the past. They preferred to provide opportunities to all students, not just those who could afford to live in affluent neighbor-hoods. When the new school board polled parents about their children's schools, more than 90 percent of the 42,000 parents who responded said that they were satisfied.

The data supporting busing, however, could be interpreted in different ways. Opponents of busing pointed out that a comparison of test scores in the Charlotte-Mecklenburg schools with those in the Wake County schools showed that black and low-income Wake students scored lower than their counterparts in the Charlotte-Mecklenburg schools. The Charlotte-Mecklenburg schools also provided more money per pupil than the Wake County schools did. A closer look at those statistics, however, revealed that the passing rates for black and low-income students were significantly lower in Charlotte-Mecklenburg's high-poverty schools than in the same system's diverse schools.

Educators had known for decades that low-income students performed better in diverse schools than in schools with high poverty rates. Re-segregation by race and income produced pernicious academic conse-quences. The North Carolina chapter of the NAACP, led by the Reverend William Barber, threatened to sue the Wake County schools if busing ended. In December 2009 Barber and the NAACP filed a civil rights complaint with the U.S. Justice and Education departments against another school system, that of Wayne County. The Goldsboro Central Attendance district had a student population almost 100 percent black, whereas another district in Goldsboro was nearly 90 percent white. The predominantly black district received more free or reduced school lunches. Additionally, the black district experienced lower graduation rates, higher suspension rates, and more and stiffer discipline for students. Six decades after *Brown v.*

Board of Education of Topeka the dream of equality in education seemed as elusive as ever.

Righting Old Wrongs

The North Carolina Legislative Black Caucus organized in 1984 to promote the passage of a bill making Martin Luther King Jr.'s birthday a state holiday. By 2009 the caucus included nine senators and twenty-one representatives. The caucus took as its mission the exercise of political power "in a unified manner" to carry out the views and concerns of African Americans. It also pledged to develop the "political consciousness" of African Americans.

That mission led the caucus to reflect on the state's history and seek to restore justice where injustice once prevailed. In 2000, under the sponsorship of two members of the Black Caucus, the North Carolina General Assembly established the Wilmington Race Riot Commission. The purpose of the commission was "to develop a historical record of the 1898 Wilmington Race Riot." With administrative and research support from the North Carolina Department of Cultural Resources, the commission issued a report in 2006, with recommendations for empowerment of the African American community in Wilmington by, among other things, extending the Voting Rights Act of 1965 to New Hanover County; economic redevelopment; education, including a curriculum requirement to teach students about the riot in the public schools; and erection of a monument near the sites of the 1898 events. The report received national attention from such media as National Public Radio and the *New York Times*.

Members of the Black Caucus joined with other legislators, both white and American Indian, to bring attention to the harrowing history of the North Carolina Eugenics Commission. The eugenics movement had originated in Great Britain with Sir Francis Galton in 1883. It spread quickly to the rest of Europe and eventually the United States. To improve the "inborn qualities" of the human race, Galton favored supplementing Charles Darwin's theory of natural selection with the sterilization of people with mental disabilities. In 1907 Indiana became the first of thirty-two states to pass eugenics sterilization laws. In the landmark U.S. Supreme Court case of *Buck v. Bell* (1927) the Court upheld Virginia's eugenics law by a vote of 8 to 1. Justice Oliver Wendell Holmes concluded harshly: "Three generations of imbeciles are enough."

In 1929 the North Carolina General Assembly authorized sterilization of patients or inmates in public institutions. That same year the county boards of commissioners received authorization to order sterilization at public expense of "any mentally defective or feebleminded resident" with the consent of the person's next of kin or legal guardian. In 1933 the General Assembly created the Eugenics Board to review sterilization requests for all individuals.

The board spent more than four decades reviewing cases from both public institutions and counties. Renamed the Eugenics Commission in 1972, the board approved more than 90 percent of the cases that came before it. In all more than 7,600 North Carolinians were sterilized between 1929 and 1974, when the Eugenics Commission ended. Many states disbanded their eugenics programs after World War II, at least in part as a response to Nazi atrocities in Europe. North Carolina, however, performed more sterilizations after the war (79 percent of the total number) than before. Although the majority of victims were white, increasingly after the war counties, not public institutions, ordered the procedures, often on young black women. Over the life of the eugenics program, blacks constituted approximately 38 percent of the victims. Women (84 percent) overwhelmingly made up the majority of the cases. Between 1929 and 1968 the reasons cited for sterilization included feeble-mindedness (71.4 percent), mental disease (23.6 percent), and epilepsy (5 percent).

In 2002 Governor Easley established a committee to investigate the eugenics program. The committee heard testimony from victims and recommended compensation with educational and health care benefits. The state also sponsored a traveling exhibit on the eugenics program and erected a highway historical marker to remember that unfortunate part of the state's history. Easley ultimately apologized for the state's role in such questionable science.

Rep. Larry Womble of Forsyth County took the lead in addressing the legacy of eugenics by seeking compensation for those who had received sterilization. He proposed $20,000 in compensation for each surviving person. In 2009 the General Assembly considered legislation to provide counseling to eugenics survivors, to establish a database to verify the status of persons who claimed to be victims, to include information on the eugenics program in the public schools' history curriculum, and to offer ethics training for state, county, and local government employees. In a difficult budget year, the bill failed to pass.

In 2008 the North Carolina General Assembly established the African American Heritage Commission. North Carolina became the tenth state in the region to establish such a program. The General Assembly directed the commission to "assist the Secretary of Cultural Resources in the preservation, interpretation, and promotion of African-American history, arts, and culture." The commission adopted an ambitious plan to fulfill its mission and hosted "listening" sessions across the state. Initial programming included participation in commemoration of the 150th anniversary of the Civil War; sponsorship of teachers' workshops on African American history; development of an African American music trail; and creation of a Roanoke River Maritime Underground Railroad Trail.

The Election of Barack Obama

Since the election of Lyndon Baines Johnson in 1964, only one other Democratic presidential candidate had carried North Carolina before the twenty-first century: Jimmy Carter in 1976. That changed on November 4, 2008.

The election of Barack Obama, the junior U.S. senator from Illinois, as the nation's first African American president produced historic repercussions in the South as elsewhere. Overall Obama received 365 electoral votes, including North Carolina's 15, whereas Arizona Republican and U.S. senator John McCain received 173 electoral votes. Besides North Carolina, Virginia and Florida also cast their electoral ballots for Obama. With the exception of Carter's victory in 1976, the South had voted solidly Republican in presidential elections since the civil rights era of the 1960s. To be sure, Obama's margin of victory in North Carolina was razor thin. Obama won 2,142,651 votes (49.2 percent) to McCain's 2,128,474 votes (48.9 percent). Only in Missouri, which McCain won, was the election closer.

Both the Democratic and Republican campaigns had targeted North Carolina as a battleground state. Obama campaigned in North Carolina into the final week of the election. He spoke in Raleigh on October 29 and in Charlotte on November 3. In all he or his wife Michelle visited the state a total of twelve times. Obama also raised more money than McCain in North Carolina, $8,569,866 to $2,888,920, and outspent the Republican senator there $15,178,674 to $7,137,289.

Obama's margin of victory came in the cities, especially along the I-85 corridor. Whereas Obama carried only 35 of North Carolina's 100 counties

Democratic presidential candidate Barack Obama addresses North Carolinians on the Halifax Mall in Raleigh on October 29, 2008, before the historic election as the first African American to be elected president of the United States. Photograph by Allison Cummings.

and only 35 percent of the white vote, those counties accounted for more than one-half of the state's population. He won the state's five largest counties—Durham, Forsyth, Guilford, Mecklenburg, and Wake—by 11 percentage points or more.

Obama fashioned a new coalition of urban and suburban voters to win North Carolina. African Americans and college students overwhelmingly supported him. He also received significant support from highly affluent and well-educated voters, many of whom had migrated to the Tar Heel State from other parts of the country. As the registration of African American voters increased in 2008 by more than 300,000 to 1,258,564, exit polls revealed that more than 95 percent of African Americans cast ballots for Obama. Even more striking, an estimated 95 percent of the state's registered African American voters turned out. Obama carried an unprecedented 100 percent of African American females and African Americans aged eighteen to twenty-nine; 93 percent of African American males voted for him. Overall turnout in the state reached 69.9 percent of the eligible electorate. In endorsing Obama for president on October 19, 2008, the *News and Observer* of Raleigh stated simply: "His time has come. And these times have come to him."

In 1903 W. E. B. Du Bois, the preeminent black intellectual of his time, declared famously: "THE PROBLEM of the twentieth century is the problem of the color-line. . . ." Barack Obama's election certainly did not signal the end of that problem, nor did it resolve all issues of race, racial prejudice, or racial equality. Much remains unfinished on the nation's racial agenda. Obama's election did represent, however, a great step forward for minorities in North Carolina and beyond. More than one hundred years after the Wilmington Race Riot and more than fifty years after the *Brown* decision, perhaps North Carolina finally had earned its reputation as the South's most progressive state.

Appendix 1

African American Legislators in the
North Carolina General Assembly, 1868–1900

Name	County	Office	Term(s)
Abbott, Israel B.	Craven	Representative	1872
Alston, Isaac	Warren (19th)	Senator	1870, 1891
Baker, Wiley	Northampton	Representative	1883
Battle, Clinton Wesley	Edgecombe	Representative	1879, 1881
Brewington, Henry	New Hanover	Representative	1874
Bridgers, Aaron R.	Edgecombe	Representative	1883
Bridgers, Edward	Edgecombe	Representative	1889
Bryant, John R.	Halifax	Representative	1870, 1872
	Halifax (4th)	Senator	1874, 1876
Bunn, Willis	Edgecombe	Representative	1870, 1872, 1874, 1876
Cale, Hugh	Pasquotank	Representative	1876, 1879, 1885, 1891
Carey (Cary), Wilson	Caswell	Representative	1868, 1874, 1876, 1879, 1889
Carter, Hawkins W.	Warren	Representative	1874, 1876, 1879
	Warren (19th)	Senator	1881, 1883
Cawthorne, William W.	Warren	Representative	1868, 1870
Cherry, Henry C.	Edgecombe	Representative	1868
Christmas, Lewis Thomas	Warren	Representative	1879
Coates, W. C.	Northampton	Representative	1899
Crawford, A. A. (H.)	Granville	Representative	1868
Crenshaw, R. C.	Edgecombe	Representative	1887
Crews, William Henry	Granville	Representative	1874, 1876, 1893
Crews, Wm. Henry, Jr.	Granville	Representative	1895, 1897
Danc(e)y, Franklin David	Edgecombe (5th)	Senator	1879
Dudley, Edward R.	Craven	Representative	1870, 1872
Eagles, John S. W.	New Hanover	Representative	1869
Eaton, Harry B.	Vance	Representative	1883, 1885
Eaton, James Youman	Vance	Representative	1899
Elliott, Richard	Chowan	Representative	1874, 1897
Ellison, Stewart	Wake	Representative	1870, 1872, 1879
Eppes, Henry	Halifax (6th)	Senator	1868, 1870
	Halifax (4th)		1872, 1879, 1887
Falkner, Henry H.	Warren	Representative	1889

Fa(u)lkner, Richard	Warren	Representative	1868, 1870
Fletcher, Robert	Richmond	Representative	1870, 1872
Fuller, Thomas Oscar	Warren (11th)	Senator	1899
Galloway, Abraham H.	New Hanover (13th)	Senator	1868
Good, John R.	Craven	Representative	1874
Grady, Luke	New Hanover	Representative	1885
Gray, Robert R.	Edgecombe (5th)	Senator	1883
Green, Eustace E.	New Hanover	Representative	1883
Harris, James Henry	Wake (18th)	Senator	1872
Hayes, W. T. J.	Halifax	Representative	1868
Hayley, Paul F.	Northampton	Representative	1881
Henderson, William B.	Vance (11th)	Senator	1893, 1897
Hewlin, Hillard J.	Halifax	Representative	1883
Hicks, Alexander	Washington	Representative	1881
Hill, Edward H.	Craven	Representative	1874
Hill, Joseph Corbin	New Hanover	Representative	1876
Holloway, John	New Hanover	Representative	1887, 1889
Howe, John T.	New Hanover	Representative	1897
Howe, Valentine	New Hanover	Representative	1887, 1889
Hudgins, Ivey	Halifax	Representative	1868
Hughes, Hanson Truman	Granville	Representative	1872, 1874
	Granville (21st)	Senator	1876
Hussey, John E.	Craven	Representative	1885, 1889
Hyman, John Adams	Warren (20th)	Senator	1868, 1870
	Warren (19th)	Senator	1872
Johnson, Daniel R.	Warren	Representative	1876, 1881
Johnson, Richard M.	Edgecombe	Representative	1870
Jones, John A.	Halifax	Representative	1874
King, George H.	Warren	Representative	1872, 1881
Leary, John Sinclair	Cumberland	Representative	1868
Lloyd, Alfred	New Hanover	Representative	1872, 1874
	Pender	Representative	1876
Mabson, George L.	New Hanover	Representative	1870
	New Hanover (12th)	Senator	1872
Mabson, William P.	Edgecombe	Representative	1872
	Edgecombe (5th)	Senator	1874, 1876
McLaurin, William H.	New Hanover	Representative	1872
Mayo, Cuffie	Granville	Representative	1868
Mebane, George Allen	Bertie (3rd)	Senator	1876, 1883
Montgomery, Jacob H.	Warren	Representative	1883
	Warren (19th)	Senator	1885

Moore, William H.	New Hanover	Representative	1874
	New Hanover (12th)	Senator	1876
Morgan, Wilson Willis	Wake	Representative	1870
Morris, Benjamin W.	Craven	Representative	1868
Newell, John	Bladen	Representative	1874, 1879, 1881, 1883
Newsome, William D.	Hertford	Representative	1870
Page, John R.	Chowan	Representative	1870
Paschall, John M.	Warren	Senator	1874
Paschall, John William H.	Warren	Representative	1872
Peace, Moses M.	Vance	Representative	1895, 1897
Person, William Lee	Edgecombe	Senator	1897
Pettipher, Willis D.	Craven	Representative	1879
Pittman, James McCoy	Halifax	Representative	1883, 1887
Poe, James	Caswell	Representative	1883
Price, George Washington, Jr.	New Hanover	Representative	1868
	New Hanover	Senator	1870
Rawls, Edward R.	Northampton	Representative	1887, 1889, 1897
Reavis (Reaves), W. H.	Granville	Representative	1870
Reynolds, John Thomas	Northampton	Representative	1868
	Halifax	Representative	1876, 1879
Robbins, Augustus	Bertie	Representative	1879, 1881
Robbins, Parker D.	Bertie	Representative	1868, 1870
Rogers, Henry Clay	Granville	Representative	1876
Scott, Henry Ephraim	New Hanover	Representative	1879
	New Hanover (12th)	Senator	1881, 1883
Simmons, Henry Hamilton	Craven	Representative	1876
Smith, Charles	Halifax	Representative	1870
Smith, Isaac Hughes	Craven	Representative	1899
Speller, Turner Ridley	Bertie	Representative	1883
Speller, Turner Roscoe (Rascoe)	Bertie	Representative	1884, 1887
Stevens, A. W.	Craven	Representative	1868
Sutton, Edward H.	Chowan	Representative	1883
Sweat, Isham S.	Cumberland	Representative	1868
Sykes, Thomas A.	Pasquotank	Representative	1868, 1870
Taylor, Robert S.	Edgecombe (5th)	Senator	1885, 1887
Taylor, Taswell L.	Granville	Representative	1893
Thorpe, Bryant Washington	Edgecombe	Representative	1885
Tilley, Hugh G.	Granville	Representative	1887, 1889

Tucker, Richard	Craven	Representative	1870
	Craven (8th)	Senator	1874
Waddell, William Henry	New Hanover	Representative	1879, 1881, 1883
Ward, R. C.	Warren	Representative	1885, 1887, 1889
Watson, James M.	Vance	Representative	1887, 1889, 1891, 1893
Watson, W. W.	Edgecombe	Representative	1881
Webster, W. P.	Caswell	Representative	1887
White, George Henry	Craven	Representative	1881
	Craven (8th)	Senator	1885
White, John A.	Halifax	Representative	1874, 1876, 1879, 1887
Williamson, John Hendrick	Franklin	Representative	1868, 1870, 1872, 1876, 1887
Williamson, Robert W.	Caswell	Representative	1893
Willis, George B.	Craven	Representative	1870
Wimberly, Dred	Edgecombe	Representative	1879, 1887
	Edgecombe (5th)	Senator	1889
Wright, J. H.	Warren	Representative	1893, 1899
Young, James Hunter	Wake	Representative	1895, 1897

Legislators Not Yet Positively Identified as African Americans

Name	County	Office	Term(s)
Belcher, William	Edgecombe	Representative	1883
Chapman, John	Craven	Representative	1891
Jacobs, A. R.	Northampton	Representative	1889
Johnson, William H.	Craven	Representative	1883
Jones, Burton H.	Northampton	Representative	1872
Justice, Daniel	Edgecombe	Representative	1889
Newby, Noah R.	Pasquotank	Representative	1883
Wilson, James	New Hanover	Representative	1876, 1881

Appendix 2

North Carolina African Americans in Major Governmental Posts (State and Federal), 1969–2011

NAME	PARTY	SERVED	TERM(S)	FROM	ADDITIONAL INFORMATION
Adams, Alma	Democrat	N.C. House	1995–present	Guilford	
Alexander, Frederick D.	Democrat	N.C. Senate	1975–1980	Mecklenburg	
Alexander, Kelly M., Jr.	Democrat	N.C. House	2008–present	Mecklenburg	
Allen, Bernard	Democrat	N.C. House	2003–2006	Wake	Died 10/13/06
Ballance, Frank W., Jr.	Democrat	N.C. House	1983–1986	Warren	Senate deputy president
		N.C. Senate	1989–2003		pro tempore, 1997
		U.S. House	2003–2004		Resigned 6/8/04
Barnhill, Howard C.	Democrat	N.C. House	1985–1994	Mecklenburg	
Beasley, Cheri		N.C. Court of Appeals	2009–present	Cumberland	
Beatty, Bryan E.	Democrat	Secretary, Crime Control and Public Safety	2001–2009	Rowan	Resigned 2009
Beatty, James A.		U.S. District Court for Middle District of N.C.	1994–present	Guilford	
Beck, Theodis	Democrat	Secretary, Correction	1999–2009	Buncombe	
Beery, Philip O.	Democrat	N.C. House	1983–1984	Mecklenburg	
Bell, Larry Moseley	Democrat	N.C. House	2001–present	Sampson	House majority whip, 2005–2011
Biggs, Loretta Copeland	Democrat	N.C. Court of Appeals	2001–2002	Forsyth	
Blue, Daniel T., Jr.	Democrat	N.C. House	1981–1998;	Wake	Speaker of N.C. House,
			2005–2009		1991–1994
		N.C. Senate	2009–present		
Bonner, Donald Allen	Democrat	N.C. House	1997–2004	Robeson	
Boyd-McIntyre, Flossie	Democrat	N.C. House	1995–2003	Guilford	
Brandon, Marcus	Democrat	N.C. House	2011–present	Guilford	

Name	Party	Office	Years	County	Notes
Braswell, Jerry	Democrat	N.C. House	1993–2000	Wayne	House minority whip, 2005–2011
Brown, Dock	Democrat	N.C. House	1993–1994	Halifax	
Bryant, Angela R.	Democrat	N.C. House	2007–present	Nash	
Bryant, Wanda G.	Democrat	N.C. Court of Appeals	2001–present	Brunswick	
Burke, Logan	Democrat	N.C. House	1987–1990	Forsyth	
Burris-Floyd, Pearl	Democrat	N.C. House	2009–2011	Rowan	
Burton, William A., III	Democrat	N.C. House	1993–1994	Guilford	
Butterfield, G. K., Jr.	Democrat	N.C. Supreme Court U.S. House	2001–2002 2003–present	Wilson	
Campbell, Ralph, Jr.	Democrat	State Auditor	1993–2004	Wake	Died 1/11/11
Carey, Moses, Jr.	Democrat	Secretary, Administration	2010–present	Orange	
Clayton, Eva M.	Democrat	U.S. House	1992–2003	Warren	
Coleman, Linda	Democrat	N.C. House Director, Office of State Personnel	2005–2009 2009–present	Wake	Resigned 1/9/09
Creecy, Charles M.	Democrat	N.C. House	1981–1986	Northampton	
Cummings, Frances M.	Republican	N.C. House	1993–1996	Robeson	
Cunningham, William Pete	Democrat	N.C. House	1987–2007	Mecklenburg	House minority whip, 1995–1996
Dannelly, Charlie Smith	Democrat	N.C. House N.C. Senate	1995–2002 2002–present	Mecklenburg	Senate deputy president pro tempore, 2003
Davis, Don	Democrat	N.C. Senate	2009–2011	Greene	
Davis, Robert E.	Democrat	N.C. House	1979–1980	Robeson	Appointed
Dorsett, Katie G.	Democrat	Secretary, Administration N.C. Senate	1993–2001 2003–2011	Guilford	Senate majority whip, 2009–2010
Earle, Beverly	Democrat	N.C. House	1995–present	Mecklenburg	House majority whip, 1999–2004

Name	Party	Office	Years	County	Notes
Edwards, Chancy Rudolph	Democrat	N.C. House N.C. Senate	1983–1990 1993–1996	Cumberland	
Erwin, Richard Cannon	Democrat	N.C. Senate N.C. Court of Appeals U.S. District Court for Middle District of N.C.	1975–1978 1978–1980 1999–2006	Forsyth	Died 11/7/06
Farmer-Butterfield, Jean	Democrat	N.C. House	2003–present	Wilson	
Fitch, Milton F., Jr.	Democrat	N.C. House	1985–2001	Wilson	House majority whip,1989–1990 House majority leader, 1993–1994 Deputy House minority leader, 1997–1998
Floyd, Elmer	Democrat	N.C. House	2009–present	Cumberland	
Ford, Jimmie Edward	Democrat	N.C. House	2000–2002	Wayne	
Foriest, Anthony E.	Democrat	N.C. Senate	2007–2011	Alamance	
Freeman, William M.	Democrat	N.C. House	1987–1988	Wake	
Frye, Henry E.	Democrat	N.C. House N.C. Senate N.C. Supreme Court N.C. Supreme Court	1969–1980 1981–1982 1983–1999 1999–2001	Guilford	First African American N.C. legislator in 20th century Associate justice Chief justice
Gill, Rosa U.	Democrat	N.C. House	2009–present	Wake	
Gist, Herman C.	Democrat	N.C. House	1983–1994	Guilford	Died 3/4/94
Graham, Malcolm	Democrat	N.C. Senate	2005–present	Mecklenburg	
Green, James P., Sr.	Democrat	N.C. House	1991–1994	Vance	
Hall, John D.	Democrat	N.C. House	2001–2005	Halifax	Died 3/17/05
Hall, Larry D.	Democrat	N.C. House	2006–present	Durham	

Name	Party	Position	Years	County	Notes
Hampton, Thurman	Democrat	Secretary, Crime Control and Public Safety	1993–1996	Chatham	
Hardaway, Thomas C.	Democrat	N.C. House	1987–1992 1997–2000	Halifax	
Harrell, Ty	Democrat	N.C. House	2007–2009	Wake	Resigned 9/20/09
Hauser, Charlie B.	Democrat	N.C. House	1983–1986	Forsyth	
Holloman, Robert Lee	Democrat	N.C. Senate	2003–2006	Hertford	
Hughes, Sandra Spalding	Democrat	N.C. House	2008–2011	New Hanover	
Hunt, Ralph Alexander	Democrat	N.C. Senate	1985–1993; 2004	Durham	
Hunter, Howard J., Jr.	Democrat	N.C. House	1989–2007	Northampton	Died 1/7/07
Jeralds, Luther R.	Democrat	N.C. House	1983–1992	Cumberland	
Johnson, Aaron	Republican	Secretary, Correction	1985–1990	Pender	
Johnson, Joy J.	Democrat	N.C. House	1971–1978	Robeson	
Jones, Earl	Democrat	N.C. House	2003–2011	Guilford	
Jones, Edward	Democrat	N.C. House N.C. Senate	2005–2007 2007–present	Halifax	
Jordan, Luther H.	Democrat	N.C. Senate	1993–2002	New Hanover	Senate majority whip, 1999–2002 Died 4/23/02
Keller, Alvin	Democrat	Secretary, Correction	2009–present	Cumberland	
Kennedy, Annie B.	Democrat	N.C. House	1979–1994	Forsyth	
Kinney, Theodore J.	Democrat	N.C. House	1993–2000	Cumberland	
Lee, Howard N.	Democrat	Secretary, Natural Resources and Community Development N.C. Senate	1977–1981 1991–1994, 1997–2003	Orange	

Name	Party	Chamber	Years	County	Notes
Linney, Larry	Republican	N.C. House	1995–1996	Buncombe	
Locks, Sidney A.	Democrat	N.C. House	1983–1990	Robeson	
Lucas, Jeanne Hopkins	Democrat	N.C. Senate	1993–2006	Durham	First African American woman in N.C. Senate. Senate majority whip, 2003–2006
Lucas, Marvin W.	Democrat	N.C. House	2001–present	Cumberland	
McAllister, Mary E.	Democrat	N.C. House	1991–present	Cumberland	
McIntire, Flossie Boyd	Democrat	N.C. House	1995–present	Guilford	
McKinney, Theodore J.	Democrat	N.C. House	1993–2000	Cumberland	
McKissick, Floyd B., Jr.	Democrat	N.C. Senate	2007–present	Durham	
McKoy, Henry E.	Republican	N.C. Senate	1995–1996	Wake	
Mackey, Nick	Democrat	N.C. House	2009–2011	Mecklenburg	
Malone, Vernon	Democrat	N.C. Senate	2003–2009	Wake	Died 4/18/09
Mansfield, Eric	Democrat	N.C. Senate	2011–present	Cumberland	
Martin, William Nelson	Democrat	N.C. Senate	1983–2002	Guilford	
Michaux, Henry M., Jr.	Democrat	N.C. House	1973–1977, 1985–present	Durham	
Miller, Paul	Democrat	N.C. House	2001–2006	Durham	House majority whip, 2003. Resigned 7/7/06
Mobley, Annie W.	Democrat	N.C. House	2007–present	Hertford	
Moore, Rodney	Democrat	N.C. House	2011–present	Mecklenburg	
Oldham, Warren Claude	Democrat	N.C. House	1991–2003	Forsyth	
Parham, Earline	Democrat	N.C. House	2003–present	Forsyth	
Pierce, Garland E.	Democrat	N.C. House	2005–present	Scotland	

Name	Party	Office	Years	County	Notes
Richardson, James Franklin	Democrat	N.C. House / N.C. Senate	1985–1986 / 1987–1992	Mecklenburg	Senate majority whip,1991–1992
Robinson, Gladys	Democrat	N.C. Senate	2011–present	Guilford	
Shaw, Larry	Democrat	N.C. House / N.C. Senate	1995–1996 / 1997–2011	Cumberland	
Spaulding, Kenneth B.	Democrat	N.C. House	1979–1980, 1981–1982	Durham	
Swinson, Gwinn	Democrat	Secretary, Administration	2000–2006	Beaufort	
Thigpen, Cressie H., Jr.		N.C. Court of Appeals	2010; 2011–present	Wake	
Timmons-Goodson, Patricia	Democrat	N.C. Court of Appeals / N.C. Supreme Court	1997–2005 / 2006–present	Cumberland	
Wainwright, William L.	Democrat	N.C. House	1991–present	Craven	Speaker pro tempore, 2007–2011
Watt, Melvin	Democrat	N.C. Senate / U.S. House	1985–1986 / 1993–present	Mecklenburg	
Willingham, Shelly	Democrat	N.C. House	2002–2003	Edgecombe	
Winters, John W.	Democrat	N.C. Senate	1975–1977	Wake	Resigned 1977
Womble, Larry W.	Democrat	N.C. House	1995–present	Forsyth	
Wright, Thomas E.	Democrat	N.C. House	1993–2008	New Hanover	Expelled 3/20/08
Wynn, James Andrew, Jr.		N.C. Court of Appeals / N.C. Supreme Court / U.S. Court of Appeals	1990–1998; 1998–2010 / 1998 / 2010–present	Martin	
Young, Reuben F.	Democrat	Secretary, Crime Control and Public Safety	2009–present	Wake	

Redistricting of Congressional Districts in North Carolina: A Chronology, 1991–2001

JULY 9, 1991
The General Assembly approves a congressional redistricting plan, based on 1990 census. The Twelfth District, extending from Durham to Gastonia, is the only majority-minority district.

DECEMBER 18, 1991
The U.S. Department of Justice objects to the congressional redistricting plan under Section 5 of the Voting Rights Act.

JANUARY 24, 1992
The General Assembly passes a new congressional redistricting plan with two majority-minority districts.

FEBRUARY 26, 1992
The U.S. Department of Justice approves the new plan.

MARCH 12, 1992
Robinson O. Everett, Durham lawyer and Duke University professor of law, files a lawsuit in federal court, challenging the constitutionality of the redistricting plan, asserting that it imposes racial quotas.

APRIL 27, 1992
A three-judge federal district court dismisses Everett's lawsuit on the ground that there is no claim on which relief can be granted. Everett appeals to the U.S. Supreme Court.

JUNE 28, 1993
The U.S. Supreme Court reverses the dismissal of Everett's lawsuit (*Shaw v. Reno*) and remands the case to federal district court. Writing for the majority in the 5–4 decision, Justice Sandra Day O'Connor characterizes the redistricting map as a "political apartheid."

AUGUST 1, 1994
The three-judge federal district court rules by a vote of 2 to 1 that while the 1992 redistricting plan is a racial gerrymander, it is carefully drawn to meet the demands of the Voting Rights Act and to remedy decades of discrimination.

JUNE 29, 1995
The U.S. Supreme Court agrees to review *Shaw v. Hunt*, Everett's appeal of the federal district court's decision of August 1994.

JUNE 13, 1996
The U.S. Supreme Court reverses the three-judge federal district court again. In another 5–4 decision, Chief Justice William Rehnquist, writing for the majority, declares the Twelfth District unconstitutional.

JULY 30, 1996
A three-judge federal district court allows North Carolina to conduct 1996 elections under the existing (1992) plan but gives the General Assembly until April 1, 1997, to propose a remedial plan.

MARCH 31, 1997
The General Assembly approves a new redistricting plan that maintains a partisan balance of six Republicans and six Democrats in Congress and two majority-minority districts.

APRIL 3, 1998
A three-judge federal district court grants summary judgment striking down the Twelfth District under the 1997 redistricting plan. The court postpones congressional primaries until September and orders the General Assembly to devise a new redistricting plan.

MAY 21, 1998
The General Assembly passes a new redistricting plan for the Twelfth District. Guilford County is removed from the district, and all of Rowan County is incorporated into it.

MAY 27, 1998
Robinson O. Everett files an objection to the 1998 redistricting plan.

MAY 17, 1999
The U.S. Supreme Court, ruling on the state's appeal of the federal district court's summary judgment of April 1998, votes 9 to 0 to uphold the appeal. The Court rules that the lower court was wrong to throw out the 1997 redistricting plan without a trial and reinstates the 1997 plan to govern the 2000 elections.

NOVEMBER 29–DECEMBER 1, 1999
A three-judge federal district court holds a trial in Raleigh to rule on the constitutionality of the First and Twelfth Districts under the 1997 redistricting plan.

MARCH 7, 2000
The three-judge federal district court rules 2 to 1 that the Twelfth District is unconstitutional because race played too large a role in its unusual configuration. The constitutionality of the First District is upheld.

JUNE 26, 2000
On appeal from the state, the U.S. Supreme Court agrees to review the 1997 version of the Twelfth District.

APRIL 18, 2001
By a vote of 5 to 4, the U.S. Supreme Court upholds the constitutionality of the Twelfth District. In reversing the lower-court decision, the Court rules that race was only one factor, not the main factor, in designing the district. *Easley v. Cromartie* marks the fourth time that the Court has ruled on North Carolina's congressional districts since 1993.

Suggested Readings

Abrams, Douglas Carl. "Irony of Reform: North Carolina Blacks and the New Deal." *North Carolina Historical Review* LXVI (April 1989).

Alexander, Roberta Sue. *North Carolina Faces the Freedmen: Race Relations during Presidential Reconstruction, 1865–1867.* Durham: Duke University Press, 1985.

Anderson, Eric. *Race and Politics in North Carolina, 1872–1901: The Black Second.* Baton Rouge: Louisiana State University Press, 1981.

Anderson, Jean Bradley. *Durham County: A History of Durham County, North Carolina.* Durham: Duke University Press, 1990.

Aptheker, Herbert. *One Continual Cry: David Walker's Appeal.* New York: Humanities Press, 1965.

Bates, Beth Tompkins. *Pullman Porters and the Rise of Protest Politics in Black America, 1925–1945.* Chapel Hill: University of North Carolina Press, 2001.

Beeby, James M. "Red Shirt Violence, Election Fraud, and the Demise of the Populist Party in North Carolina's Third Congressional District, 1900." *North Carolina Historical Review,* LXXXV (January 2008).

Berlin, Ira. "Time, Space, and the Evolution of Afro-American Society in British Mainland North America." *American Historical Review* 85 (February 1980).

Bishir, Catherine W. "Black Builders in Antebellum North Carolina." *North Carolina Historical Review* LXI (October 1984).

Blassingame, John W. *The Slave Community: Plantation Life in the Antebellum South.* New York: Oxford University Press, 1972.

Brisson, Jim D. " 'Civil Government Was Crumbling Around Me': The Kirk-Holden War of 1870." *North Carolina Historical Review,* LXXXVIII (April 2011).

Butchart, Ronald E. *Schooling of the Freed People: Teaching, Learning, and the Struggle for Black Freedom, 1861–1876.* Chapel Hill: University of North Carolina Press, 2010.

Carter, Wilmoth A. *The Urban Negro in the South.* New York: Vantage Press, 1961.

Cecelski, David S. *Along Freedom Road: Hyde County, North Carolina, and the Fate of Black Schools in the South.* Chapel Hill: University of North Carolina Press, 1994.

_____. *The Waterman's Song: Slavery and Freedom in Maritime North Carolina.* Chapel Hill: University of North Carolina Press, 2001.

Cecelski, David S., and Timothy B. Tyson. *Democracy Betrayed: The Wilmington Race Riot of 1898 and Its Legacy.* Chapel Hill: University of North Carolina Press, 1998.

Chafe, William H. *Civilities and Civil Rights: Greensboro, North Carolina, and the Black Struggle for Freedom.* New York: Oxford University Press, 1980.

Click, Patricia. *Time Full of Trial: The Roanoke Island Freedmen's Colony, 1862–1867.* Chapel Hill: University of North Carolina Press, 2001.

Cohen, William. *At Freedom's Edge: Black Mobility and the Southern White Quest for Racial Control, 1861–1915.* Baton Rouge: Louisiana State University Press, 1991.

Crow, Jeffrey J. "An Apartheid for the South: Clarence Poe's Crusade for Rural Segregation." In *Race, Class, and Politics in Southern History: Essays in Honor of Robert F. Durden,* edited by Jeffrey J. Crow, Paul D. Escott, and Charles L. Flynn Jr. Baton Rouge: Louisiana State University Press, 1989.

_____. *The Black Experience in Revolutionary North Carolina.* Raleigh: Division of Archives and History, Department of Cultural Resources, 1977.

_____. "Slave Rebelliousness and Social Conflict in North Carolina, 1775 to 1802." *William and Mary Quarterly* XXXVII (January 1980).

Daniel, Pete. "Going among Strangers: Southern Reactions to World War II." *Journal of American History* 77 (December 1990).

Escott, Paul D. *Many Excellent People: Power and Privilege in North Carolina, 1850–1900.* Chapel Hill: University of North Carolina Press, 1985.

_____. *Slavery Remembered: A Record of Twentieth-Century Slave Narratives.* Chapel Hill: University of North Carolina Press, 1979.

Fenn, Elizabeth A. " 'A Perfect Equality Seemed to Reign': Slave Society and Jonkonnu." *North Carolina Historical Review* LXV (April 1988).

Franklin, John Hope. *The Free Negro in North Carolina, 1790–1860.* Chapel Hill: University of North Carolina Press, 1943.

_____. *From Slavery to Freedom: A History of Negro Americans.* New York: Knopf, sixth edition, 1988.

Gavins, Raymond. "Fighting for Civil Rights in the Age of Segregation: The NAACP in North Carolina to 1955." In *New Directions in Civil Rights Studies,* edited by Armstead L. Robinson and Patricia Sullivan. Charlottesville: University Press of Virginia, 1991.

_____. "The Meaning of Freedom: Black North Carolina in the Nadir, 1880–1900." In *Race, Class, and Politics in Southern History: Essays in Honor of Robert F. Durden*, edited by Jeffrey J. Crow, Paul D. Escott, and Charles L. Flynn Jr. Baton Rouge: Louisiana State University Press, 1989.

_____. "North Carolina Black Folklore and Song in the Age of Segregation: Toward Another Meaning of Survival." *North Carolina Historical Review* LXVI (October 1989).

Genovese, Eugene D. *Roll, Jordan, Roll: The World the Slaves Made.* New York: Pantheon Books, 1974.

Gershenhorn, Jerry. "A Courageous Voice for Black Freedom: Louis Austin and the *Carolina Times* in Depression-Era North Carolina." *North Carolina Historical Review,* LXXXVII (January 2010).

Gutman, Herbert G. *The Black Family in Slavery and Freedom, 1750–1925.* New York: Pantheon Books, 1976.

Haley, John H. *Charles N. Hunter and Race Relations in North Carolina.* Chapel Hill: University of North Carolina Press, 1987.

Hanchett, Thomas W. "The Rosenwald Schools and Black Education in North Carolina." *North Carolina Historical Review* LXV (October 1988).

Harding, Vincent. *There Is a River: The Black Struggle for Freedom in America.* New York: Harcourt Brace Jovanovich, Publishers, 1981.

Henri, Florette. *Black Migration: Movement Northward, 1900–1920.* Garden City, NY: Anchor Press, 1975.

Hogan, Wesley C. *Many Minds, One Heart: SNCC's Dream for a New America.* Chapel Hill: University of North Carolina Press, 2007.

Jacobs, Harriet. *Incidents in the Life of a Slave Girl.* Edited by Jean Fagan Yellin. Cambridge, Mass.: Harvard University Press, 1987.

Johnson, Charles S. *Negro in American Civilization.* New York: Henry Holt and Company, 1930.

Johnson, Guion Griffis. *Ante-Bellum North Carolina: A Social History.* Chapel Hill: University of North Carolina Press, 1937.

Justesen, Benjamin R. " 'The Class of '83': Black Watershed in the North Carolina General Assembly." *North Carolina Historical Review,* LXXXVI (July 2009).

_____. *George Henry White: An Even Chance in the Race of Life.* Baton Rouge: Louisiana State University Press, 2001.

Kay, Marvin L. Michael, and Lorin Lee Cary. "A Demographic Analysis of Colonial North Carolina with Special Emphasis upon the Slave and Black Populations." In *Black Americans in North Carolina and the South,* edited by Jeffrey J. Crow and Flora J. Hatley. Chapel Hill: University of North Carolina Press, 1984.

_____. "Slave Runaways in Colonial North Carolina, 1748–1775." *North Carolina Historical Review* LXIII (January 1986).

Kelly, Blair M. *Right to Ride: Streetcar Boycotts and African American Citizenship in the Era of Plessy v. Ferguson.* Chapel Hill: University of North Carolina Press, 2010.

Kirby, Jack Temple. "The Southern Exodus, 1910–1960: A Primer for Historians." *Journal of Southern History* XLIX (November 1983).

Kluger, Richard. *Simple Justice: The History of Brown v. Board of Education and Black America's Struggle for Equality.* New York: Knopf, 1975.

Korstad, Robert. *Civil Rights Unionism: Tobacco Workers and the Struggle for Democracy in the Mid-Twentieth-Century South.* Chapel Hill: University of North Carolina Press, 2003.

Korstad, Robert, and Nelson Lichtenstein. "Opportunities Found and Lost: Labor, Radicals, and the Early Civil Rights Movement." *Journal of American History* 75 (December 1988).

Kousser, J. Morgan. *Colorblind Injustice: Minority Voting Rights and the Undoing of the Second Reconstruction.* Chapel Hill: University of North Carolina Press, 1999.

Krause, Bonnie J. " 'We Did Move Mountains!': Lucy Saunders Herring, North Carolina Jeanes Supervisor and African American Educator, 1916–1968." *North Carolina Historical Review,* LXXX (April 2003).

Larkins, John R. *The Negro Population of North Carolina: Social and Economic,* Special Bulletin No. 23. Raleigh: State Board of Charities and Public Welfare, 1944.

Lawson, Steven F. *Black Ballots: Voting Rights in the South, 1944–1969.* New York: Columbia University Press, 1976.

Meier, August, and Elliott Rudwick. *Along the Color Line: Explorations in the Black Experience.* Urbana: University of Illinois Press, 1976.

_____. *CORE: A Study of the Civil Rights Movement, 1942–1968.* New York: Oxford University Press, 1973.

Mobley, Joe A. "In the Shadow of White Society: Princeville, a Black Town in North Carolina, 1865–1915." *North Carolina Historical Review* LXIII (July 1986).

_____. *James City: A Black Community in North Carolina, 1863–1900.* Raleigh: Division of Archives and History, Department of Cultural Resources, 1981.

Morris, Charles Edward. "Panic and Reprisal: Reaction in North Carolina to the Nat Turner Insurrection, 1831." *North Carolina Historical Review* LXII (January 1985).

Murray, Pauli. *Proud Shoes: The Story of an American Family.* New York: Harper and Row, 1956, 1978.

Murray, Percy E. *History of the North Carolina Teachers Association.* Washington, D.C.: National Education Association, 1985.

Pearson, Reggie L. " 'There Are Many Sick, Feeble, and Suffering Freedmen': The Freedmen's Bureau's Health-Care Activities during Reconstruction in North Carolina, 1865–1868." LXXIX (April 2002).

Perman, Michael. *Struggle for Mastery: Disfranchisement in the South, 1888–1908.* Chapel Hill: University of North Carolina Press, 2001.

Prather, H. Leon, Sr. *We Have Taken a City: Wilmington Racial Massacre and Coup of 1898.* Rutherford, N. J. : Fairleigh Dickinson University Press, 1984.

Quarles, Benjamin. *The Negro in the American Revolution.* Chapel Hill: University of North Carolina Press, 1961.

Rabinowitz, Howard. *Race Relations in the Urban South, 1865–1890.* New York: Oxford University Press, 1978.

_____, ed. *Southern Black Leaders of the Reconstruction Era.* Urbana: University of Illinois Press, 1982.

Richardson, Michael B. " 'Not Gradually . . . But Now': Reginald Hawkins, Black Leadership, and Desegregation in Charlotte, North Carolina." *North Carolina Historical Review,* LXXXII (July 2005).

Ritterhouse, Jennifer. *Growing Up Jim Crow: How Black and White Southern Children Learned Race.* Chapel Hill: University of North Carolina Press, 2006.

Schoen, Johanna. *Choice and Coercion: Birth Control, Sterilization, and Abortion in Public Health and Welfare.* Chapel Hill: University of North Carolina Press, 2005.

Schweninger, Loren. *Black Property Owners in the South, 1790–1915.* Urbana: University of Illinois Press, 1990.

_____. "John Carruthers Stanly and the Anomaly of Black Slaveholding." *North Carolina Historical Review* LXVII (April 1990).

[Scott, Emmett J.]. "Letters of Negro Migrants of 1916–1918." *Journal of Negro History* IV (July 1919).

Tindall, George B. *Emergence of the New South, 1913–1945.* Baton Rouge: Louisiana State University Press, 1967.

Troxler, Carole Watterson. " 'To Look More Closely at the Man': Wyatt Outlaw, a Nexus of National, Local, and Personal History." *North Carolina Historical Review* LXXVII (October 2000).

Tyson, Timothy B. *Radio Free Dixie: Robert F. Williams and the Roots of Black Power.* Chapel Hill: University of North Carolina Press, 1999.

Umfleet, LeRae S. *A Day of Blood: The 1898 Wilmington Race Riot.* Raleigh: North Carolina Office of Archives and History, Department of Cultural Resources, 2009.

[U.S. Department of Labor, Division of Negro Economics]. *Negro Migration in 1916–17.* Washington, D.C.: Government Printing Office, 1919.

Waynick, Capus M., John C. Brooks, and Elsie W. Pitts, eds. *North Carolina and the Negro*. Raleigh: Mayors' Cooperating Committee, 1964.

Weare, Walter B. *Black Business in the New South: A Social History of the North Carolina Mutual Life Insurance Company*. Urbana: University of Illinois Press, 1973.

Wood, Peter H. *Black Majority: Negroes in Colonial South Carolina from 1670 through the Stono Rebellion*. New York: Alfred A. Knopf, 1974.

_____. " 'The Dream Deferred': Black Freedom Struggles on the Eve of White Independence." In *In Resistance: Studies in African, Caribbean, and Afro-American History*, edited by Gary Y. Okihiro. Amherst: University of Massachusetts Press, 1986.

Zipf, Karin L. *Labor of Innocents: Forced Apprenticeship in North Carolina, 1715–1919*. Baton Rouge: Louisiana State University Press, 2005.

Index